RACIAL RECKONING

Prosecuting America's Civil Rights Murders

RENEE C. ROMANO

Harvard University Press

Cambridge, Massachusetts
London, England
2014

Library of Congress Cataloging-in-Publication Data

Romano, Renee Christine, author.
Racial reckoning : prosecuting America's civil rights murders / Renee C.
Romano.
pages cm
Includes bibliographical references and index.
ISBN 978-0-674-05042-6 (alk. paper)
1.   Trials (Murder)—United States—History.   2.   Civil rights
movements—United States—History.   3.   African Americans—Civil rights—
History—20th century.   4.   United States—Race relations.   I. Title.
KF221.M8R66 2014
345.73'02523—dc23   2014003227

For my parents

Contents

Racial Reckoning

Introduction

Exhuming the Past

> Americans, unhappily, have the most remarkable ability to alchemize all bitter truths into an innocuous but piquant confection and to transform their moral contradictions, or public discussion of such contradictions, into a proud decoration, such as are given for heroism on the field of battle.
>
> —James Baldwin, 1951

JUNE 1, 2005, dawned warm and sunny in Alsip, Illinois, a suburb twenty miles south of Chicago, but the mood at Burr Oak Cemetery, a historic black burial ground, was somber. A few relatives, a preacher, and a group of FBI agents had gathered to exhume the body of Emmett Till, a fourteen-year-old black Chicagoan who had been killed in Mississippi almost exactly fifty years earlier. Till had gone to the tiny town of Money in August 1955 to spend some time with his extended family. Just a week after his arrival, he was brutally murdered, a punishment for supposedly sassing a young white female clerk in a small local store. Stories differ on whether Till actually whistled at twenty-one-year-old Carolyn Bryant, but whatever had transpired, Bryant's husband, Roy, decided that the teenager from Chicago needed to be taught a lesson.[1] Several days after the fateful encounter in the store, Bryant and his half brother, J. W. Milam, kidnapped Till from his great-uncle's house and took him to a barn where they and several others beat him, gouged out one of his eyes, and shot him in the head before dumping his body in the Tallahatchie River.

In 1955, there was no justice for Emmett Till. Bryant and Milam were charged with the murder, but an all-white jury acquitted them after a five-day trial and a sixty-seven-minute deliberation. Emboldened by their acquittal, the two men confessed to the murder on the pages of *Look* magazine in exchange for $4,000. They would both die of old age never having served a day in jail for the crime. Till's brutal murder and the complete failure of the criminal justice system to hold anyone accountable for it galvanized many young African Americans to join the struggle against the southern racial caste system.[2]

Fifty years later, in response to years of lobbying to reinvestigate the murder by relatives and activists, state and federal authorities reopened the case. Their efforts to determine whether anyone else could be charged with Till's murder prompted the exhumation of his body so that an autopsy could be conducted. The backhoe that dug up the earth around Till's casket was, quite literally, excavating the past. And that excavation did not begin or end with the case of Emmett Till. Since the late 1980s, state and federal authorities have reinvestigated over one hundred killings that took place during the struggle to uphold the racial order in the 1950s and 1960s. Legal proceedings related to nine incidents of violence have resulted in, to date, thirteen contemporary trials and the sentencing of more than twenty men to jail time for racially motivated murders they committed in the years between 1955 and 1970.

Racial Reckoning seeks to understand the phenomenon of the contemporary prosecution of civil rights–era crimes. It explores the forces that drove the legal system to revisit these decades-old murders, what happened in the courtroom when they came before a jury, and how reopenings and trials have been represented in the media and popular culture. Most centrally, it uses these modern civil rights trials to explore the dramatic evolution in the operation of race in American society, as a legally enforced caste system based on claims of white biological superiority has been rapidly replaced by ideologies that instead maintain inequalities by insisting that the United States has effectively ended discrimination and thus public policy should be "colorblind." Trials became a key site of contestation between those who wanted to harness them to the project of declaring and celebrating the end of racism in a "postracial" nation and those who saw in them the potential to challenge the denial of the significance of race that was at the foundation of the new racial order.

While many domestic forces have contributed to the interest in revisiting civil rights–era violence, exhumations like those of Emmett Till reflect much broader international trends. In the years since 1945, and especially since 1990 with the end of the Cold War, a growing number of communities and nations have revisited and tried to address historical injustices. Stemming in large part from the new human rights norms that developed after the Holocaust and reflecting the growth of political power of minority groups, nations around the globe have begun to acknowledge guilt for their wrongdoings, from their complicity with the Holocaust to their persecution of native peoples. The appearance of restitution cases all over the world, where nations voluntarily offer acknowledgment of or reparations for a historical injustice, marks one manifestation of the new moral standards in international politics. So do efforts to hold state officials accountable for genocide and gross human rights violations through war crimes tribunals or international or domestic prosecutions, which since the 1990s have exploded in what one scholar has called a "justice cascade." The prevalence of truth commissions—since the 1980s, there have been nearly thirty international or national commissions established around the world to explore past atrocities—reflects this unprecedented historical moment as well. Indeed, as legal scholar and human rights advocate Martha Minow argues, what is truly distinctive about the twentieth century is not its infamous record of human rights abuses and genocides, but the ways in which nations have been moved to formally respond to these atrocities.[3]

The exhumation of Emmett Till's body offers some clues as to the particular nature of the American manifestation of this broader international trend. For one, it highlights the fact that the nation's history of racial violence, especially that which was directed at African Americans in the Jim Crow era of the 1890s through the 1970s, remains an unsettled past that has demanded some kind of formal response. Jim Crow–era racial violence is not the only history that the United States has been moved to address in the past thirty years—other examples include federal reparations for victims of the World War II Japanese internment and some apologies and legal restitution directed at Native Americans. But the racial violence symbolized by a figure like Emmett Till has been at the forefront of the histories that garnered national media and political attention. Some pasts, South African Archbishop Desmond Tutu has said, "refuse to lie down quietly."[4] The racial violence of the Jim Crow era is such a past. Murders like Till's were committed in the pursuit of the political end of maintaining a system of white supremacy. Their history did not "lie down quietly" because the murders, while committed by a relative few, were enabled and condoned by the larger community and its institutions, a story encapsulated in the failure of the legal system to hold anyone responsible for the crimes at the time. When Jim Crow gave way to a new racial system characterized by the principle of formal legal equality, the racial violence of that era became even more restive, symbolizing as it did the near-total failure of the law to protect blacks and their white allies.

The exhumation of Emmett Till also makes clear that bringing these unsettling pasts into the present required effort. Till's case would not have been reopened if not for the persistence and dedication of his mother, Mamie Till Mobley. Till Mobley had died by 2005, but she was still near Emmett, buried in the same cemetery as her son. From the time of his death fifty years earlier, she had dedicated her life to making sure that he not be forgotten, going on speaking tours, collaborating with playwrights and filmmakers to tell Emmett's story, and starting youth groups dedicated to his memory. Emmett's murder became a national touchstone because his mother insisted that his body be displayed in a glass-topped casket for his funeral; the photos of his mutilated corpse, circulated in the black press and internationally, vividly uncovered the evil at the heart of the Jim Crow system.[5] Mamie Till Mobley did everything in her power to ensure that the day would come when Emmett's murder might be revisited. Fittingly, the unique casket she chose preserved her son's remains exceptionally well, making it possible for FBI forensic scientists to uncover new evidence about his death.[6] Through her activism, she both preserved the past so that it could be revisited and lobbied and fought to ensure that it would be.

The fact that the FBI exhumed Emmett Till's body as part of a criminal investigation highlights another important aspect of America's racial reckoning: much of it has taken place through the legal process, and especially in the arena of criminal courts. While many countries around the world have created truth commissions or ordered official investigations

Mamie Till grieving at her son's 1955 funeral. She chose the unique glass-topped casket to ensure that the world could see Emmett's brutalized body. Till dedicated her life to keeping her son's memory alive and fought for decades to see his murder investigation reopened. (AP Photo/*Chicago Sun-Times*, File)

to explore and redress their histories of violence, there has never been an official truth commission in the United States, and there have only been a very few official commissions appointed at the state level charged with examining episodes of racial violence, such as those appointed by state legislatures in Oklahoma and North Carolina to address, respectively, the 1921 Tulsa Race Riot and the 1898 race riot in Wilmington.[7] More commonly, the United States has revisited its historic violence in criminal proceedings designed to hold perpetrators accountable for their crimes. The criminal legal process was the earliest site of any official accounting for the history of the Jim Crow era; the first civil rights trial took place in 1977, with many others following the 1994 trial of Byron De La Beckwith for the 1963 murder of Medgar Evers. Arguably these prosecutions, which have focused national attention on dramatic incidents of historic racial violence, helped generate the political support that resulted in one of the few other official acts revisiting the nation's racial history, the apologies issued by the U.S. Congress in 2005 and 2009 expressing regret and remorse for slavery and for lynching.[8]

The very widespread media coverage of reopened murder investigations and criminal trials, moreover, has made civil rights trials into the most widely publicized site for a national reckoning with the nation's history of racial violence. In criminal trials, reporters, documentarians, and feature filmmakers found ready-made dramas that could be used to tell powerful stories. The bevy of reporters standing just outside the cemetery gate as Till's body was exhumed serves as testament to the importance of media coverage in making the legal arena the most important public site of racial reckoning.

Every form of redress for historic violence has different strengths and limitations; contemporary civil rights trials offer a way to explore the ways in which the legal process has shaped the nature of America's racial reckoning. What, for example, does a trial in a decades-old case mean to family members of victims? Can trials offer healing and closure? In what ways, if any, can the criminal legal process help repair the rifts left by the failure of communities and states to acknowledge the social value of the victims of historic violence? And can criminal prosecutions explore community or state complicity in historic violence? It is especially important to understand the effects of addressing civil rights–era violence through criminal law because efforts to prosecute these murders have gained official approval and support since the 1990s, not only on the federal level, but also among southern states. In recent decades, many southern political leaders who once publicly opposed efforts to revisit the region's history of racial violence have openly endorsed attempts to bring civil rights crimes into the courtroom. Why have governmental bodies in the United States favored trials over truth commissions or other mechanisms as its formal response to historic atrocities?

The attention paid to the Till case signals another key feature of America's racial reckoning: it has focused primarily on southern racial violence rather than the type of violence that structured race relations outside the South. Just as Martin Luther King Jr.'s failed attempt to bring his brand of nonviolent protest to Chicago has little place in the mainstream representations of the civil rights struggle, the racial reckoning that began in the 1990s would do little to explore the nature of racism and racial violence outside the South.[9] While the racial system in the North and West did not rely as openly on segregation laws or voting restrictions against blacks, blacks outside the South faced poor housing conditions in racially segregated, run-down neighborhoods, economic discrimination, inadequate segregated schools, and police brutality. When black residents in northern and western cities erupted in frustration and rage in race riots that became common in the last five years of the 1960s, police and National Guardsmen sent to quell the disorder killed rioters and black bystanders in numbers that rivaled the violence unleashed in the South during the struggle to uphold segregation.[10]

Civil rights trials could have focused attention on the particular nature and extent of racial violence outside the South since one of the cases that has been reopened and that has resulted in trials involved deaths that took place during the course of riots in York, Pennsylvania, in 1969. Two people were killed during the York riots: Henry Schaad, a white police officer shot as he rode in an armored car in a black neighborhood, and Lillie Belle Allen, an African American woman from South Carolina, who died when a white mob opened fire on her family's car when it ventured into a white neighborhood. No one faced charges for either murder at the time, but in 2001, legal proceedings resulted in the conviction of twelve men, nine whites for the murder of Allen and three blacks for the murder of Schaad.[11]

While media coverage of civil rights trials almost always notes that there have been twenty-three contemporary convictions, journalists almost never explain that twelve of those convictions took place for a crime that occurred outside the South, and almost none of the many articles written about the various southern civil rights murders have brought in the York case as comparison or context. Instead of raising questions about racial violence outside the South, national coverage of the York trials took pains to pointedly remind readers that York was only barely a northern city. "York lies near Gettysburg, close to the Mason-Dixon line," the *Washington Post* helpfully explained, while a *New York Times* feature described York as "nearer to Baltimore than to Philadelphia."[12] When one York native complained that all of the coverage of the Allen and Schaad trials "makes us look like we're a redneck town in Mississippi," it revealed his sense that the kind of racial violence that had occurred in York was only supposed to happen down South. Rather than leading to a discussion of racial segregation in the North, the workings of the racial caste system outside the South, or the role of violence, both official and unofficial, in maintaining racial order, the York case was instead marginalized or "southernized" so it could fit within the typical dichotomies of America's racial understanding: North versus South, de facto versus de jure, and pre-1970 and after.[13]

That typical framing would be adopted too by the federal government when it formally sanctioned the goal of seeking new trials as part of America's racial reckoning. In 2008, when the U.S. Congress approved legislation that authorized $10 million over ten years to fund units in the Department of Justice and the FBI dedicated to investigating racially motivated murders committed before 1970, it named the law the "Emmett Till Unsolved Civil Rights Crimes Act." The "Till Bill," as it was commonly described even after it became law, did not exclude murders committed outside the South. But the discussion of the bill in Congress and before the House Judiciary Committee made clear that most supporters understood racial violence as a southern phenomenon. Moreover, of the 125 murders that have been investigated under the act to date, all but two took place in the South.[14] The FBI's list of cases to reinvestigate failed to include those of victims who were killed by police during urban riots or those of murdered black radicals, such as slain Black Panther Fred Hampton. The framing of the law, historian David Garrow has publicly charged, "limits itself to the kinds of easy cases that fit our expectations and everyone can agree on—while ignoring the cases that cut against our wistful, nostalgic desire to see civil rights history as just a Deep South morality play featuring drooling racists versus Gandhian victims."[15] Naming the law after Emmett Till, the most iconic symbol of that Deep Southern morality play, framed racial violence as both a problem of the South and a problem of the past.

The exhumation of Emmett Till that June morning offers one final insight into the nature of America's racial reckoning: it has inspired debate and contestation over what kind of attention to the past the trials should generate and, ultimately, over what might constitute "justice" in response to the nation's racial history. The Reverend Jesse Jackson, who worked alongside Martin Luther King Jr. during the civil rights movement, responded to the exhumation of Till's body by asking why it had taken so long for authorities to act. "Justice delayed is justice denied," he charged, a claim that suggested whatever legal justice might come from reopening the case would not equal the injustice that the crime and the failure to punish anyone for it at the time represented. FBI agent Arthur Everett, who witnessed the exhumation as the assistant special agent in charge of Chicago's FBI office, offered a different message. For him, the exhumation signified "that even though the system of justice sometimes turns very slowly, it still turns." Justice delayed was not, in his view, a sign of justice denied.[16] Their disagreement illustrates the foundational questions raised by the contemporary reopening of civil rights–era murders: what exactly should constitute "justice" in terms of revisiting the nation's history of racial violence, and could a criminal prosecution deliver it?

Emmett Till was only one of over a hundred victims of racially motivated violence from the 1950s and 1960s whose murders have been reinvestigated in the years since 1990. These "cold cases" were either not fully solved at the time or perpetrators escaped punishment because of racism within the criminal justice system. They include the murders of activists who played a leading role in the civil rights struggle, those of individuals like Till whose deaths highlighted the brutality of the racial system in a way that galvanized the movement, as well as those who were targeted, sometimes randomly, in efforts to intimidate blacks and quell social protest. Most of the reopenings have not resulted in any formal charges. The passage of time, loss of evidence, and death of witnesses and suspects have made it difficult, if not impossible, to pursue further legal action in many cases. Only a handful of cases have proceeded from investigation to indictments. While *Racial Reckoning* analyzes the broader phenomenon of the reopening of civil rights cold cases, it necessarily pays particular attention to the eight southern cases that have proceeded furthest in the legal process to indictments and to resolution through trial or plea bargain.

In 1991, in the case that would spark a wave of reopenings, Mississippi state authorities indicted Byron De La Beckwith for the 1963 murder of Medgar Evers. Evers, a Mississippi native and a World War II veteran, served as the Mississippi state field secretary of the National Association of Colored People (NAACP). Over the course of his civil rights career, he fought to desegregate the University of Mississippi, led boycotts against Jim Crow stores in Jackson, organized local NAACP chapters, and investigated racial murders like that of Emmett Till. On July 12, 1963, just hours after President Kennedy addressed the nation to call for a national law to desegregate public accommodations, Evers was gunned down in his driveway as he returned home from an evening meeting. Two state juries failed to convict Byron De La Beckwith of murder charges in 1964. Thirty years later, in 1994, a Mississippi jury finally sent Beckwith to jail.

In 1998, another well-known civil rights murder came back into the courtroom when Mississippi authorities indicted three men for the 1966 killing of Vernon Dahmer. Dahmer, a successful black farmer and businessman in Forrest County, Mississippi, served as president of the local NAACP and was active in voter registration campaigns. Late on the evening of January 10, 1966, Klansmen angered by Dahmer's political activities and economic success came to Dahmer's farm and set his house on fire. Although Dahmer was able to hold off the attackers with a gun so his family could escape the burning house, he died of smoke inhalation the next day. The state tried thirteen men on charges of arson or murder in the 1960s, and won convictions against four of them. The federal government brought conspiracy charges against eleven men in relation to the murder; all of the federal trials ended in acquittals or hung juries. In 1998, the state brought new charges against three men involved in the killing, and Sam Bowers, the Klan leader who ordered the killing and who had escaped punishment in four different mistrials in the 1960s, was finally convicted of Dahmer's murder.[17]

That same year, authorities reopened the case of Rainey Pool, a fifty-four-year-old sharecropper from Humphries County, Mississippi. On April 12, 1970, a group of seven white men gathered at a bar beat Pool after one thought they saw him with his hand in a white man's truck. They then loaded an unconscious Pool into the truck, drove to the Sunflower River, and threw him in. In 1970, the state indicted four men for the killing, but the prosecutor dismissed the charges. In 1999, the state brought charges against all five living suspects in the case. One pled guilty to manslaughter and agreed to testify against the others, resulting in three convictions and one acquittal.

One of the most famous crimes of the civil rights era, the September 15, 1963, bombing of Birmingham's Sixteenth Street Baptist Church, resulted in trials in 2001 and 2002. Klansmen targeted the church because civil rights protestors were using it as a staging ground for marches demanding an end to segregation in Birmingham. The bomb went off on a Sunday morning, killing four black girls: Denise McNair, eleven years old, and Carole Robertson, Addie Mae Collins, and Cynthia Wesley, all fourteen. No one was charged in connection with the bombing in the 1960s. In 1977, a committed Alabama attorney general successfully prosecuted one of the bombers in the first effort to redress unresolved civil rights–era violence. Twenty-five years later, in 2001 and 2002, Alabama juries convicted Thomas Blanton and Bobby Frank Cherry for their roles in the church bombing.

Legal justice would come next for Ben Chester White, a sixty-seven-year-old Natchez, Mississippi, farmhand, killed by Klansmen in 1966. Described by relatives as a quiet and humble man who never missed work or church, White had steered clear of the civil rights marches, boycotts, and strikes that engulfed Natchez in 1965. But he became a target when local Klansmen decided something must be done to detract attention from activist James Meredith, who was conducting a Freedom March across Mississippi. The Klansmen hoped too that a brutal murder might lure Martin Luther King Jr. to Natchez so that they could assassinate him. So on June 10, 1966, James Jones, Claude Fuller, and Ernest Avants drove White to a bridge over a creek in the Homochitto National Forest. Fuller shot White at least fifteen times with a rifle; Avants then fired a single shotgun blast that blew off the top of White's head.[18] Jones's trial ended in a hung jury, while Fuller was charged but never tried. A state jury acquitted Avants of murder in 1966, but in 2003, he was convicted of federal charges of murder after authorities discovered that White had been killed on federal land.

The 1964 triple murder of three activists, one black and two white, in Neshoba County, Mississippi, became the subject of a 2005 trial. Mickey Schwerner, a native white New Yorker, came to Meridian in early 1964 with his wife, Rita, to direct the activities of the Congress of Racial Equality in one of their five Mississippi districts. James Chaney, a twenty-one-year-old black resident of Meridian, befriended the Schwerners and began working with them to organize voter registration campaigns and Freedom Schools. Andrew Goodman, a twenty-year-old white Queens College student, came south as a volunteer for Freedom Summer, a well-publicized coordinated campaign to register black voters in Mississippi in 1964. All three men died on June 21, 1964, when Klansmen angered by the voting campaign shot them at point-blank range. The state did nothing. Federal authorities brought conspiracy charges against eighteen men—the federal government could not charge them with murder—and seven were convicted in 1967. The state did not act until 2005, when a Mississippi jury convicted Edgar Ray Killen, one of the then ten remaining living suspects, of manslaughter.

In 2007, the murders of two Meadville, Mississippi, nineteen-year-olds killed just a few weeks before Goodman, Chaney, and Schwerner became the focus of the next contemporary trial. Charles Moore, a student at Alcorn College, and Henry Dee, a laborer at the local sawmill, were walking along the road on May 2, 1964, when some members of the local Ku Klux Klan decided that the pair might know something about rumors that blacks in the county were importing and stockpiling guns.[19] Klansmen abducted the two young men and took them to a secluded spot in Homochitto National Forest where they were beaten and interrogated. They then drove them to an isolated spot along the Louisiana side of the Mississippi river, chained them to engine blocks and railroad ties, and threw the teenagers—both still alive—into the river. Two months later, in July 1964, FBI agents combing the Mississippi looking for the bodies of Goodman, Chaney, and Schwerner would find the lower halves of Dee and Moore's bodies. Their torsos, still attached to the weights, would not be recovered until October. Neither state nor federal authorities pursued the case at the time. Thirty years later, state authorities could not assemble a strong enough case to try the remaining living suspects for murder, but federal prosecutors proved able to secure the conviction of James Ford Seale on federal charges related to the kidnapping of the teenagers.

In 2007, the same year as Seale's trial, Alabama authorities handed down an indictment in the case of Jimmie Lee Jackson, a twenty-six-year-old native of Marion, Alabama, who died after the police responded violently to civil rights demonstrations there in February 1965. Jackson had joined about five hundred others in a peaceful march to the county jail to protest the arrest of a civil rights worker. When police began to beat protestors, Jackson ran away with his mother and eighty-two-year-old grandfather. When an unarmed Jackson tried to shield his mother from being beaten by an Alabama state trooper, trooper James Bonard Fowler shot him twice in the stomach. Jackson died of his wounds two weeks later. His death inspired what would become one of the most famous events of the movement, the 1965 Selma to Montgomery march in support of voting rights. Fowler faced no consequences for the fatal shooting in 1965, but in 2007, a grand jury charged him with murder. In 2010, after a series of delays, Fowler avoided a trial by pleading guilty to the lesser charge of manslaughter and agreeing to serve a six-month jail sentence. As this book goes to press, the Jimmie Lee Jackson case stands as the last civil rights murder to result in new criminal charges.

Racial Reckoning explores the larger processes at work behind these contemporary legal actions and the more general impetus to reinvestigate and reopen civil rights–era murders. Any one of the contemporary trials could serve as the subject for an entire book, and indeed, a few of them have.[20] Even an excellent book focused on a single case, however, cannot fully explore the larger phenomenon of reopening cold civil rights murder cases, which has gained momentum and widening circles of support since the 1990s. While a more general analysis of the contemporary trials and reopenings sacrifices some of the fascinating and poignant details about any single crime that a more narrowly focused study would permit, it allows for an analysis of the patterns that emerge when these cases are brought together and put in conversation with each other.

That broader view offers evidence of why the racial terrorism of the civil rights era went unpunished and why it was possible to reopen investigations and bring new charges decades after the murders took place. It illustrates how the rules and format of a criminal trial shaped the portrayal of civil rights crimes in the courtroom and how the conventions of the media influenced the coverage of the contemporary trials. Most powerfully, it reveals how different groups—including prosecutors, southern political elites, journalists, relatives of victims, and contemporary racial justice activists—understood the importance of the legal process and the political stakes of shaping the kind of stories the trials told about the nation's racial history and its racial present. Those stories would help to define the nature of America's racial reckoning. They would determine whether the "bitter truths" of the nation's racial past would, as James Baldwin predicted, be turned into an "innocuous but piquant confection" or would instead lead Americans towards a deeper understanding of their history and a serious consideration of what might constitute racial justice in relation to it.

1

———————————

Crimes and Complicity during the Civil Rights Era

> Nations and communities, by the standards of conduct they
> establish and which their citizens stand up and speak up to
> defend, create the social atmosphere which can breed atroci-
> ties—or respect for fellow man.
>
> —Charles Morgan Jr., *A Time to Speak*, 1964

O N MARCH 15, 1965, Martin Luther King Jr. took the stage at the
packed Brown Chapel in Selma, Alabama, to deliver a eulogy for
Reverend James Reeb. Reeb, a thirty-five-year-old white Boston minister, had come to Alabama to participate in the 1965 voting rights march
from Selma to Montgomery. He died after being attacked by a group of
white men outside a Selma restaurant. Addressing the grieving audience
at the memorial ceremony, King insisted that the important question
was not *who* killed Reeb; the answer was clearly a "few sick, demented,
and misguided men who have the strange notion that you express dis-
sent through murder." The more desperate question, King argued, was
what killed James Reeb. "When we move from the who to the what, the
blame is wide and the responsibility grows." King had made this point
before. Two years earlier, at the funeral for the four young victims of
the 1963 Birmingham church bombing, he laid the responsibility for the
murders at the feet of ministers who remained silent in the face of injustice, politicians who spewed racial hatred, and a federal government
that compromised with segregationists. Society must focus not only on

catching the murderers, he insisted, but also "the system, the way of life, the philosophy which produced the murderers."[1]

Few whites in the South actually planted bombs in churches or committed acts of violence themselves. But as King recognized, the endemic violence of the civil rights era was not best understood as the acts of a few bad men. Those who bombed churches and beat and killed protestors were produced and enabled by a social and political environment in, and often beyond, the South that tolerated violence directed at blacks and their white allies. The terror campaign that took place in the South in the civil rights era reflected a much broader community willingness to condone violence in the name of defending and maintaining the system of segregation.

Most white Southerners refused to consider the ways in which the racial violence of the era was supported by the institutions of white society or the defensiveness of southern communities in response to any criticism of their racial practices. More typically, whites assumed the mantle of aggrieved victims, blaming protestors for instigating violence or outsiders for exposing it, rather than considering the ways in which they may have contributed to a political environment that cultivated it. "All of us are victims, and most of us are innocent victims," Birmingham mayor Albert Boutwell declared in the aftermath of the 1963 church bombing.[2] But the terror campaign that took place in the South in the 1950s and 1960s could not have continued without the tacit, and often open, support of police, political officials, community leaders, and white bystanders, who did little to rein in violence or to condemn murder.

In the twenty-first century, terrorism has become nearly synonymous with Islamic fundamentalism, associated almost unconsciously by many Americans with turbans and burkas. But for most of this nation's history, violence served as a crucial means to construct, maintain, and uphold white supremacy. During the colonial era, the violent treatment of blacks through whippings, brandings, torture, and castration—brutalization that by the mid-eighteenth century was no longer socially acceptable for whites—became one of the key markers of racial status and a cornerstone of slavery. After the Civil War, violence became one of the most important tools in southern whites' struggle to reassert economic and political domination over a newly freed labor force. Violence served not only as a tool for seeking power, but as a symbolic act with cultural meanings that helped whites "mark the inferiority of blackness."[3] Lynching, the form of racial violence most associated with the period between the end of Reconstruction and the beginnings of the civil rights movement, served as a practical and symbolic tool of racial domination. Lynchings offered theatrical spectacles of white supremacy, as whites claimed their economic, cultural, and social dominance over blacks through ritualized forms of mob violence often carried out in official public spaces. This was a systematic form of racial terrorism, an assertion of whites' power and their economic, social, political, and psychological domination over African Americans.[4]

In the 1950s and 1960s, the bombings, beatings, and murders of the civil rights era would, like earlier articulations of racial violence, serve both the instrumental and symbolic ends of asserting white supremacy at a time of racial flux and challenge. A host of changes in the wake of World War II threatened to undermine the South's system for maintaining white supremacy. Claims about the biological superiority of whites and of black genetic inferiority lost respectability and legitimacy in the wake of the racial genocide of the Holocaust. The mass migration of black Southerners to northern and western cities helped create a new political dynamic as more African Americans could vote and exert some influence on national political parties. The Cold War with the Soviet Union stifled many forms of radical activism, but it also held a mirror up to U.S. practices that failed to live up to the nation's rhetoric about democracy and equality. These intellectual, political, and global shifts would begin to undermine the legitimacy of an order based on essentialist claims of black inferiority and government-sanctioned discrimination, reflected in early Supreme Court rulings like the 1944 *Smith v. Allwright* decision, which ended the white primary, and *Brown v. Board of Education*, which declared segregation of public schools unconstitutional in 1954.

African Americans responded to the changing dynamics by intensifying their struggle to overturn the Jim Crow system and to gain full economic and political equality. Black veterans who came back to the South after World War II, a war supposedly fought to guarantee freedom around the world, became more insistent in their demands for racial equality and the right to vote. In Montgomery, Alabama, in 1955, Martin Luther King Jr. would emerge as a charismatic spokesperson and leader of what would become a nonviolent movement to win blacks' civil rights. Black students emerged as a powerful force for change in 1960 as they staged sit-ins across the South to demand the integration of stores and restaurants. The Student Nonviolent Coordinating Committee, borne of the sit-in movement, would pioneer new forms of community organizing in grassroots campaigns to challenge the racial caste system. African Americans outside the South joined in as well, demanding an end to discrimination in employment and housing, to segregation in schools, and to the violence inflicted on them by police in their everyday lives. Although not all of the goals of the movement would be achieved, by the mid-1960s protestors had succeeded in forcing passage of new federal laws that outlawed segregation in public accommodations and that protected blacks' right to vote.

Many whites fought back against this challenge to the laws and customs that protected their privileges. They staged political revolts, bolting from the Democratic Party to support their own third-party candidates. Community leaders organized themselves to resist what they saw as unwarranted federal encroachments on southern customs and traditions. Within months of the *Brown* decision, whites in Indianola, Mississippi, created the first White Citizens' Council, hoping "to stop desegregation before it begins."[5] Blacks who tried to start or revive branches of the NAACP, who fought for better conditions in their schools, or who tried to register to vote found themselves facing a newly energized wall of white resistance. And the Ku Klux Klan, a group that had been somewhat dormant in the South in previous decades, reemerged and gained new members as it took on the role of violent guardians of the racial status quo, men who would use whatever means necessary, from burning churches to bombing houses to murder, to protect the privileges accorded whites. White Southerners understood that economic intimidation, legal persecution, and political counterorganizing would not be enough to stem the burgeoning movement among blacks. As John Satterfield, the president of the Mississippi Bar Association, explained in a speech after the *Brown* decision, Southerners would likely have to turn to "the gun and torch" in order to protect segregation.[6]

No one knows for sure how many people were killed during the terror campaigns of the civil rights era. The FBI estimates that approximately one hundred people died in politically and racially motivated murders in the years from 1950 to 1970, while advocacy organizations point to as many as 200 killings that they believe were part of an effort to uphold and maintain the racial order in the South.[7] The scope and nature of civil rights–era violence has sometimes been hard to see, in part because the killings of the 1950s and 1960s took place at a time when the number of lynchings—a special category of racial crimes usually defined as ritualized public murder by a mob—was decreasing. The language of lynching had provided a familiar way to understand violence as a tool of racial intimidation and terror; without it, many Americans assumed that violence was falling out of favor as a means of enforcing racial subordination.[8] But like lynchings, the racial murders of the 1950s and '60s operated as a tool of racial terrorism, driven by a desire to stifle black protest and to uphold white supremacy. And although the number of perpetrators was fewer than in traditional lynchings, the relatively small group of men who committed most of these racially motivated murders could not have acted with such impunity without the broader implicit, and sometimes explicit, support of the white community.

The murders of the civil rights era were not random acts of violence, even if the victims were sometimes chosen randomly. Some of the killings are best understood as assassinations—the murder of someone regarded as a leader to further a political cause. Many of the people who first demanded political and economic equality in the years after World War II died at the hands of whites. A bomb placed under their house killed Harry Moore and his wife, Harriette, as they slept on Christmas night 1951. As leader of the Florida state NAACP, Moore had led efforts to register black voters and to equalize pay for black teachers. In a state with a very active Ku Klux Klan, Moore's activities were, in the words of a later Florida NAACP chapter president, "extremely suicidal."[9] Others who shared Moore's fate included voting rights advocate Reverend George Lee, who was murdered in Belzoni, Mississippi, in May 1955, and Lamar Smith, gunned down on the lawn of the local courthouse in Brookhaven, Mississippi, in 1955 after encouraging local blacks to vote. Herbert Lee, a local leader who helped the Student Nonviolent Coordinating Committee organize a voting rights campaign in Amite, Mississippi, died after being shot by a Mississippi state legislator in 1961. The lone witness to that murder was killed three years later. As the movement gained national attention and some legislative successes, more leaders would be assassinated, including not only Medgar Evers and Vernon Dahmer, but most famously, Dr. Martin Luther King Jr., gunned down on the balcony of a Memphis hotel in 1968.

Whites who came to the South to join the fight for civil rights in the 1960s, like slain Freedom Summer volunteers Mickey Schwerner and Andrew Goodman, frequently became targets of those fighting to maintain segregation. In April 1963, New York postal worker William Moore was gunned down on an Alabama highway while on a one-man crusade to hand the Mississippi governor a letter urging him to support integration. Two other white volunteers in the 1965 Selma-to-Montgomery voting rights march suffered the same fate as the murdered Boston minister James Reeb. Two weeks after Reeb's murder, Klansmen shot and killed Viola Liuzzo, a white housewife from Detroit, as she ferried marchers in her car between Selma and Montgomery. Jonathan Daniels, a young seminary student from Vermont who had also come for the Selma march, decided to stay in Alabama after the murders of Reeb and Liuzzo. He became the first white volunteer in Lowndes County, an area known for its particularly violent resistance to integration. On August 20, 1965, after being released from jail following a protest, Daniels and several other civil rights workers went to the general store in Fort Armstrong, Alabama, to buy some sodas. Tom Coleman, a local man rumored to be a member of the Klan, met them at the door and shot Daniels at point-blank range.

But it was not just those who were actively engaged in the fight against segregation who proved vulnerable. Many others got caught up in the violence unleashed by black protests and the challenges to the racial order. A group of white men in Gregg County in east Texas, intent on sending a message to blacks who might expect to go to school with whites as a result of the *Brown* decision, killed sixteen-year-old John Earl Reese when they sprayed gunfire at a local café crowded with dancing black teenagers one night in October 1955. In 1963, on the same day four black girls died in the Birmingham church bombing, two other black teenagers were killed in Birmingham. Two white teenagers seeking to "scare" someone on their way home from a segregationist rally shot and killed thirteen-year-old Virgil Ware as he rode on the handlebars of his brother's bike.[10] Birmingham police shot sixteen-year-old Johnny Robinson in the back when they fired into a crowd of black teenagers who were throwing stones at a white segregationist's car.

Birmingham authorities remove the body of one of the four girls killed in the bombing of the Sixteenth Street Baptist Church on September 15, 1963. That bombing, like many other acts of racial terror in the 1950s and 1960s, aimed to suppress civil rights protest. (AP Photo)

An unknown number of African Americans became victims of Klan "nightriders," Klansmen who went out at night looking to terrorize black communities. Perhaps the best-known victim of nightriders was Lemuel Penn, a forty-nine-year-old army reservist from Washington, D.C., who was killed on July 11, 1964, while driving back home from two weeks of reserve training at Fort Benning, Georgia. Penn, an assistant superintendent of schools in D.C., had not left the army base during his two-week stay specifically because he wanted to avoid any "racial unpleasantness." Klansmen saw Penn and his two companions on the road and targeted them because of their Washington, D.C., license plates. They shot into the car, one later explained, because they thought that the "out-of-town niggers" might be there to stir up trouble. "We thought he might've been one of President Johnson's boys."[11] Other victims of nightriders included Willie Brewster, gunned down on a July night in 1965 on his way home from his shift at an Anniston, Alabama, foundry, and Johnnie

Mae Chappell, a mother of ten shot by white men in a passing car as she walked along the road in Florida in 1964.

Blacks perceived as transgressing customary racial boundaries—like the rules that barred any intimacy between black men and white women, or customs that demanded blacks be subservient or that they not seek jobs traditionally reserved for whites—also became common victims of violent retaliation, reflecting the ways in which violence served as a tool of racial and social control to maintain whites' status and privilege. Emmett Till's murderers defended their brutal slaying of the teenager on the grounds that they needed to make an example of what happened to blacks who didn't remember their place. "It was time a few people got put on notice," one of them insisted, " . . . just so everybody can know how me and my folks stand."[12] Two years after Till's 1955 murder, Klansmen forced twenty-five-year-old truck driver Willie Edwards to jump to his death off an Alabama bridge because they mistakenly believed he was having an affair with a white woman. Oneal Moore and Wharlest Jackson became targets after taking jobs that had traditionally been reserved for whites. Moore, killed in a drive-by shooting in 1965, was the first black deputy sheriff appointed in Washington Parish, Louisiana, while Jackson died in a car bombing in Natchez, Mississippi, in 1967 after accepting a promotion at the tire and rubber plant where he worked. Frank Morris, a black man who ran his own shoe-repair shop in Ferriday, Louisiana, died in 1964 after two men set his shop on fire and prevented him from exiting. Morris had refused to fix shoes for a white man who had not paid him for earlier work.[13]

This very incomplete list of the victims of violence does not begin to express the extent to which the "gun and torch" was used to shore up segregation and the southern racial order as it crumbled under outside pressures and intensified activism. The pervasive violence of these years affected all African Americans, not just those who openly challenged the racial system. As the Student Nonviolent Coordinating Committee Freedom Singers recognized in a song written after the FBI discovered three other black bodies in the Mississippi River while searching for those of Chaney, Goodman, and Schwerner, anyone with black skin was vulnerable to the terror campaign. In the Mississippi River, "you can count them one by one, it may be your son," they sang. "You can count them two by two, it may be me or you."[14] And numbers cannot fully convey what it felt like to live under the weight of this violence, a time when, as the widow of slain civil rights leader Medgar Evers explained, you were "afraid to sit in your living room on a sofa because there was a window." It was, one white Mississippi newspaperman noted in 1955, an era of "naked racially-inspired terror."[15] As a tool of terror, racial violence cut a wide swath.

The brute force behind much of the racial terrorism of the civil rights era came from a relatively small group of men, many of whom were members of the white supremacist group the Ku Klux Klan. White Tennesseans founded the Klan after the Civil War as they sought to restore political and economic control over blacks. The organization's popularity waxed and waned in subsequent decades, but it would reemerge as a major force in the South when segregation was threatened after World War II. A diffuse organization, the Klan had as many as nineteen different member groups operating in southern states by the late 1950s. The Klan had a public, palpable presence in many southern communities; sociologist David Cunningham notes that in 1960s North Carolina, there was a Klan rally somewhere in the state almost every night. In Mississippi, local Klan units, or Klaverns, could be found in more than fifty of the state's eighty-two counties by the early 1960s.[16]

These various Klan organizations differed in their approaches to violence. Some, like the United Klans of America (UKA), a group based in Tuscaloosa, Alabama, engaged in large public rallies and claimed to be nonviolent, but pointedly looked the other way when affiliated Klaverns chose to commit bombing and murders. UKA members murdered Viola Liuzzo and Lemuel Penn, among many others.[17] The White Knights of the Ku Klux Klan, a branch of the Klan headquartered in Laurel, Mississippi, eschewed public rallies in favor of secrecy. Sam Bowers, a thirty-nine-year-old World War II navy veteran who had studied engineering at Tulane and USC, founded the White Knights in 1964. Bowers earned his living running Sambo Amusements, a vending machine business. But his real love was the Klan, and his real job, as he saw it, was to preserve the white man's birthright. Described by one journalist as a "Klan leader out of central casting," Bowers descended from some of the South's best families—one grandfather had been a wealthy planter in Louisiana and another served as a congressman in Mississippi's Seventh District in the early twentieth century. Bowers ran the White Knights like a hierarchical military organization. He divided racial violence into four categories, with the most extreme being the third (arson) and the fourth (elimination), and made clear that he had to personally approve any acts of murder. Eliminations, he told his followers, should be done without malice, in silence, as a Christian act. As head of the White Knights, Bowers oversaw as many as three hundred bombings and assaults, as well as nine murders, including those of Mickey Schwerner and Vernon Dahmer.[18]

Some of the worst violence was carried out by secret Klan splinter groups, which consisted of small groups of men who had insulated themselves from the larger Klan in order to maintain secrecy about their acts of arson, bombings, beatings, and killings. The Cahaba Boys, a separate secret group in Birmingham that decided the mainstream Klan was not violent enough, committed many of the bombings that made Birmingham infamous, including the Sixteenth Street Baptist Church bombing. In the area around Athens, Georgia, a group of probably fewer than thirty Klansmen terrorized the local population; nightriders there went out about three nights a week in 1964. The Silver Dollar Group, a small group of Klansmen who identified themselves by carrying silver dollars minted in their birth years, committed many of the murders in southwest Mississippi and Louisiana, including those of Frank Morris and Wharlest Jackson.[19]

Not everyone who committed murder in the name of white supremacy was an active Klan member. J. W. Milam and Roy Bryant, who murdered Emmett Till in 1955, did not belong to the Klan, which did not become active in Mississippi until some time later. Byron De La Beckwith joined the Klan only after he murdered Medgar Evers, although rumors persisted that the Klan had ordered Evers's murder.[20] Yet whether officially Klan members or not, the white men behind the region's racial violence feared the loss of the world they knew as they saw blacks challenging the status quo and demanding a political voice and economic opportunity. They blamed Communists and outside agitators for riling up local blacks and fomenting disorder. Some wrote letters to their local papers railing about the Communist conspiracy to integrate the schools and the dangers of racial "mongrelization." And, most tellingly, they understood their terror tactics as justified to stem the tide of change. These were not men given to remorse, even when violence resulted in the death of children. As a speaker at a Florida Klan rally declared in 1964, whoever had planted the bomb in Birmingham that killed four black girls deserved a medal. "When I go out to kill rattlesnakes, I don't make no difference between little rattlesnakes and big rattlesnakes," he told the crowd. "I say, good for whoever planted the bomb."[21]

Although the Klan stood out for its rituals and white robes, it represented an extreme form of southern nationalism that was widely shared. Historian Jeff Woods argues that white southern identity had "at its core a regional desire to protect the southern way of life" from outside threats. In the 1950s and the first half of the 1960s, the "black menace," often coupled with a sense of a "red menace," would be viewed by many whites as powerful threats to a society that had long held that white rule was necessary for civic peace. Many white Southerners saw the civil rights movement as a threat to the existing order, to white authority, and to an economic system that had long relied on a subordinate black labor force. Many also felt that the real instigators of the protests were Communists who wanted to overthrow the United States or outside agitators who secretly favored racial amalgamation. The black protests taking place in the midst of a tense Cold War with the Soviet Union only fueled Southerners' fears that "the forces of Communism and integration had signed a devil's pact to destroy the region's way of life."[22] It was a mindset that helped justify a violent response to the perceived threat presented by black activism.

Southern law enforcement agencies certainly shared this mindset. For many southern police officers, county sheriffs, and state security forces, black protest posed a far greater threat to the social order than any violence perpetrated by whites to uphold the caste system. Since the beginnings of the Jim Crow era, the police had served as the guardians of the socio-legal order; their main function was not to protect blacks from harm but to keep blacks in their place.[23] Civil rights activists knew all too well that police forces throughout the South shared the Klan's goal of maintaining segregation and preserving white supremacy. The line between extralegal enforcement of racial mores undertaken by the Klan and the "legal" maintenance of white supremacy undertaken by police was muddy at best.

Many murders from this era can in fact be traced back to sheriffs and police officers who beat and killed blacks they viewed as insubordinate.

From the fire hoses and snarling dogs that Birmingham's Bull Conner turned on protestors there, it was a short step to murder. In the four years Lawrence Rainey served as a police officer in Philadelphia, Mississippi before becoming the sheriff of Neshoba County, he shot and killed two black men. In 1959, Rainey killed Luther Jackson after ordering him out of his car. Rainey claimed a drunken Jackson lunged at him, a charge that an eyewitness denied. Three years later, Rainey killed a young handcuffed black man sitting in the back of his patrol car. Coroner's juries ruled both deaths as "justifiable homicides." In 1963, Neshoba county voters elected Rainey sheriff; he campaigned as "the man who can cope with any situations that may arise." Rainey would later be alleged to have conspired in the 1964 murders of Goodman, Chaney, and Schwerner. The deputy sheriff in Concordia Parish, Louisiana, meanwhile, was linked by the FBI to two racially motivated murders, along with numerous other acts of police brutality. FBI agents viewed the corruption in the Concordia Parish sheriff's office as the major cause of violence there; one agent who worked there in 1965 described it as "a maggot-infested mess."[24]

That police would react with violence to black protest was taken for granted. When confrontations erupted between police and student demonstrators at Jackson State College (now Jackson State University) in 1967, Jackson police and the Mississippi Highway Patrol used live ammunition to quell student protest, fatally shooting twenty-two-year-old bystander Ben Brown. The investigation into the shooting lasted only a week and resulted in no charges. When Alabama State police officer James Fowler shot and killed an unarmed Jimmie Lee Jackson during a civil rights demonstration in Marion, Alabama, in 1965, he wasn't even reprimanded.[25] Police brutality and the racial terror campaign of the Klan blended rather seamlessly.

Many local police departments, moreover, had ties to the Klan. In Natchez, in Neshoba County, in Birmingham, Alabama—and the list goes on—members of the county sheriff's office or the local police department belonged to the Klan. Both of the two paid Neshoba County law officers belonged to the Klan. In southwest Mississippi, the Ku Klux Klan managed to infiltrate police forces in every county. Informants reported that the sheriffs of Adams County and Franklin County were both Klan members.[26] Klansmen not surprisingly saw the police as allies in their struggle to contain black protest. When Charles Moore and Henry Dee, subjects of a brutal Klan interrogation about blacks stockpiling guns, placated their tormentors by telling them that the guns were being hidden at a local church, Klansmen took the information to the sheriff, who joined them in a fruitless search of the building. At the time, the two young men were still alive, but the sheriff did not investigate where the Klansmen had gotten their information.[27]

Law enforcement could also use its official position to provide information and assistance to the Klan. Edgar Ray Killen, who would eventually be tried for coordinating the murders of James Chaney, Andrew Goodman, and Mickey Schwerner, described it as a "policy" for the police in Neshoba County to "call the boys" when they arrested blacks. "If it was our local boys, our own local niggers," explained Killen, "they'd let the boys beat their . . . butts good." Neshoba County deputy sheriff Cecil Price made such a call after he arrested Goodman, Chaney, and Schwerner on June 21, 1964, allegedly for speeding, while they were driving back to Meridian after inspecting a burned church. Price got in touch with Killen and held the three men while Killen organized a response. Late that night, Price released the three men, only to arrest them again on a deserted highway in order to turn them over to waiting Klansmen. Although Price insisted that he had thought the Klan intended only to whip the three men, not to murder them, he eventually admitted to witnessing the murders and to helping the Klansmen cover up evidence of the crime.[28]

Even when they were not directly involved in committing racial violence, police made it clear they condoned violence against blacks by ignoring or dismissing it. The fires that engulfed five black churches in Albany, Georgia, used for voting registration rallies were due to lightning, claimed the sheriff. Those who wanted to know who was responsible for shooting and wounding two young black women working on the voting registration campaign in Ruleville in 1962 should investigate activists who were trying to "create trouble," the sheriff argued. And even as McComb, Mississippi, witnessed a spree of fifteen bombings in less than five months in 1964, the sheriff accused one victim of bombing her own home while her children were inside.[29]

By ignoring the violence that was taking place around them, local police sent a clear signal to the Klan and other like-minded individuals that they could use whatever means they chose to preserve white supremacy. Inaction encouraged the Klan to escalate their campaign of violence. Eleven other racially motivated bombings that had not resulted in fatalities preceded the bombing that killed Harry and Harriette Moore in 1951. Similarly, the over two dozen unsolved bombings in Birmingham that police had not fully investigated created the environment for the Sixteenth Street Baptist Church bombing in 1963. And perhaps if police had actually investigated the beatings and whippings of sixteen black men that preceded the beating and murder of Charles Moore and Henry Dee, the men who killed them would have been more circumspect about their use of violence. But local police had done nothing. Cecil Briggs, the minister whose church was searched by police based on the information Dee and Moore fabricated to try to stop their beating, lamented in his journal that no arrests had been made for any of the earlier reports of violence, "although each of them was reported to law officers of Franklin County, Miss."[30] No arrests would be made after the murders of Dee and Moore, either. The police either allowed the Klan to terrorize blacks or, worse, actively helped them to do so.

Just as Klan violence could not have continued unabated without the implicit, or even open, permission of law enforcement, neither could the police inaction and active complicity with the Klan occur without tacit approval from higher authorities. The intransigence of local law officials who allowed Klan violence to continue was enabled by the support of others who were more powerful than local sheriffs or city police. In his history of white Southerners in the civil rights era, Jason Sokol notes that "a cadre of powerful men stood behind every brutal southern sheriff and every vicious purveyor of prejudice. Politicians, businessmen, lawyers, professors, and otherwise 'respectable' leaders of southern communities gave the requisite winks and nods to the enforcers of segregation—and quite often they gave much more." Karl Fleming, a *Newsweek* reporter stationed in Atlanta in the 1960s, quickly found out that the local police "were only as good—or bad—as their bosses—the white power structure." Cops, Klansmen, and "ordinary racists" behaved brutally towards blacks only "when they had the tacit or real approval—and sometimes active encouragement—from political and business leaders."[31] Southerners from all social and economic classes shared the goal of protecting the southern way of life.

Community and business leaders in the South responded quickly to what they saw as the threat to segregation, founding the new organization the White Citizens' Council (later shortened to the Citizens' Council or CC) in 1954 to bring community elites together with the goal of preventing integration in the schools and elsewhere, theoretically without resorting to violence. The CC preferred more "respectable" means of pressuring local blacks who sought change, particularly relying on economic intimidation to encourage those who fought the status quo to give up and, ideally, leave town. The CC spread rapidly throughout the South. By 1956, Mississippi's statewide Association of Citizens' Councils had perhaps 65,000 members; the Citizens' Council of America became a national organization that same year. By 1957, it could count 250,000 to 300,000 members in its five hundred local chapters across the region.[32]

The Citizens' Councils relied on a more elite constituency than the Klan, and they eschewed the Klan's reliance on brute violence, preferring economic and political intimidation as a way to keep local blacks in check. But they shared the Klan's broad goal of defending white supremacy, and at least some members recognized that their more "respectable" resistance depended on the violence performed by groups like the Klan. As one Citizens' Council leader noted during a debate about how to prevent integration at a local swimming pool, if blacks got near the pool, "we can let some redneck take care of him for us." This kind of symbiotic relationship could serve both racial vigilantes and local elites. In her sweeping work on Birmingham during the civil rights era, Diane McWhorter traces how the city's elite sought to maintain their economic and racial supremacy through vigilantism. She discovered "that the elite establishment of the city itself had nurtured the Ku Klux Klan"; they provided the "respectable underpinnings of their violent resistance." The Citizens' Councils' efforts "to create a resistance mentality through extralegal as well as legal means," historian Neil McMillen concludes, made it "more than a little accountable" for the racial turmoil of the period.[33]

Local and state politicians too must be held accountable for the ways in which their actions heightened resistance and excused racial terrorism. For much of the 1950s and 1960s, political authorities in southern states failed to rein in or criticize the violence directed at African Americans. Their rhetoric and policies helped fan the flames of racial hatred, further contributing to an atmosphere of racial terror. In the wake of the

1954 *Brown* decision, political rhetoric surrounding race became more extreme as politicians tried to outdo each other in their segregation-ist credentials.[34] In Arkansas, former moderate governor Orval Faubus insisted that even the token integration of Little Rock's Central High in 1955 would lead to bloodshed and violence, statements that galvanized a mob to threaten the nine students who had been chosen to integrate the school. In Alabama, after the gubernatorial candidate endorsed by the Klan defeated a more moderate George Wallace in 1958, Wallace learned his lesson. "No other son-of-a-bitch will ever outnigger me again," he declared after his loss.[35] In 1962, Wallace ran as a staunch segregationist, infamously pledging to uphold "segregation today, seg-regation tomorrow, segregation forever" in his inaugural address. Ross Barnett, governor of Mississippi between 1960 and 1964 and perhaps the most extreme segregationist politician of the era, urged citizens of Mississippi to ignore federal court orders and to stand up against fed-eral encroachment. He publicly defied the Supreme Court in resisting the court-ordered desegregation of the University of Mississippi in 1962. Through their actions and rhetoric, southern politicians made clear that extreme measures were justified in the defense of segregation.

Many states, in fact, created state-funded agencies specifically dedi-cated to the preservation of segregation. Mississippi led the way with the creation of the Mississippi Sovereignty Commission (MSC) in 1956. The MSC hired investigators and informants to infiltrate civil rights orga-nizations, harass activists, and monitor challenges to the racial status quo. It also launched an ambitious public relations campaign to defend Mississippi and its racial practices to outsiders. When hardliner Ross Bar-nett assumed the governorship of Mississippi, the MSC became closely linked with the Citizens' Council; from 1959 until the end of 1964, the MSC funneled nearly $200,000 in state funds to the private prosegre-gation organization. In Alabama, George Wallace created both the Ala-bama Peace Commission and the Alabama Sovereignty Commission to investigate "all known integrationists and subversives." Staff from the sovereignty commission traveled the state telling local officials how best to prevent blacks from registering to vote.[36]

The work of government agencies like the Mississippi Sovereignty Commission contributed to an environment that bred violent resistance to the black struggle by targeting and seeking to intimidate those who were fighting for integration. Medgar Evers died at the hands of rogue killer Byron De La Beckwith, but the MSC had long kept Evers under surveillance, hoping to catch him violating state law. Evers's assassin had in fact applied for a job as an MSC investigator in 1956, claiming that he was qualified because of his war record and his membership on the Greenwood Citizens' Council and because he was "expert with a pistol, good with a rifle and fair with a shotgun—and—RABID ON THE SUBJECT OF SEGREGATION."[37] The Sovereignty Commission regularly insisted that civil rights groups were themselves responsible for acts of violence directed at blacks, and MSC investigators sometimes provided local law enforcement the tools they needed to harass civil rights workers. Neshoba County sheriff Cecil Price could be on the lookout for Mickey Schwerner because the MSC had sent his office a dossier that included Schwerner's address, telephone number, car license plate number, and driver's license number.[38] Instead of trying to put a stop to rampant violence in their state, officials at the MSC conducted public relations campaigns to discredit Mississippi's critics. When a civil rights volunteer appeared on a Seattle television talk show and spoke about the murders of two black men during Freedom Summer, for example, the Sovereignty Commission retained an attorney to contest what they called "false information" and pressured the station to give equal time to state officials to "offset" the claims.[39]

With their racist rhetoric and their public policies aimed at stifling black protest, political leaders in the South created an environment ripe for political violence and racial terrorism. Many followed the example of southern police who refused to even recognize that crimes had been committed when whites targeted blacks. When a rash of bombings struck McComb, Mississippi, the mayor wondered whether "the incidents" were "instigated by white or colored." When Goodman, Chaney, and Schwerner disappeared in Neshoba County, Mississippi Governor Paul Johnson insisted that "any incident of strife or civil disorder comes from the professional visiting troublemaker" and claimed that the whole thing was likely a publicity stunt undertaken by civil rights groups to bring attention to Freedom Summer. For all he knew, he told reporters, the three men "could be in Cuba," in a not-so-subtle attempt to tar the civil rights struggle with communism.[40] Even after the trio's bodies were finally found, the state remained reluctant to admit they had been murdered. When Mickey Schwerner's widow, Rita, received a death certificate from the state several months after his murder, it declared the cause of death unknown. Such acts and rhetoric, as civil rights activists charged, created "a moral climate" that nurtured the Klan.[41]

The responsibility for that "moral climate" lay not just with the police who actively aided and abetted the Klan or with elected political leaders whose rhetoric suggested that segregation must be defended at all costs. It lay too with the broader white community—the religious leaders who failed to condemn racial violence, the journalists who spouted racial hatred, and ultimately white community members who ostracized those who advocated for change. The Klan may have been extreme in their beliefs, but their views resonated with many Southerners who never belonged to the organization. Racial violence, one white ally of the movement charged, was the product of a "community heritage of racial intolerance," a heritage that led whites to believe that they were superior to blacks and deserved to be treated as such.[42]

Whites in Montgomery, Alabama, protest court-ordered school integration in September 1963. Protestors' signs reflect the frequent linking of civil rights and communism. (Flip Schulke/Corbis)

Religious leaders, despite their positions as moral guardians, did little to challenge the violent status quo in the 1950s and 1960s. Most religious leaders and the major white congregations in the region actively supported segregation, and the handful of white southern clergy who expressed support for the movement did not last long in their posts. The Southern Baptist Convention, the largest denominational institution in the South, feared that civil rights protests fostered disorder and a dangerous disrespect for authority. Like many southern whites, Baptist leaders worried that the black protests were part of a larger Communist plot to undermine southern society. They were particularly critical of Martin Luther King Jr. and of northern clergymen who insisted that the struggle for civil rights should be understood as a Christian movement seeking justice. These misguided activist ministers, Baptist leaders argued, had forgotten that the path to righteousness was individual salvation of souls, not political or civil rights.[43]

With a handful of exceptions, southern clergy failed to take a strong public stand against racial terrorism. Some suggested that activists themselves should be held responsible for fostering disorder that ended in violence. An Alabama Baptist pastor thus argued that Martin Luther King Jr. "loaded the gun of his own destruction by making himself the symbol of resistance to law and order." Others simply remained silent. Charles Marsh, who grew up in Laurel, Mississippi—the hometown of Sam Bowers—recalled that while his minister father loathed the Klan, he never talked about it in his sermons. The terror and violence were, "to a good Baptist preacher like him, finally matters of politics, having little or nothing to do with the spiritual geography of a pilgrim's journey to Paradise." Similarly, when an old seminary school friend asked Douglas Hudgins, the pastor of the largest Baptist church in Jackson, Mississippi, how the city could be so violent when he was preaching the gospel every Sunday, Hudgins insisted that Baptists had "no business tinkering in political matters." Hudgins, widely recognized as the leader of the state's most influential religious institution, offered only a tepid statement when Klan members bombed the home of a Jackson rabbi in 1967. Rabbi Perry Nussbaum, incensed after the bombing, held Christian leaders like Hudgins who had not criticized the atmosphere of violence in Mississippi as responsible for the crime as the Klansmen who had placed the bomb.[44]

Few southern journalists proved willing to publicly condemn the racial terror campaign either. While there were a perhaps a dozen southern newspapers that supported gradual integration, most southern newspapers provided little leadership on issues of race, either because they feared offending their white customer base or, more commonly, because editors or publishers shared a desire to protect segregation. The publishers of two of the South's major papers, the *Clarion-Ledger* of Jackson and the *Jackson Daily News*, belonged to the Citizens' Council, while the editor of the *Franklin Advocate* in Franklin, Mississippi, served as the publicity director for Americans for the Preservation of the White Race, a group funded by the Ku Klux Klan.[45]

Not surprisingly, many southern newspapers reflected the racist orthodoxy of the era, adding to the volatile environment that encouraged a violent response to threats to the status quo. The *Clarion-Ledger* and other papers described civil rights activists as "race-mixing invaders" and "dirty beatniks." They printed racist propaganda provided to them by the Mississippi Sovereignty Commission and agreed to requests by the MSC not to run certain stories about racial violence that might scare potential investors from outside the state. Newspapers reacted defensively when outsiders questioned or criticized the South's racial practices. When NAACP Executive Secretary Roy Wilkins described Emmett Till's murder as a racially motivated lynching, the local media charged the NAACP with fanning the flames of racial hatred for its own gain and trying to "create a false impression by labeling it as an act of race hatred which whites in Mississippi might condone." Ten years later, the *Meridian Star* insisted that civil rights organizations should be considered at least partially responsible for the Goodman, Chaney, and Schwerner murders "inasmuch as they care nothing for how much violence they provoke."[46] Hodding Carter III, the son of one of the few racially moderate southern newspaper editors, condemned much of the coverage of southern papers during the movement. "There was an absolute willingness to submerge all journalism values in service of the status quo," he claimed.[47]

Such coverage undoubtedly played a role in shaping community views of the violence directed at blacks. Charles Marsh, a ten-year-old in 1967, recalled learning from the local paper in Laurel, Mississippi, that Communists, Leninists, beatniks, and subversives had invaded the state. Birmingham lawyer Charles Morgan, a racial moderate who would eventually be driven from Birmingham by death threats after repeatedly defending those advocating for civil rights, argued that the media skewed its coverage so as not to offend the "extremist elements" in Birmingham. As a result, the "most extreme elements" were able to set "the standards for community acceptance or rejection of information and even entertainment."[48] The southern press did not directly engage in racial violence, but their coverage helped create a climate where it could thrive.

Of course, institutions like the church and the press reflect, to some extent, the mindset and values of the people in their communities. Most white Southerners did not belong to the Klan or even to the Citizens' Councils, but they elected the political leaders who condoned violence; they bought the newspapers that blamed protestors; and they harassed and ostracized whites who dared to criticize segregation. While white Southerners might recoil at the brutal crimes committed by the Klan, they generally agreed with the Klan's basic goals to maintain the racial status quo and to prevent integration. White Southerners might disagree about what methods should be used to maintain white supremacy, but precious few disagreed about the importance of preserving their status and privilege; the threat represented by black protest only made whites more inclined to accept violent acts like those of the Klan. David Chalmers suggests that in the 1950s and '60s "the enhanced specter of a black menace gave the Klan a degree of approval that it had lacked for many years," a view echoed by *New York Times* reporter Claude Sitton in a 1963 feature on race relations in Mississippi. "In the current emotional atmosphere the unscrupulous have virtual immunity so long as they act in the name of segregation," Sitton wrote. "Charlatans who would be laughed off the streets in normal times find a receptive audience."[49] Instead of challenging Klansmen who committed murder, local whites ostracized those few whites willing to speak out against racial violence or to voice even hesitant support for civil rights.

When civil rights crimes attracted attention or criticism from outside the South, communities typically responded defensively, circling the wagons and rallying behind the men believed responsible. When Emmett Till was killed, local whites initially distanced themselves from the accused murderers. The murder, one newspaper declared, was the work of "sick"

men with "depraved minds" who "did not represent or reflect a majority
sentiment in the community."[50] But when the crime attracted national
attention and some criticized it as a lynching, the community quickly ral-
lied to support the two men accused of the crime. Newspapers shifted their
sympathy to J. W. Milam and Roy Bryant, $10,000 poured into a campaign
to raise funds for the defense, and all five of the county's defense lawyers—
men who had originally refused to take the case—agreed to represent the
two accused. As Hugh Whitaker put it in his exhaustively researched 1963
thesis on the Till case, the "power structure of Tallahatchie County" had
"decided to 'go to bat'" for Milam and Bryant.[51] Byron De La Beckwith, the
man accused of killing Medgar Evers, was embraced by the larger white
community as well. While in a prison cell awaiting his trial, Beckwith was
treated "like visiting royalty," brought special meals by housewives, sent
boxes of cigars, and allowed to keep a TV in his cell. A group of prominent
citizens of Greenwood, Beckwith's hometown, founded the White Citizen's Legal Fund to raise money for his defense, and when he returned
home after a mistrial, it was an occasion for celebration.[52]

Instead of condemning murder, white communities turned on the
few whites who challenged the racial status quo. Ira Harkey, the editor and publisher of the Pascagoula, Mississippi, *Chronicle-Star* and the
only newspaper editor in all of Mississippi who called himself an "inte-
grationist," discovered firsthand what happened to whites who criticized segregation. In 1962, Harkey, who had written several editorials
supporting the integration of the University of Mississippi, became the
target of a group of men, led by the sheriff, who had taken it upon
themselves to rid Pascagoula of any "niggerlovers." Harkey's critics shot
up the newspaper's office, threatened the paper's advertisers until they
dropped their ads, and roughed up newspaper delivery boys. Harkey
found that "there was no power to which I could turn for help." Local
leaders refused to speak out in his defense, police refused to provide protection to the newspaper offices, and, although advertisers and subscrib-
ers eventually returned, Harkey himself remained a social pariah. By
July 1963, Harkey had left his position with the *Chronicle-Star*, despite
winning national accolades for his coverage, including a Pulitzer Prize.
"We failed to arouse anyone to the danger of allowing organized terrorists to exercise hegemony over the community," Harkey later lamented.
He was appalled that no political, business, or religious leaders had stood

In this cartoon, the Council of Federated Organizations, the civil rights umbrella group that sponsored Freedom Summer, ridicules white Southerners for criticizing northern racial practices while ignoring the racial violence in their own backyard. "Ain't it awful what's going on up the'ah in New Yawk," one white man says to another even as they stand behind three coffins labeled with the names of Goodman, Chaney, and Schwerner. The image in the top corner shows three pairs of hands—representing the three slain workers—breaking chains and encouraging blacks to vote. (Zeman Freedom Summer Collection, McCain Library and Archives, University of Southern Mississippi)

up to suggest that it was dangerous for Pascagoula to allow itself "to be ruled by the least responsible and most vicious element among its citizenry." Their silence ensured that those who terrorized Harkey could operate freely and openly.[53]

Many other whites across the South who dared to even question the unyielding defense of segregation shared Harkey's fate. Juliette Morgan, one of the handful of whites who publicly supported the Montgomery Bus Boycott, killed herself after she lost her job and became the target of threatening phone calls.[54] When the family of 1964's Miss Mississippi overstepped traditional racial boundaries by inviting white civil rights volunteers to dinner in an effort to preserve peace in the community, they became the subject of a vicious intimidation campaign. As was the case for Ira Harkey, no one came to their defense, not "their newspaper editor friend, the mayor, the police chief, the sheriff, their business friends, their Country Club friends."[55] The family soon moved. Florence Mars, a longtime resident of Neshoba County, Mississippi, became a target after she cooperated with the FBI investigation into the murders of James Chaney, Andrew Goodman, and Mickey Schwerner. The Klan led a successful boycott of her business and turned the community and her church against her. The atmosphere in Neshoba County, Mars wrote in 1965, "made me understand how Nazi Germany was possible."[56] The willingness to cast out whites who dared to question the violent defense of segregation suggests the depth of many whites' commitment to protecting a southern way of life premised on white privilege.

That Florence Mars faced ostracism after speaking with the FBI attests to the fact that the federal government was not completely absent in the South. Although federal authorities would have preferred to stay out of the southern struggle, they often found themselves forced to take steps to maintain order and to uphold federal law. Protestors, after all, were fighting for basic constitutional rights. Civil rights activists tried to pressure the federal government to uphold the law by targeting areas where the courts had ruled in their favor. The 1961 Freedom Rides, for example, were designed to test a court ruling that had struck down segregation in interstate transportation. Politicians outside the South, moreover, had to answer to the growing number of black voters living in states where they could vote. And the federal government had broader interests to keep in mind, like how incidents of racial violence made the United States look on the international stage. All of these concerns contributed to occasional decisions by President Eisenhower and President Kennedy to send federal forces to protect protestors, as Kennedy did when he ordered federal marshals to quell violence against Freedom Riders in 1961.

But until at least the mid-1960s, federal authorities proved unwilling to take the kind of steps that would have been necessary to protect blacks from racial terrorism, especially the ongoing and everyday violence that took place in the South. The FBI frequently came in to investigate racially motivated killings, but those investigations did little to prevent racial violence or help those who were threatened by it. The FBI had only limited jurisdiction in most cases and often refused to become involved if jurisdiction was not clear. When friends and relatives of Emmett Till went to the FBI in Chicago only four hours after he was kidnapped—and probably while Till was still alive—they were told that unless Till was brought by his kidnappers across state lines, there was nothing that federal authorities could do.[57]

While federal authorities did not have free rein to prevent racial terrorism, their inaction attested to a broadly shared racial consensus. An agency with its own history of racist exclusions, the FBI shared the larger national tendency to compromise with southern white supremacists for the sake of political expediency. Many FBI agents came from the very communities where these crimes took place, and they often had outlooks similar to local whites. Many agents, including FBI Director J. Edgar Hoover, also shared the common view of civil rights activists as troublemakers who were probably the tool of the Communists. J. Edgar Hoover famously sought to discredit Martin Luther King Jr., and he considered civil rights activists subversives. As a result, southern whites understood that their distaste for civil rights activists was shared "by no less an authority than J. Edgar Hoover."[58]

Presidential administrations for most of the civil rights era adopted a policy of nonintervention in southern violence. Convinced that the federal government could not serve as a police force without an extreme expansion of federal power, both Eisenhower and Kennedy administration officials insisted that state and local authorities, not the federal government, were responsible for preventing racial terrorism. "There is no substitute under the federal system for the failure of local law enforcement," Assistant Attorney General Burke Marshall argued in 1963. Attorney General Robert Kennedy admitted that it was "unfortunate" that federal inaction might lead to more deaths, but he defended the Kennedy administration's failure to take steps to curb racial violence in the South. "Maybe it's going to take a decade, and maybe a lot of people are going to be killed in the meantime," Kennedy explained, "but in the long run I think it's best for the health of the country and the stability of this [the federal] system."[59]

Activists watching friends die blamed not just the men who committed murder or the state politicians and communities that tolerated racial violence, but also the federal government, which many involved in the movement believed could have done far more to prevent racial terrorism. The U.S. government, civil rights activist and Tougaloo College chaplain Ed King insisted at James Chaney's 1964 funeral, bore responsibility for Chaney's death, for it had allowed "white Mississippians to kill black Mississippians at will." Speaking at the same funeral, Congress of Racial Equality activist Dave Dennis angrily told the mourners that he blamed the president of the United States for Chaney's death as much as he did the men who pulled the trigger.[60]

As levels of violence intensified in the mid-1960s, the federal government began to reconsider what was really necessary to preserve the country's stability. In 1964, after the killings of the three civil rights workers in Mississippi and the slaying of National Guardsman Lemuel Penn, federal authorities finally took meaningful steps to challenge the reign of racial terror in southern states. The FBI launched massive investigations into both Lemuel Penn's murder and the Freedom Summer killings, involving more than two hundred agents and tens of thousands of man-hours. Prodded by President Johnson, the Bureau opened a field office in Jackson, Mississippi, and launched a major counterintelligence program designed to harass and disrupt the Klan. These FBI efforts would eventually help end the unchecked racial terrorism of the 1950s and 1960s.[61]

Yet for much of the civil rights era, the infamous image of an FBI agent observing and taking notes while white mobs attacked civil rights protestors epitomized the failure of the federal government to step in to protect American citizens from racial violence. Even decades later, this hands-off approach incensed former activists. "The FBI could not be counted on and it was not the friend of the civil rights movement. The FBI stood by with their suits and ties . . . and took notes while people were being beaten in front of them. This happened again, and again, and again," radical historian and civil rights supporter Howard Zinn recalled.[62] From his perspective, the federal government condoned the use of violence to maintain the racial status quo.

For twenty years after World War II, racial terror served as one of the primary tools of maintaining the racial system. The rhetoric and actions of police, politicians, and community elites created an environment that made it permissible to use violence for the larger good of the white community. In an impassioned speech before a group of white businessmen the day after the Sixteenth Street Baptist Church bombing, white lawyer and civil rights supporter Charles Morgan blamed all of white Birmingham for planting the bomb that killed four black girls. "We all" threw the bomb, he told his audience. The answer to "who" threw the bomb is "every little individual who talks about the 'niggers' and spreads the seeds of his hate to his neighbor and his son," Morgan charged. It is "every Governor who ever shouted for lawlessness and became a law violator," the courts "that move ever so slowly," newspapers that "defend the law," white ministers, the timid mayor, and the distant business community. "Every person in this community who has, in any way, contributed during the past several years to the popularity of hatred is at least as guilty, or more so, than the demented fool who threw that bomb." The community, he charged, had created a social atmosphere that bred atrocities.[63] And nothing offered clearer evidence of the ways in which those who committed racial violence were excused or even encouraged by southern whites, and to a lesser extent, by federal authorities, than the failings of the criminal justice system during the civil rights era. The police, the politicians, and the larger community not only produced murderers; they would protect them from punishment too.

2

"Jim Crow" Justice

In too many places, the Negro cannot depend on the police for protection and, when an occasional terrorist is arrested and brought to trial, the Negro can be confident that the white court will turn the offender loose or punish him so lightly that the penalty is interpreted as quiet approval of terrorism.

—"Southern Justice: An Indictment,"
Southern Regional Council, 1965

WHEN A BOMB placed under the steps of Birmingham, Alabama's Sixteenth Street Baptist Church exploded as the church prepared for its 1963 "Youth Day" services, killing four black teenage girls and seriously wounding a fifth, city leaders expressed shock and disgust. The city council called the bombing a "barbaric and senseless atrocity" and pledged its full resources to finding those responsible. Mayor Albert Boutwell insisted that "no stone" would be left unturned, "no effort or expense . . . spared" in the search for the bombers. While violence of this sort was nothing new in Birmingham—so many black homes and churches had been bombed there since the 1940s that the city had been nicknamed "Bombingham"— this bombing was different. The *Birmingham News*, a newspaper that had sharply criticized black demonstrators, insisted that the church bombers must be brought to justice. If whites wanted blacks to take their grievances to court rather than to the streets, whites too must follow the law, an editorial explained: "It all comes down to law."[1]

The law, however, would fail the four girls killed in Birmingham. Despite their public pledges to find the bombers, Alabama state authorities did not bring any charges in the case. Neither did the federal government, even though the FBI quickly identified the same men who would be convicted of the bombing decades later. Characteristic of many of the racial killings in the South in the civil rights era, no one would be charged at the time, let alone punished, for killing four girls as they prepared for Sunday services in the downstairs' ladies lounge.

Even when racially motivated killings generated widespread censure and condemnation, as happened in the case of the Birmingham church bombing, the southern criminal justice system nearly always failed to hold perpetrators accountable. Most incidents of racial violence during the civil rights era did not result in any criminal charges at all. When grand juries did hand down indictments, prosecutors or judges sometimes took steps to ensure that cases did not proceed further. The few cases that went to trial commonly ended in acquittals or mistrials. When the rare jury did convict, those found guilty received sentences so token that, in the words of the Southern Regional Council, a small organization of white southern liberals committed to ending racial injustice, even penalties signaled "quiet approval of terrorism."[2]

The failure of the legal system to adequately address the racial terror of the civil rights era highlights how racism operated at many different levels to protect whites who committed racial violence. A shared interest in protecting the Jim Crow system by police and legal officials contributed to an unwillingness to bring charges, shoddy investigations, and lackluster prosecutions. The racism institutionalized within the southern political system ensured that few blacks would serve on the juries deciding whether to bring indictments or on those hearing cases. And many of the whites on those juries proved receptive to the argument that defendants were simply doing what was needed as white men to protect the southern way of life from the forces that threatened to destroy it. Even committed prosecutors who worked to present a fair and thorough case to a jury typically failed to win convictions in the face of these obstacles. And the federal government, reluctant to usurp state authority, proved hesitant to prosecute racially motivated murders under federal law despite the failure of states to take effective action to hold perpetrators accountable.

The fact that at least through the late 1960s, white men could murder blacks and their allies without fearing any meaningful retribution illustrates again the myriad ways in which the state—reflected here in the actions of police, prosecutors, and judges—shared some responsibility for the racial violence of the era. And the unwillingness of juries to convict shows that many whites understood that upholding the racial status quo necessitated turning a blind eye to murder. Convictions, they knew, would be hugely symbolic at a time when blacks were openly challenging the racial system. As long as many whites felt that finding white men guilty in racial killings would undermine the racial order, there was little hope that the law would offer anything resembling justice.

The denial of legal justice to blacks in the South has a long history. Since the era of Reconstruction, the venerable black scholar and activist W. E. B. Du Bois wrote in 1948, "the courts in the South have been used largely as instruments for enforcing caste rather than securing justice."[3] Enforcing caste required harsh treatment of blacks who committed crimes against whites and lenient treatment of whites who committed crimes against blacks. In the Jim Crow era, blacks accused of harming whites faced quick retribution and harsh punishments, but whites who injured or murdered blacks typically escaped trial or, if tried, received minimal punishments that symbolized the low value whites accorded to black life. The southern justice system, like other institutions in the Jim Crow South, served the larger purpose of subordinating blacks.

The legal response to racially motivated murders in the civil rights era throws into sharp relief the many factors and everyday practices that made it possible, as a 1965 Southern Regional Council report put it, "for a white man to murder a Negro without fear of serious retribution." Few of the racially motivated murders that took place during the civil rights era resulted in charges at all, and not all of those led to state or federal trials. Indictments were the exception rather than the norm. Neither Southerners nor outside observers expected these cases to go to trial. As a reporter for the *Wall Street Journal* noted sardonically in 1965, "civil rights crimes are looked on with a great deal of tolerance in these parts."[4]

Local police committed to preserving the Jim Crow social and political order often failed to conduct the kinds of investigations of racially motivated murders that could lead to indictments. Police refused to even investigate the 1955 murder of George Lee. Although he died after being shot, the Humphreys County sheriff insisted that Lee had been killed

"...DON'T WORRY. YOU'RE IN GOOD HANDS!"

This 1962 *Atlanta-Constitution* cartoon by Clifford Baldowski, who was well known for his racially moderate views, lampoons the southern criminal justice system. Here members of the Klan and southern lawmen kidnap "justice" while reassuring her that she is "in good hands." (*Atlanta Constitution*, Clifford H. "Baldy" Baldowski Editorial Cartoons, courtesy of the Richard B. Russell Library for Political Research and Studies, University of Georgia Libraries) in a car crash and that the metal fragments in Lee's jaw came from the fillings in his teeth. No one was ever arrested or charged with the crime. That same year in Brookhaven, Mississippi, the sheriff failed to arrest the white man with "blood all over him" he saw leaving the scene after voting rights activist Lamar Smith was killed in broad daylight on the lawn of the courthouse in 1955. No one would ever be tried in the case.[5]

Even if the local authorities sought charges, the legal process could come to an abrupt end if a grand jury—the body in the American justice system responsible for deciding whether there is enough evidence to warrant criminal charges—failed to return indictments. In 1955, a Leflore County grand jury refused to bring charges of kidnapping against J. W. Milam and Roy Bryant, despite the fact that the two had already admitted to abducting Emmett Till during their earlier trial for his murder. An Alabama grand jury disregarded seemingly strong evidence when it refused to return any indictments in the 1963 murder of William Moore, a white civil rights activist shot dead in Etowah County, Alabama, during a one-man trek to Jackson, Mississippi, to protest segregation. In this case, Roy McDowell, an Alabama Bureau of Investigation agent, had retraced Moore's route, interviewed people who had seen him, and read through Moore's diary, and investigators had matched the bullets that killed Moore to a .22 caliber rifle they seized from a nearby house. But after four hours of deliberation, the grand jury chose not to indict the gun's owner, Floyd Simpson. McDowell felt "let down by the grand jury. We felt like that was the gun that did it."[6] A grand jury in Neshoba County examining the 1964 murders of Andrew Goodman, James Chaney, and Mickey Schwerner acted to protect the accused rather than to seek justice for the victims. Rather than handing down indictments in the Freedom Summer murders, a grand jury instead issued a report praising the work of Neshoba County Sheriff Lawrence Rainey and Deputy Sheriff Cecil Price—men who later faced federal charges in relation to the murder—for doing "an exceptional job of maintaining law and order in this county, even in the face of drastic provocation by outside agitators."[7] In the Jim Crow justice system, the secretive grand jury process could easily work to protect perpetrators.

Even when indictments were handed down, there was no guarantee that cases would proceed further. The 1970 case of the murder of sharecropper Rainey Pool languished for years after a judge at the time ruled that the confession by one of the men involved in the killing was not admissible in court. Shortly after the murder, Joe Oliver Watson gave a written confession to a Highway Patrol investigator, detailing how he and four other men had beaten Pool in the parking lot of a bar in Louisville, Mississippi, and then thrown his body into the Sunflower River. But Watson later insisted he had not been read his rights and the judge quashed the confession. Three months later, the district attorney dismissed the case. Yet the investigator who took Watson's confession was never called in to testify about it, and charges were dropped against all five men despite the existence of other statements and confessions. Years later, a new Belzoni district attorney charged that the prosecution "was never serious. One confession gets suppressed and they dismiss the case against everybody. . . . There was never any real attempt to secure justice at that time by the State."[8]

Given the widespread failure of southern authorities to indict any-one in most cases of racially motivated murderers, it is not surprising that supporters of civil rights pressed the federal government to step in to act when southern states failed to pursue legal justice. That pressure, coupled with concerns about the potential of racial violence in the South to undermine federal authority and harm America's international rep-utation, led President Truman's Presidential Committee on Civil Rights to call on the FBI to investigate racial killings more systematically.[9] That was no easy task. Many Southerners, both black and white, feared what would happen if they talked to the FBI. As J. Edgar Hoover noted in a 1956 memo, "Invariably, when atrocious acts of violence break out we run into a curtain of silence. . . . The difficulties which our Agents face at times are almost indescribable."[10] Nevertheless, FBI investiga-tions demonstrated that many of these cases could be solved with the typical tools of police work: ballistics and explosions tests, widespread interviewing, wiretaps, and rewards for information. The agency, for example, undertook what the biographer of Harry Moore described as an "exhaustive, full-throttled, no-holds-barred investigation" into the bombing that killed Moore and his wife in Florida in 1951. Seventeen agents researched the case for months, going so far as to build and blow up replicas of the Moores' house to better understand what explosive had been used in the bombing.[11] FBI investigations would prove instru-mental in identifying suspects in many of these civil rights–era murder cases, including the 1963 Birmingham church bombing, the 1964 Lemuel Penn and Freedom Summer murders, and the 1965 murder of Viola Liuzzo. The thick files the FBI gathered on some of these crimes have proven invaluable to legal authorities who began to reopen cases in the 1990s and 2000s.

Yet whatever the quality of many of the FBI investigations, they rarely translated into any actions to hold the suspects they identified accountable for their crimes. Given that southern state authorities had shown that they were more interested in defending segregation than punishing racial violence, the agency could not simply turn its information over to state authorities and expect them to act on what they had found. And if police were complicit in these murders, the FBI could not expect them to protect their informants or witnesses. The murder of Louis Allen, a black World War II veteran who ran a small timber business in Liberty, Mississippi, offers a vivid demonstration of the dangers of the FBI passing information to local authorities. In 1961, Allen had seen Mississippi state legislator E. H. Hurst shoot an unarmed Herbert Lee, a NAACP member who had been working for voting rights. Under pressure from the local sheriff, Allen swore that Hurst shot Lee in self-defense, but he later approached the FBI to tell them the truth of what he knew. Even though the FBI recognized in its internal memos that the local sheriff might be plotting to kill Allen, they referred Allen's reports of death threats to the same sheriff's office. The night before Allen planned to flee Mississippi for good, he was shot in the head, most likely by the sheriff. But no one knows, since it was that same sheriff who "investigated" Allen's killing.[12]

When southern state authorities failed to act on the information uncovered by the FBI, federal authorities argued that there was little they could do about it. Under the federalist system in the United States, states hold the responsibility for prosecuting most crimes. Murder is only considered a federal crime under limited circumstances—if a killing takes place on federal property, for example. As a result, federal officials had only very limited tools at their disposal to bring federal charges in cases of racial violence. Two Reconstruction-era statutes theoretically gave the federal government authority to punish racial violence as long as they could prove that there had been a conspiracy to deny victims of their civil rights or that the crime had involved state officials.

Subsequent Supreme Court rulings, however, had severely limited the scope of those statutes to the point that by the 1950s, a Justice Department official admitted that the department's authority to act in cases of racial violence was "meager and hedged with technicalities." Even so, neither the Eisenhower nor the Kennedy administrations even tried to use these existing statutes. Nor did either seek the legislative authority to do more.[13]

The FBI had its own reasons for being reluctant to pursue legal charges, since doing so might reveal the identity of informants or uncover the agency's potentially embarrassing investigative methods. The FBI needed informants, especially those who were members of the Klan, to provide them with information about these murders if they hoped to identify suspects. But if cases went to court, the identity of their informants would be exposed and the agency would lose valuable access to information. Faced with this dilemma, the agency often chose protecting its assets over prosecution. When the most notorious FBI Klan informant, Gary Thomas Rowe, attacked Freedom Riders along with other Klan members on Mother's Day 1961 in Birmingham, the Bureau tried to cover up his involvement and did not discipline him. Their reluctance to try to build a case against the Klan attackers stemmed in part from their desire to protect Rowe's position in the Klan. When Rowe told his handlers that he had killed a black man in Birmingham in 1963, supposedly in an act of self-defense, he claimed that the agency instructed him to just keep quiet about it. In an explosive investigation in 1978, the Justice Department harshly criticized the FBI for condoning Rowe's violent role as an "agent provocateur" in the Klan; FBI officials insisted that Rowe "couldn't be an angel and be a good informant." Yet in working to cover up Rowe's violent actions so that he could continue to be of use as an informant, the agency not only handcuffed some of its own investigations, but also may have encouraged further violence. Rowe was in the car of the Klansmen who shot and killed Viola Liuzzo in 1965 and may even have been the triggerman.[14]

No case better epitomizes the absolute failures of both federal and state authorities to aggressively pursue legal justice in racial murders than the 1963 Birmingham church bombing. Despite the shocked condemnation of the city's establishment and their offer of a substantial reward for information, no charges were filed in the case. Local and state authorities ceded the investigation to the FBI, which quickly identified a small, especially violent, group of Klansmen as the likely bombers. But even as the FBI assembled evidence in the bombing case, Alabama's commissioner of public safety, Al Lingo, likely in collusion with the Klan, arrested three of the suspects on a lesser and unrelated charge of possession of dynamite, a move that many at the time saw as an effort to derail the federal investigation by tying up evidence and taking the suspects off the streets.[15] The three were fined $1,000 and given six-month sentences, which were later suspended. Those charges would prove the only ones the state would bring in the 1960s.

Federal authorities could have moved forward with conspiracy charges, and FBI agents leading the investigation pressed Hoover to take the case to trial before the five-year statute of limitations on civil rights violations expired. But Hoover balked, perhaps because he believed that there was no chance for a successful prosecution. Moving forward, moreover, would have required the testimony of Gary Thomas Rowe, the violent FBI informant who belonged to the same Klavern as the suspects. Once he was identified, the FBI would lose Rowe's access to the Klan; worse, the agency might be tarnished by its association with a man who had likely been involved in other bombings in Birmingham, and may have even played a role in the church bombing himself.[16] Elizabeth Cobbs, the niece of one of the suspects, who cooperated with the FBI, described the years after the bombing as a time of "frustration and waiting. Waiting for the other shoe to drop. Waiting for the FBI agents to call and say they finally had Justice Department approval to make arrests or that there would be evidence presented to the federal grand jury."[17] But Cobbs would wait in vain. The Justice Department allowed the case to close without pressing charges.

Chris McNair, whose daughter Denise died in the Sixteenth Street Baptist Church bombing, could only conclude that authorities had condoned the crime. Although McNair believed he could possibly forgive the men who bombed the church, he could not imagine how he could ever forgive "a society that permits it."[18] As McNair recognized, the failure to even indict anyone for most of the racially motivated killings that took place in these violent decades reflected not only on the handful of men who committed these crimes but also on the society that permitted them to do so.

That complicity was reflected not only in the failure to charge anyone with murder in instances like that of the Birmingham church bombing, but also in the failure to convict perpetrators or to punish them in accordance with their crimes in those cases that proceeded further in the legal process. Some civil rights–era murders did result in indictments and trials, but most men accused of racially motivated murders walked free after mistrials or, more commonly, acquittals. States brought at least thirty-three men to trial for twenty different civil rights–era murders at the time the crimes were committed. But seventeen, or more than half of those state trials, ended in acquittals, and nearly another quarter of the cases ended with hung juries and were not tried again.[19] Klan leader Sam Bowers only exaggerated slightly when he told his followers, "There ain't no jury in the State of Mississippi gonna convict a white man for killing a nigger." It was an era, white activist Virginia Durr lamented, of "murder without penalty, murder without pain, and the victims get no sympathy at all."[20]

The fact that so few were convicted or punished for racially motivated murders reflected racism endemic to all levels of the southern criminal justice system. Police sympathetic to the murders sometimes openly obstructed justice. H. C. Strider, the sheriff responsible for the investigating Emmett Till's murder, refused to collect evidence in the case. At the trial, he testified that he could not tell if the body that had been pulled from the river was Till's, or even that of a black person, despite the fact that the corpse was wearing Till's ring.[21] A few local black activists and black journalists had to undertake the investigation that the sheriff failed to pursue. They found several people who had seen Till in J. W. Milam's truck and at a plantation owned by Milam's brother and convinced them to testify.[22] But Sheriff Strider ensured that the most potentially damning witnesses—two black men who were in the truck with Till and who reportedly washed blood out of the bed—would not be found by locking them up in a Mississippi jail under false names for the duration of the trial.[23] Byron De La Beckwith also escaped punishment in part because of policemen who lied on his behalf by testifying that they had seen Beckwith miles away from the crime scene at the time Evers was shot. That testimony, now known to be fabricated, significantly weakened the case since the prosecution couldn't prove that Beckwith was in Jackson at the time of the crime, even though they successfully traced the murder weapon back to Beckwith.[24]

The lackluster performance of many of the prosecuting attorneys and trial judges made clear that they had little desire to see the defendants charged in racially motivated murders serve any jail time. Ben Chester White's killers all remained free because of rulings by the trial judge and questionable decisions by the prosecution. Although three men were indicted after White was killed in 1966, only two would ever be tried. The trial judge dismissed charges against Claude Fuller after he complained that he suffered from ulcers and arthritis. The trial of James Jones resulted in a hung jury, but he was not retried after he too told the judge that he suffered from ulcers. The third defendant, Ernest Avants, escaped punishment even though he told FBI agents that he could not be found guilty of murder since White was already dead by the time he blew off the top of his head with a shotgun. Avants effectively admitted to participating in White's murder. But state prosecutors did not use the information available to them to build a strong case. They chose not to introduce a confession that Jones had given naming Avants as one of the killers, they decided against bringing in Avants's statement to the FBI, they presented no motive for the killing, and they failed to even raise the charge of aiding and abetting a murder. Even though the defense did not call a single witness and the jury had two black members, all twelve jurors agreed they had not heard enough evidence to convict Avants.[25]

The trial of the three men accused of inflicting a fatal beating on white minister James Reeb on the streets of Selma in 1965 offers a textbook example of how to lose a case. The prosecutors did not object when the defense challenged the mental competency of a key witness for the state on the basis of the testimony of a doctor who was not a psychiatrist and who had not even examined the man in question. They did nothing when a material witness for the state refused to come to Alabama to testify.[26] And they saw no reason to seek a mistrial when it was discovered that one of the jurors was the brother of a key defense witness. To trial observer Reverend Walter Royal Jones of the Unitarian Universalist Commission, it was clear that the prosecution presented only the evidence "it could not help presenting."[27] The jury took only ninety-seven minutes to find all three men not guilty.

Prosecutors arguing these cases in court often shared the racial outlook of the men standing trial. Lowndes County Solicitor Carleton Perdue, who acted as prosecutor in the trials of the men accused of

murdering Viola Liuzzo and Jonathan Daniels, openly expressed his segregationist views to the press. There were better ways of keeping "nigras"
in their place than murdering them, he told journalists. He did not object
when United Klans of America Imperial Wizard Robert Shelton sat at
the defense table during opening arguments in the Liuzzo trial.[28] During
Tom Coleman's trial on charges of murdering white civil rights volunteer Jonathan Daniels in Lowndes County, Alabama, in 1965, Perdue
put more energy into attacking Daniels than he did into prosecuting the
man who murdered him. Coleman had shot seminary student Daniels
and Father Richard Morrisroe, a white priest, when they stopped at a
store to buy soda after being released from jail for being involved in
nonviolent protests. Before the trial began, Perdue told reporters that
if the two white men "had been tending to their business like I tend
to mine, they'd be living and enjoying themselves today." He failed to
contest most aspects of the defense case, which one observer called "a
calm choreography of perjury." Perdue accepted without question the
defense team's lie that Daniels had been armed with a knife. Perdue also
suggested on his own that Daniels had been trying to force his way into
the store and decided not to call eight African Americans who had seen
the shooting because, in his opinion, it would have "destroyed whatever
good feeling we might have had with the jury by calling up a bunch of
niggers (who were) 100 yards away so they couldn't see anything."[29] A
jury quickly acquitted Coleman on the grounds that he had shot Daniels
and Morrisroe in self-defense.

Even dedicated and fair legal officials could have trouble influencing
the outcome in a system that was so rigged in favor of the white defendants. Alabama Attorney General Richmond Flowers, a vocal critic of
the Klan and of Alabama's Governor George Wallace, tried to intervene
to prevent Coleman's quick acquittal. Flowers had allowed Perdue to
move forward with the case, believing that a conviction might be more
likely if the jury knew that the prosecutor was a strict segregationist. But
as he watched the train wreck unfold, he decided to take over the prosecution himself. Unfortunately for Flowers, the judge in charge proved
to be as biased as Perdue. When Flowers sought a delay in the proceedings so that Father Morrisroe could recover enough to testify, the
judge denied his request. And when he asked the judge to stop the proceedings so he could seek murder charges instead of the manslaughter

charges Perdue was willing to settle for, the judge put Perdue back on the case. In the farce of a trial and the acquittal, Richmond Flowers saw the "democratic process going down the drain of irrationality, bigotry and improper enforcement of the law."[30]

The juries that heard these weak and often blatantly racist prosecutions further reflected the ways in which racism influenced every level of the southern criminal justice system. Since southern states typically limited jury service to "qualified electors," defendants could rest assured that they would likely be judged only by other whites, and often only by other white men. Voting restrictions shut most blacks out of the political process and ensured that few blacks were even eligible to serve on juries. Although the exclusions of blacks from juries began to come under federal scrutiny as early as the mid-1940s, for several more decades, states were able to use all-white juries as long as local authorities were willing to deny that there had been any racial discrimination in jury selection.[31]

Defense teams, moreover, found state authorities were often willing to help them choose jurors who would be unwilling to convict their clients. In the Emmett Till trial, the sheriff-elect pointed out men he considered "safe" to the defendants' lawyers. By the time thirteen jurors had been chosen, the defense felt confident that they could not lose the case. Just to make sure, members of the Citizens' Councils reportedly found a way to visit every member of the sequestered jury during its deliberations to confirm that each juror planned to vote "the right way." A lawyer defending Byron De La Beckwith asked an investigator with the Mississippi Sovereignty Commission to "check out" a list of eleven prospective jurors; the investigator talked to the jurors' employers and submitted a written report. He identified one juror as a member of the Citizens' Council and described him as "stable and well respected." Another he suggested was not suitable for the jury based on the report of a man who "knew his thinking."[32] In this case, even as Beckwith was being tried by the state of Mississippi, a state agency did legwork for the defense that helped result in a mistrial.

Segregationist judges could make it difficult, if not impossible, for prosecutors to keep even people who were openly biased in favor of the defendants off the jury. Jurors who expressed open disdain or hatred towards blacks and white civil rights workers weren't typically dismissed from juries in these trials. When the state of Georgia tried two men for

The all-white, all-male jury that acquitted Roy Bryant and J. W. Milam in the 1955 murder of Emmett Till was typical of most southern juries that heard civil rights murder cases. The jury, pictured here in the Sumner, Mississippi, courthouse on September 21, 1955, took only sixty-seven minutes to reach its verdict of not guilty. (© Bettmann/Corbis)

the murder of Lemuel Penn in 1964, the judge decided not to call a mistrial after he learned that the jury foreman had told people that he could never convict white men for killing a black man.[33] The few dedicated prosecutors like Richmond Flowers found it nearly impossible to keep open supporters of segregation off juries. Although Flowers tried to assemble a jury as free of racial bias as possible when he prosecuted Collie Wilkins in the murder of Viola Liuzzo, the judge would not let him excuse eleven prospective jurors who admitted that they believed white integrationists were inferior. The jury that ultimately acquitted Wilkins included six "self-described white supremacists and eight present or former members of the Citizens Council." No wonder that a Mississippi district attorney could boast to Attorney General Robert Kennedy in

1964 that as long as white Southerners had the right to a jury trial, "you cannot whip us."[34]

As a last resort, Klansmen could try to rig juries to guarantee that some jurors would not vote to convict. Sam Bowers, head of the White Knights of the Ku Klux Klan, ensured hung juries in two trials on charges of arson stemming from the 1966 Dahmer killing by successfully persuading one or two jurors to vote not guilty before the prosecutions even started.[35] But these instances of jury tampering were relatively rare. For most of the 1950s and 1960s, the Klan did not need to worry about fixing juries because the system effectively did it for them.

The rarity of convictions in the case of racially motivated murders not only reflected the racism endemic to the criminal justice system, which contributed to weak cases being presented before all-white juries, but it also exposed the ideologies of racism shared by so many whites and their common interest in maintaining a racial order that privileged whites, especially white males. Juries regularly acquitted whites accused of murdering blacks because they knew that seriously punishing racially motivated murders might weaken a social system based on white supremacy and black subordination. In most of these trials, it mattered little whether the case was weak or strong, evidence flimsy or compelling. Trials became a referendum on white supremacy, and most jurors did what they thought necessary to protect the racial status quo.

Defense teams often put the victims on trial, constructing cases that implied that murder had been justified because of the political activities of those who had been killed. During one of Byron De La Beckwith's trials for the murder of Medgar Evers—he would be tried twice in quick succession by the state in 1964, with both cases ending with hung juries—the defense team did everything they could to emphasize Evers's political activism. "Was he very active in the integration movement?" defense attorney Hardy Lott asked Evers's widow, Myrlie. Had he filed a suit to integrate the Jackson schools? Wasn't their son's middle name Kenyatta? Prosecutor William Waller argued that it wasn't appropriate to ask such questions of Myrlie Evers, a housewife who "wasn't in the movement," and insisted that whether or not Evers was seeking to integrate schools "had nothing to do with this slaying at the time, in the middle of the night at his home."[36] Of course, Waller could not have been more wrong. Evers's slaying had everything to do with his civil rights organizing, and the defense played that to their advantage. Even in cases where the victims had not been actively challenging the southern order, astute questioning by the defense could subtly stigmatize victims as agitators. When Alabama tried two men for the 1964 murder of Lemuel Penn, the black army reservist shot while driving back to Washington, D.C., after training in Georgia, the defense pointedly asked one of the men who had been in the car with Penn if they had used the "regular restrooms" when they stopped at a service station in Atlanta. Given the passage of the Civil Rights Act weeks before, it was keeping a separate white restroom, not Penn's alleged use of it, that was illegal. But implying that Penn had transgressed a traditional racial boundary ensured he could not be portrayed as an innocent victim.[37]

When possible, defense attorneys argued that the murdered victims represented a threat to the sexual order that served as one of the foundations of segregation. White Southerners had long justified extreme racial measures, from segregated public spaces to lynchings, as necessary to protect white women from the sexual threat posed by black men. Any kind of intimacy between black men and white women represented a challenge in a society premised on black inequality and white privilege. That privilege allowed white men to have exploitative sexual relationships with black women as long as those relationships were not perceived to be intimate ones between equals. A white man could have sex with a black woman, but he was not supposed to kiss her.[38]

Defense teams clearly believed that jurors would acquit if the murdered victim could be portrayed as transgressing these sexual rules. During the Emmett Till murder trial, the defense team argued that the case was not about whether the two men on trial had murdered the black teenager, but whether Till had been a sexual threat to an innocent white woman. Defense attorneys noted repeatedly that despite his age, Emmett Till looked like a "pretty good sized man." C. Sidney Carlton asked Deputy Sheriff Cothran, on the stand to testify about the condition of the body, whether Till had "well developed privates." Milam and Bryant, sitting up front next to their pretty wives with their young sons on their laps, had only been performing their duties as white men to protect white womanhood, the defense suggested. Ten years later, defense lawyers for Tom Coleman stigmatized the young seminary student Jonathan Daniels, whom Coleman had shot at point-blank range, by suggesting that he had kissed one of the black women he was with shortly before he was killed, had written letters to her in jail, and had worn red underpants (although what this indicated remained unsaid). Coleman, they argued, had gone to the store in the first place to protect the white female owner; he was, they insisted, defending southern white womanhood from a radical outsider.[39]

Special venom was directed at white women who willingly violated the ultimate southern taboo by treating black men as their equals. In the 1965 state trial of Collie Leroy Wilkins for the murder of Viola Liuzzo, it was really Liuzzo who was put on trial for her open transgression of racial and gender boundaries. Liuzzo, a thirty-nine-year-old Detroit mother of five, proved an easy target because her decision to leave her family to volunteer in the southern movement immediately marked her as a woman who refused to conform to gender expectations and the role of a stereotypical housewife. Reflecting the cultural anxiety about the proper role of women and mothers, Liuzzo could be stigmatized as a sexual pervert who had deserted her children so she could come south and sleep with black men.[40] FBI Director J. Edgar Hoover, eager to deflect attention from the role informant Gary Rowe had played in Liuzzo's murder, circulated lurid memos claiming that she was a drug user and that Liuzzo had been sitting "very, very close" to black teenager Leroy Moton when she was killed, giving "all the appearances of a necking party." These innuendos, leaked via Klan informants to the press, became the basis of the defense. What, the lead defense attorney asked the jury, did they think Moton was doing "all that time, in that car, *alone* with that woman?" Unlike Liuzzo, defense lawyer Matt Murphy charged, he was proud to stand up "for white supremacy, not the mixing and mongrelization of the races." After a first trial ended in a hung jury, Murphy was confident he could win an acquittal in the next trial if he spent more time talking about Liuzzo's alleged sexual improprieties. "All I need to use is the fact that Liuzzo was in the car with a nigger man and that she wore no underpants." Unfortunately for Murphy, he would never get to make that argument. He died in a car crash before Wilkins's second state trial, which again ended with a hung jury.[41]

Both defense and prosecution teams assumed that jurors would feel contempt for victims who had challenged the racial status quo. Prosecutors committed to putting on the best case they could had to convince jurors that convicting a few men of murder would not destabilize the entire racial order. Even the best prosecutors in the 1960s reassured jurors that they too shared a commitment to segregation. During the Beckwith trials, prosecutor William Waller asked potential jurors whether they could decide the case as any other, despite the fact that "the deceased worked in a way obnoxious and emotionally repulsive to you as a businessman and me as a lawyer."[42] Similarly, the prosecutors in the Viola Liuzzo murder trial assured jurors that they were segregationists too who didn't "agree with the purpose of this woman either."[43] Prosecutors did not try to foster sympathy for murder victims among the jurors. They instead tried to convince jurors that convicting the defendants did not represent a betrayal of the racial system.

Defense teams hammered home the need for racial loyalty and white solidarity, especially at a time when segregation was under attack. That message came through in a variety of ways. It was evident in the special venom defense lawyers directed at the few whites who acted as informants by providing information about the actions of the men on trial. The defense spent hours in the many arson and murder trials that resulted from Vernon Dahmer's murder attacking the character and racial loyalties of star witness Billy Roy Pitts, a Klansman who had been involved in the firebombing of Dahmer's house. Defense lawyers sought to paint Pitts as a traitor who was making up testimony for money, a "paid liar of the government."[44] Gary Rowe, the key witness in the Viola Liuzzo murder case, was a traitor, defense lawyer Matt Murphy insisted, a two-faced witness for hire who sold his soul "for thirty pieces of silver." How could you believe any man who took money from Communists and the NAACP, Murphy asked the jury? Rowe was "worse than a white nigger," Murphy declared. He had abandoned his people and betrayed his heritage at a time of crisis.[45]

Defense teams also appealed to jurors by trying to turn state cases of murder into referenda on the federal government and its policies towards the South. Even in cases brought by state authorities, defense teams suggested that the trial showed that an overreaching federal government was threatening the southern way of life. Defense teams frequently framed the federal government in terms southern juries would relate to historically—as a carpetbagger, trying to impose itself and its will on the South.[46] Putting the federal government on trial proved a powerful way to rile up the resentment of southern white jurors. When Georgia put two Klansmen accused of killing Lemuel Penn on trial in 1964, the defense team secured its acquittal in part by directing its ire at the "carpetbagging administration of justice" and the "swarms" of FBI agents who had supposedly been sent to "infiltrate the land" and told not to come back "until you bring us white meat."[47] Byron De La Beckwith's attorney also tried to harness jurors' resentment of the federal government to secure Beckwith's freedom in his Mississippi state trials by asking the jury in his closing argument not to "render a verdict to satisfy the Attorney General of the United States."[48] White Southerners, defense arguments made clear, needed to stand together against outsiders, whether they be civil rights activists, traitors willing to inform on their friends, or the federal government.

Defense attorneys openly appealed to jurors' sense of racial heritage, loyalty, and pride in asking them to free their clients. "Every last Anglo-Saxon one of you men has the courage to set these men free," one of the lawyers defending Emmett Till's killers insisted. If they didn't, another defense lawyer warned, their forefathers would "absolutely turn over in their graves."[49] A lawyer defending the men accused of shooting Lemuel Penn also pointedly appealed to jurors' racial pride, reminding them of their Anglo-Saxon heritage five times during his closing arguments.[50] Defense teams expressed the underlying contract in the courtroom in stark terms: whites who wanted to maintain their way of life had to be willing to tolerate some violence committed on their behalf. The man who shot seminary student Jonathan Daniels, his defense team told the jury, was "protecting all of us." The South needed more men like him, "men with great hearts, strong minds, pure souls—and ready hands."[51] Viola Liuzzo's accused killers were "white Christian patriots," their Klan lawyer insisted. And the two men accused of killing Lemuel Penn "weren't doing it for money," like those Klan informers. "They were doing it for you."[52] Civil rights–era murders were understood here to serve the needs of the entire white society.

Reverend Walter Jones, a Unitarian minister who watched in despair as a jury acquitted the men who fatally beat Reverend James Reeb, recognized the fundamental problem with prosecuting racial violence in the Jim Crow South: "Murder is not murder except in the community that regards it as so."[53] And indeed, even in the rare instances where juries did hold defendants accountable for their crimes, they almost never treated the killing of a black person as they would have murders of whites by other whites, or certainly murders of whites by blacks. Over the course of these two decades, southern courts did convict eleven white men—or about a third of those who faced charges—in eight different instances of racial murders. Yet the pattern of convictions in state courts illustrates the limitations of Jim Crow justice even at its most effective. Only one of the cases that led to convictions, that of the firebombing of Vernon Dahmer, involved a victim who was a recognized civil rights activist.[54] All of the other cases that resulted in convictions were random murders of a black victim who could not in any way be portrayed as challenging the racial order. The handful of victims who received even the veneer of justice through the courts were those like Johnnie Mae Chappell, the mother of ten gunned down in Florida while searching for her wallet along the side of the road, or James Earl Reese, a sixteen-year-old black boy shot through a window while dancing with other black teens. Such random killings proved almost the only scenario where southern juries would draw a line about what level of violence was unacceptable in service of the racial order.

Those convicted, moreover, served very little actual jail time. In all but two of these cases, defendants who had been charged with murder were sentenced only to the lesser crime of manslaughter, a crime that does not involve premeditation and where deaths may even be considered accidental. And even for these lesser charges, judges imposed exceptionally light sentences. A man who threw a rock that killed a seventy-three-year-old black minister walking down the street in Huntsville, Alabama, in 1956 was sentenced to only one year in jail. William Zantzinger, who struck and killed fifty-one-year-old barmaid Hattie Carroll with his cane when she didn't serve him his drink fast enough at a charity ball in Baltimore in 1963, served a six-month sentence for his manslaughter conviction.[55] Those sent to jail, moreover, typically served only a fraction of even these short sentences. Only four men convicted in state courts in racially motivated killings ended up serving more than one year in jail. Three of those men had been sentenced to life in prison for the 1966 murder of Vernon Dahmer, but all three would be released within ten years. J. W. Rich would serve only three years of his ten-year sentence for the murder of Johnnie Mae Chappell.

Many convicted in state trials served no time in jail at all. Perry Dean Ross was convicted of "murder with malice" for killing John Earl Reese and wounding two other black teenagers when he shot into a café in Mayflower, Texas, in 1957. But the judge suspended his five-year sentence, apparently accepting the defense's argument to "call it a bad day and let the boy go on in life."[56] Neither of the two teenagers who were found guilty of or pled guilty to manslaughter in the 1963 murder of thirteen-year-old Virgil Ware served a day in jail, since the judge suspended their seven-month sentences. "You could get more time back then for killing a good hunting dog," Ware's brother lamented years after the original crime.[57]

By the mid-1960s, the repeated failures of the criminal justice system in the South to offer a modicum of justice in even the most publicized crimes were attracting widespread censure and condemnation in the press. The brutal murders, sham trials, and short sentences of the civil rights era garnered the attention of journalists from around the country, who painted vivid portraits of the South as a racist, backwards region that showed little respect for human life or the rule of law. When Tom Coleman was acquitted of the murder of Jonathan Daniels, newspapers outside the South described it as a "travesty of American justice," a brazen exhibit of "contempt for justice," and a "flimsy conspiracy of the white community . . . to officially exonerate" a murderer. That last story ran under the headline "Alabama Court Charade Cries Out for Intervention."[58] White Southerners pointed out, not unfairly, that northern journalists seemed far more interested in racial crimes taking place in the South than those taking place in their own backyards, but the courageous black struggle in the 1950s and 1960s and the growth of new media like television, which made news more immediate and violence more visceral, led northern reporters to condemn the travesties of justice taking place in the South's "strange, tight little" towns that had a "nearly pathological" fear of outsiders.[59]

As the coverage of the crimes increased—and racial violence intensified in response to Freedom Summer and other civil rights protests—the federal government faced growing pressure to intervene, not only to uphold law and order by disrupting the Klan, but also to ensure that the murderers be brought to justice if the southern courts failed to act. After the 1964 murder of Lemuel Penn, Justice Department officials made clear that if southern authorities failed to bring charges, the federal government would figure out a way to do so. Still hopeful that a southern jury might convict in a racially charged murder case if it was presented strong evidence, federal authorities assisted the state in preparing its case. But a Georgia jury acquitted the three men on trial for Penn's murder after hearing a defense that railed against federal intervention in the South. Other southern juries responded similarly in a series of other high profile cases that ended in acquittals, including the 1965 trials for the murders of James Reeb, Viola Liuzzo, and Jonathan Daniels. Moreover, even the keen interest of the federal government in the Goodman, Chaney, and Schwerner murders did not lead state authorities to charge anyone with that crime.

The Department of Justice responded to these acquittals and failures to prosecute by pursuing indictments in both the Penn and the Freedom Summer murders based on the limited federal statutes they had at their disposal. When southern judges threw out federal indictments on the grounds that the federal government had no jurisdiction to bring charges in these cases, the Department of Justice appealed to the Supreme Court. In two 1966 decisions, *U.S. v. Guest* and *U.S. v. Price*, the Supreme Court expanded the federal government's jurisdiction to charge those engaged in racially motivated murders with conspiring to violate the civil rights of their victims.[60] Armed with court legitimacy for its authority, the Justice Department launched federal prosecutions in four notorious civil rights murder cases: those of Lemuel Penn, Viola Liuzzo, Vernon Dahmer, and Goodman, Chaney, and Schwerner.

Defense attorneys sought to win these federal cases by acting as they had in state trials. They demonized the victims, appealed to whites' racial loyalties, and, especially since these were federal trials, attacked the federal government for trying to take over the South. In the federal trial stemming from the Freedom Summer triple murder, defense attorney H. C. Watkins argued that Mississippians rightfully resented "some hairy beatnik" from another state who came to Mississippi to defy state custom. Civil rights activists, Watkins told the jury, were "low class riff-raff, that are misfits in our own land." One lawyer repeatedly asked witnesses whether Mickey Schwerner was an atheist and suggested that he had tried to get young black men to sign a pledge to rape one white woman a week, a charge that even presiding judge

Harold Cox—who had once called blacks a "bunch of chimpanzees" in his courtroom—ruled was out of line.[61] Federal prosecutors made concerted efforts to localize these cases by stressing the active participation of local people and the ultimate control the state had over the verdict, and they had some success. Federal juries returned convictions against two of the six men brought up on charges of conspiracy for the murder of Lemuel Penn, three of Viola Liuzzo's killers, and seven men involved in the murders of Goodman, Chaney, and Schwerner.

But many men tried in federal court also walked free: twenty-five federal cases related to these four murders ended in acquittals or mistrials, including those of ten defendants in the Freedom Summer murders and—despite the limited success in state courts—all eleven defendants tried in connection with Vernon Dahmer's murder. Defendants in these cases, moreover, could only be convicted on federal charges that carried maximum sentences of ten years. And few would serve even that long. Of the seven men convicted of federal charges in the 1964 Freedom Summer murders, only two received the full punishment of ten years, and only one ended up actually spending more than six years in federal prison. Judge Cox, the man in charge of sentencing, defended his decision to mete out lighter punishments than allowed by law by explaining, "They killed one nigger, one Jew, and a white man. I gave them all what I thought they deserved."[62]

Federal intervention did not signal the end of racism in the criminal justice system. Throughout the 1950s and much of the 1960s, the Jim Crow justice system protected almost all whites who turned to violence in their efforts to uphold white supremacy in the South. Even after some states began to take tentative steps to hold a few murderers accountable—most notably when the state of Mississippi convicted four men for arson and murder in the 1966 killing of Vernon Dahmer—whites who murdered blacks could remain sympathetic figures. Just three years after Clifford Wilson was sentenced to life in prison for his part in the killing, which included firing his gun into Dahmer's burning house so the targeted man could not escape, Mississippi's governor could justify his decision to commute Wilson's sentence on the grounds that the convicted murderer was "even-tempered, mild, timid and nonviolent" and his family needed him at home. Ellie Dahmer, Vernon Dahmer's widow, would have liked her husband at home too. And she would have liked his murderers to be punished in accordance with their crime. "Had black people done what they did," she charged, "the black people would still be in jail and everyone knows that."[63]

Ellie Dahmer was not satisfied with the results of the few trials in her husband's murder case or with the exceptionally lenient treatment accorded to those who had been convicted for the crime. But there was little she could do in the late 1960s or 1970s to generate further interest in or attention to the case. In ensuing years, whites sought to distance themselves from the violence of the civil rights era, confident, as the federal prosecutor in the Freedom Summer murders explained, that the handful of convictions in racial crimes in the 1960s meant that "they could move away from their past."[64] But white southerners would find that the unchecked violence of the civil rights era proved not so easily silenced or contained. Within decades, a new media, political, and cultural climate would offer Ellie Dahmer and others like her the opportunity to demand that now-old men finally be brought to justice. And just as in the 1960s, debates would again emerge about how the crimes should be understood and who, ultimately, bore responsibility for them.

3

Reopening Civil Rights–Era Murder Cases

Emmett Till is dead. I don't know why he can't just stay dead.

—Roy Bryant, 1991

O N OCTOBER 1, 1989, Jackson *Clarion-Ledger* reporter Jerry Mitchell called Myrlie Evers, the widow of Medgar Evers, the Jackson civil rights leader who had been killed in 1963. Mitchell had just published a story in the paper based on information he had found in files of the Mississippi Sovereignty Commission, the state-spying agency that finally closed its doors in 1973. Although the state legislature had sealed the commission's records for fifty years in an attempt to prevent embarrassing and potentially incriminating information from becoming public, a confidential source had leaked copies of many files to Mitchell, then a thirty-year-old reporter on the courts' beat. Among those documents, Mitchell would find evidence that the Sovereignty Commission had secretly aided the defense during one of Byron De La Beckwith's 1964 murder trials. On that October morning, he called Evers to ask if she thought this new evidence should be cause for reopening the case.[1]

For Myrlie Evers, Mitchell's story offered an opportunity to pressure authorities in Mississippi to finally put the man she knew had murdered her husband in jail, a goal that she had been working towards for decades. She had watched Byron De La Beckwith escape punishment in two state trials in 1964, trials in which a confident Beckwith testified that his gun, which had been found at the murder scene, had been stolen from his car just days before the shooting; in which two policemen provided him with an alibi that contradicted the testimony of other witnesses; and, worst of all, in which Mississippi Governor Ross Barnett came into the courtroom and shook Beckwith's hand in full view of the jury.[2] When she heard about the potential jury tampering, she immediately issued a public call for authorities to reprosecute the case, and she arranged a meeting with the Hinds County district attorney to demand action.[3]

At that meeting, Myrlie Evers encountered a young Hinds County assistant district attorney named Bobby DeLaughter. The son of Mississippi elites, DeLaughter knew little about the history of Jim Crow violence, and he feared that the meeting with Myrlie Evers would be an "in-your-face confrontation" with a black political activist pursuing a civil rights case.[4] But he became more sympathetic as he began to see the case as the cold-blooded murder of a man his own age who, like him, had three young children. The idea of any man being shot in the back in his own driveway in front of his family appalled him. DeLaughter would come to see the failure to punish Beckwith as a stain on the reputation of the state he loved, and he would become a vocal advocate for the need to show that Mississippi courts could treat blacks and whites equally.

Thirty years earlier, the state of Mississippi had helped Byron De La Beckwith get away with murder. In subsequent decades, political authorities and southern communities silenced or denied their histories of racial violence. A few isolated efforts to revisit civil rights–era murders in the 1970s won little public support. But within days of the reopening of the Evers case, relatives of other victims began pressing authorities to examine other unresolved racially-motivated killings from the 1950s and 1960s. In the years since Mississippi authorities reopened the Beckwith case, over one hundred murders committed in the South during the 1950s and 1960s have become the subject of new legal investigations.

The figures of Myrlie Evers, Bobby DeLaughter, and Jerry Mitchell encapsulate the three most important forces generating this new momentum for prosecuting civil rights–era violence. Reopenings would not have taken place without the political efforts of committed activists like Myrlie Evers, who had a deeply personal interest in preserving the memory of their loved ones and in seeing perpetrators held accountable. Their struggle bore new fruit in the years after 1989 because changes in the political and media climate fostered an environment that enabled them to win broader support for their efforts to bring decades-old cases back to the courtroom. Those committed to reopening cases found new allies among the growing number of black officials elected to public office once African Americans gained political power as a result of new civil rights laws. They found too that some white political and legal officials—people like Bobby DeLaughter—became more open to the idea of revisiting these unresolved murders as colorblindness emerged as the dominant racial discourse in the United States. In a political environment that insisted that society should not recognize or treat anyone differently on the basis of race, some white officials became more concerned about the denial of justice that had taken place during the civil rights era, and more worried about the potential damage to the reputation of their communities and states of failing to address it. That concern would only be heightened by the extensive coverage of these crimes in the media. Activists could not have been successful without the help of journalists like Jerry Mitchell. Journalists began to report on civil rights cold cases with a new intensity in the 1990s, and their coverage helped make cases relevant, humanized the victims, and energized investigations. The media's interest would create new pressures on authorities to act and would provide a new vocabulary for understanding why it was important to spend time and money on pursuing elderly men for their now decades-old crimes.

The drive to reopen civil rights–era murders gained momentum in the years after the Beckwith trial because the pursuit of legal justice could bring together people with a wide range of interests across the political spectrum. Within a decade, a range of new activists—who were dedicated to uncovering the full extent of the racial terrorism of the 1950s and 1960s as well as state complicity with it—embraced the project of seeking prosecutions. But conservative southern politicians who had little interest in a broad examination of the extent of racial violence or the state's responsibility for it could also support reopenings. For them, bringing individual perpetrators to justice offered a way to close the door on a troublesome past. Legal justice proved compelling both to activists who hoped to open a discussion of the past and to politicians who hoped to move beyond it.

There was little hope that relatives or activists could succeed in getting any unresolved cases into a courtroom in the first three decades after the murders were committed. Neither southern authorities nor the federal government expressed interest in revisiting these cases. White Southerners wanted the racial violence of the civil rights era to recede into the past and be quickly forgotten so that the region could move forward unencumbered by its history. Political authorities and local communities spent much of the three decades after the murders trying to prevent discussion of the racial violence of the civil rights era. They were not subtle about their attempts to wipe civil rights murders from the historical record or to ensure that they faded into obscurity. State authorities in Mississippi sought to quickly bury Emmett Till's brutalized body before his mother could even see it and then tried to prevent her from opening his casket before burying him. The sites of civil rights killings were not marked with memorials, and vandals regularly desecrated the graves of victims.[5] The desire to repressively erase the history of the era reached its apex in 1977, when the Mississippi House of Representatives approved the destruction of the files of the Mississippi Sovereignty Commission. Destroying the files, one House member argued, would serve to "forever erase them from Mississippi," while another saw it as the best way "to close the book on this chapter" of the state's history. Only the intervention of historians who appealed to the State Senate not to destroy such rich sources for future research kept the Senate from approving the House plan. The Senate instead ordered the files sealed until 2027.[6]

In the communities where crimes had taken place, an unwillingness to discuss civil rights murders reflected both the levels of fear generated by the racial terror campaign and the awareness that blacks and whites remained sharply divided about the crimes. Around Money, Mississippi, Emmett Till's murder became a taboo subject. "People didn't want to talk about it, not blacks and not whites," one black man recalled. That was "the way everyone got along with each other out in this rural area. You had to deal with each other." Carolyn Maull, a fourteen-year-old who was in the sanctuary when the bomb exploded at Birmingham Baptist Church, recalled the silence that descended on her community after the bombing. No one mentioned the four dead girls after the funeral, she wrote in 2011. "It was like the word *cancer*. No one wanted to say it out loud or acknowledge it. . . . It was almost as if it never happened."[7] In Philadelphia, Mississippi, the local schools did not teach anything about the 1964 triple murder that had taken place there, and few reminders of Goodman, Chaney, and Schwerner or, indeed, of the civil rights struggle could be found in Neshoba County. Donna Ladd, a white native of Philadelphia who would eventually embrace the cause of reopening these cases, didn't even know that the killings had taken place in her hometown until she was fourteen. "We didn't talk about it in school. Our parents didn't tell us about it," she later wrote. "There was a conspiracy of silence to pretend that all that ugliness, set off by 'outsider agitators,' would just stay in the past where it belonged." Twenty years later, there had never been a community-wide commemoration for the three victims. The local paper, the *Neshoba Democrat*, did not acknowledge the twentieth anniversary of the murders.[8]

Family members or friends of victims would take the lead in countering this campaign to eradicate these crimes from the historical record. They recognized that these repressive efforts to silence discussion of the victims of civil rights violence was in many ways a continuation, in less violent form, of the politics of terror that had prevailed during the movement. Mamie Till Mobley, who had defied authorities by allowing the black press to publish photos of her son's mutilated corpse, describes "making a commitment to rip the covers off Mississippi, USA," to reveal to the world "the horrible face of race hatred." She became a regular speaker for the NAACP in order to tell the world about Emmett's murder. In 1973, she founded the Emmett Till Players, a performance group where black children could learn about their history. And on every anniversary of the murder, she willingly "relived the tragedy" whenever reporters asked her about it.[9] Her work helped ensure that Emmett could not be forgotten; indeed, many years after his death, seeing the photos of Till's corpse in *Jet* magazine would spur an aspiring black filmmaker to tackle the project of getting the murder case reopened.

Myrlie Evers too dedicated herself to ensuring her slain husband was not forgotten. After her husband's death, she began to travel around the country as a regular speaker for the NAACP. Although initially reluctant to become a public figure, she had, she said, "a strong desire not to have him forgotten in a month or two the way so many others had been." Her lectures became her way of "working to keep his name alive in people's memories."[10] Both Till Mobley and Evers-Williams drew on the limited cultural capital they had, as mother and widow, to use their private grief to fuel public remembrance.

In Neshoba County, a handful of people worked to keep residents from effacing the memory of the 1964 triple murder there, or, as slain civil rights worker James Chaney's younger brother Ben put it, to prevent whites from sweeping "all the dirt under their carpet." Cornelius and Mabel Steele, members of the church the Klan burned to lure Mickey Schwerner out to rural Neshoba County, refused to let the murders fade completely from the community's memory. From 1964 on, Cornelius Steele organized an annual memorial ceremony at the church in the hopes that commemorating the slain activists each year would help lead to justice some day. Some years, there were only a few people there, but Cornelius Steele persisted, sometimes even paying a preacher for the memorial ceremony out of his own pocket. For years, the Longdale commemoration represented the only local acknowledgment of the murders.[11] Ben Chaney, only ten years old when his brother James was murdered, joined the struggle to keep his memory alive when he became an adult. He, along with representatives from the Goodman and Schwerner families, organized a Freedom Ride bus tour to Mississippi to commemorate the three slain men on the twentieth anniversary of the murders in 1984. It marked the first time he had returned to the state since fleeing with his family as a child. Soon after, Chaney established the James Earl Chaney Foundation to conduct voter registration campaigns, to investigate allegations of racism in the court system, and to raise money to protect his brother's frequently vandalized gravestone.[12]

In this environment of repressive silence, there was little hope of persuading authorities to reopen investigations into civil rights murders despite the efforts of some relatives. Although Myrlie Evers moved to California to rebuild her life after her husband's murder, she returned to Mississippi three times a year to keep tabs on Beckwith, hoping that he would eventually incriminate himself. She subscribed to Mississippi newspapers to keep watch for information that she could use to get the case reopened. When friends told her she should just let it go, she insisted that she had promised Medgar that if anything ever happened to him, she would pursue justice. Mamie Till Mobley too wanted justice for her son; she described new legal action in her son's murder as "a dream I have had since I left the courtroom." Vernon Dahmer's family, who had seen at least a few of the men involved in their father's murder serve some jail time in the 1960s, was not satisfied with that outcome.

"We're not vindictive folks," Vernon Dahmer Jr. insisted, but "we won't be satisfied until the judicial process works for us as a black family."[13]

Relatives of victims proved the most insistent advocates because these cases had such deep personal and political meaning for them. The failures of the justice system in the 1960s and efforts to erase these crimes from the historical record only added to the intense pain and grief they experienced when their loved ones were murdered. However much others around them might want to put this history to rest, their own wounds had never healed. As Vernon Dahmer's widow explained, "It may be the in past for them, but it's not in the past for us." Ben Chaney constantly met people in Philadelphia, Mississippi, who told him, "It's 40 years later, let bygones be bygones. Why open up dead wounds, you know?" But for him, the wound was "still there . . . knowing that my brother lost his life in that community, and yet still, a lot of the attitudes have not changed." The long failure to bring charges only exacerbated his personal pain. Myrlie Evers did not believe Beckwith's conviction would end all of her pain, but she was certain that legal justice would allow her and her children to heal in a way they could not while Medgar Evers's assassin remained free.[14]

Their quest for legal justice reflected an ongoing political struggle to ensure that African Americans be recognized as first-class citizens of the United States. Legal scholar Mark Weiner argues that for a group to achieve full civic membership in the United States, they must be perceived as "people of law," which requires both that they "be deemed worthy of the law and its protection" and that they "demonstrate a commitment to the law in its culture and everyday practices."[15] In pursuing criminal prosecution decades after the original crimes, relatives of victims demanded that southern states compensate for their failure to grant blacks legal protection in the past. They did so in a way that made clear their own commitment to the legal process and the very idea of legal justice. Myrlie Evers always understood that the quest to reopen her husband's case was part of a "larger and truly more important" mission. For her, Beckwith's continued freedom symbolized "the sad reality that the American justice system doesn't work for all of its citizens." It represented "everything Medgar fought so hard against." Shelton Chappell, son of Johnnie Mae Chappell, too insisted that his mother deserved her day in court. "We could have let this go, but it would have been a slap in the face to my mother." Chappell saw the pursuit of legal justice as a way to affirm the value of the life of his mother.[16]

Many of these relatives sought legal justice not just as an affirmation of the worth of their loved ones, but also as a way to expose the systemic racism that had led to their deaths in the first place. Those closest to these crimes knew full well that the responsibility for their loved ones' deaths went well beyond the Klan. Myrlie Evers described her husband's murder as "an official act." As she saw it, Byron De La Beckwith "had been appointed by the state to carry out the execution of an enemy of the state, an execution that the state could not, in all good public relations, openly carry out itself." For her, getting Beckwith back in court was a way to put Mississippi on trial. The widow of Mickey Schwerner would be unwavering in her insistence that any meaningful justice for her husband would have to expose the complicity that the state had played in enabling his murder; the men who killed her husband "didn't act in a vacuum," she insisted. The state, she charged, was "complicit in these crimes and all the crimes that occurred, and that has to be opened up." Wasn't it time, she asked when Jerry Mitchell discovered new evidence in the case in 1998, for the state to take a real look at the role it had played, "instead of continuing to duck responsibility?"[17]

Despite the commitment of relatives to securing legal justice for their loved ones, only one civil rights–era murder case was successfully brought back into the courtroom before 1989. That reopening took place because the same person who had a passionate commitment to legal justice happened to be in a political position to pursue it on his own authority. In 1975, the attorney general of Alabama, Bill Baxley, reopened an investigation into the Sixteenth Street Baptist Church bombing, and in 1977 won a conviction of Robert Chambliss for murder. Baxley took on the bombing case as a political crusade knowing that it would likely hurt his career. The lack of support he received in the process ensured that few other southern legal officials would be eager to follow in his footsteps.

Of all the racially motivated crimes that took place in the 1950s and 1960s, few had shaken the nation as powerfully as the 1963 bombing that left four black girls dead as they prepared for Sunday school. The victims became immortalized under the moniker "four little girls," a label that emphasized their youth, gender, and innocence.[18] Bill Baxley, a law student at the University of Alabama in 1963, had been horrified by the bombing. "It just made me sick," he recalled. "I wondered who could do something like that, kill four kids." Baxley had long been uncomfortable with the racial status quo. Singing songs about racial equality at his Methodist church, he had taken them seriously. Baxley hoped that, as a law student, he could volunteer to help out with the prosecution once the FBI arrested suspects.[19] But the FBI never arrested any suspects; J. Edgar Hoover ordered the investigation shelved and Alabama state authorities scuttled their own inquiry.

When Baxley became the youngest attorney general in the state's history, just twenty-eight when he was elected in 1970, he saw it as an opportunity to do something about a crime that had long obsessed him. The plaque he hung behind his desk paraphrased Dante: "The hottest places in hell are reserved for those who in times of great moral crisis maintain their neutrality." Almost as soon as he was sworn in, he assigned an investigator to the case and requested the FBI files on the bombing. It would take Baxley five years to convince a very suspicious FBI to share the information with him; to do so, he had to threaten to expose their efforts to hinder the case in the national press and to bring the families of the victims to Washington for a press conference. The FBI begrudgingly relented, and by 1977, Baxley's team had assembled enough evidence to press charges against Bob "Dynamite" Chambliss.[20] After a five-day trial that hinged on the testimony of several of Chambliss's white female relatives, a jury found Chambliss guilty and sentenced him to life in prison.

In this case, Baxley had to place pressure on the FBI, not on state authorities, since he was the state authority leading the case. The tools he used to do so—planning to bring in the families to win sympathy and threatening embarrassing press coverage—would be the same kind that activists would later use to win support for reopening other cases. But Baxley was operating within a political climate very different from that of later activists. Baxley had hoped that his office would be able to investigate other civil rights–era murders and to bring more charges in the bombing case.[21] Yet Chambliss's conviction proved not the first salvo in a crusade, but an anomaly. No one else would be indicted for the bombing for another twenty-five years.

The FBI deserves some of the blame for the failure of the conviction to spark any further trials. Like southern states that had little interest in revisiting their histories of racial violence, the bureau was not eager in the mid-1970s to see its activities in the 1960s exposed to public view. Under intense scrutiny from Congress for its domestic surveillance programs in the wake of the Watergate scandal, the FBI was already fighting civil charges that its informant Gary Thomas Rowe had failed to prevent the murder of Viola Liuzzo.[22] It wanted to limit any further disclosures of its unsavory relationship with Klan informants. As a result, the bureau not only delayed Baxley's investigation of Chambliss, but also failed to inform him that they had audiotapes that implicated Tom Blanton in the bombing. When the tapes were finally turned over to Alabama prosecutors in 1997, a livid Baxley argued that their actions had allowed Blanton to avoid prosecution. The FBI, he charged, had given Blanton a twenty-year "get out of jail free card."[23]

While FBI foot-dragging slowed him down, Bill Baxley's efforts fizzled because it really was, for the most part, a one-man crusade. Baxley received hate mail from around the country, and even his friends wondered why he was "dragging" this old civil rights case back into the light. Digging up the past would only rekindle old racial animosities and lead to negative publicity about the city, Baxley was told. But Baxley saw it differently. This case, he insisted, must be revisited because it was fundamentally immoral to treat black children as less deserving of legal justice than white children. He asked whites who opposed his investigation why they didn't treat this murder the way they would that of four little white girls. If four white girls were murdered, "you would want that case pursued to the ends of the earth." Why couldn't "good people" feel the same way about the church bombing? he asked. And far from hurting Birmingham by focusing attention on the church bombing, revisiting the bombing, Baxley insisted, was instead "a means to cleanse a black mark from his state's history." Finding Chambliss guilty would help change Birmingham's still-negative national image. A conviction, he told the jury, would "show the world that this murder case has been solved by the people of Alabama."[24] Baxley argued that the city would gain more by confronting its history in the courtroom than by ignoring it.

While the Birmingham press described the conviction as bringing an "unashamed sense of relief" and for easing the "nagging civic frustration" left by the unresolved nature of the church bombing, few in the city shared Baxley's zeal for revisiting the city's history of racial violence.[25] Many at the time questioned his political motives, suggesting that he only pushed the investigation because he wanted to woo newly enfranchised black voters, a charge Baxley considered ridiculous. Only fools thought that appealing to African Americans would help someone win a political election in 1970s Alabama, Baxley insisted. And, in fact, when Baxley ran for governor in 1978, he attributed his loss to his role in pushing for the church bombing trial: "Every day, every town, every plant gate, a dozen people a day, at least, would not shake hands or would say 'I would have voted for you. I liked you. I thought you were my kind, but you put that old man in jail.'"[26] Putting other old men in jail for the racial crimes of the civil rights era held little interest for the man who succeeded Baxley as attorney general, and Alabama authorities quietly closed ongoing investigations.

The first reopening of a civil rights–era murder did not spur others and it did not seem to change the city of Birmingham's orientation towards the bombing. Six years after the trial, bombing victim Denise McNair's father, Chris, expressed frustration that convicting Chambliss had not led to more substantive change in Birmingham or to more open conversation about the crime. The only memorial to the girls remained a stained glass window, donated to the Sixteenth Street Baptist Church by the people of Wales. "People want you to forget that 16th Street happened," he charged. "Why do you want to sweep it under the rug?"[27] In 1977, the forces arrayed against remembering these crimes or revisiting them through the criminal justice system remained very powerful. By 1990, however, when a Mississippi grand jury indicted Byron De La Beckwith for the murder of Medgar Evers, political and cultural forces had converged to draw new and more intense attention to these unresolved crimes, and to create the conditions that would enable those committed to seeing legal justice to achieve greater success.

In the 1970s and 1980s, whites' attitudes about race underwent a dramatic shift. In the wake of the civil rights movement, the idea of biological racism lost legitimacy, as did expressions of overt racial bigotry. With the passage of the 1964 and 1965 Civil Rights Acts, government-sanctioned racial discrimination became impermissible. The demise of Jim Crow–type racial thinking had a major impact in the arena of the law, and especially in the growth of support for the principle of formal legal equality. That principle, which legal scholar Roy Brooks claims has become the nation's "fundamental public policy on civil rights" since the 1960s, held that since there were no "legally material" differences between the races, blacks and whites were "entitled to equal legal treatment." This discrediting of caste thinking has led to the ascendance of liberal universalism, an ideology that stresses the equal legal protection of individuals, as the foundation of the nation's shared legal values and in many ways its shared identity.[28]

Poll data since the 1970s reflect the widespread acceptance of the principle of legal equality. Although changes in racial attitudes came slowest to the Deep South, polls since the 1970s have shown a steady increase among whites for the principle of racial integration and formal equal opportunity. By the 1980s, white Americans from a range of political backgrounds had accepted the position that the government should not discriminate on the basis of race. Critics have been quick to note that embracing formal legal equality was not the same as supporting government policies that might help to make racial equality a meaningful reality, such as busing or affirmative action. Indeed, embracing the idea of equality before the law could easily lead to the claim that public policy designed to redress racial inequalities was as dangerous as public policies that had explicitly discriminated against people because of their race, an ideology often referred to as "colorblindness."[29]

But the emerging consensus about the importance of formal legal equality served to make the murders of the civil rights era more unsettling and disturbing to many Americans; civil rights crimes became more offensive to an American sensibility and identity founded on a belief in legal equality for all. Racially motivated murders ignored by the political and legal system called into question one of the basic tenets of liberal civil ideology that had become widely accepted by the 1980s—that everyone, black or white, deserved equal protection of the law. As a result, a quarter century or more after the crimes had taken place, victims of the racial violence of the civil rights era resurfaced in public consciousness with a new intensity. Mamie Till Mobley noticed the change in 1985, at the thirtieth anniversary of Emmett's murder. While a few local newspapers and media outlets typically contacted her on the five-year anniversaries of his death, 1985 was different: "There was a spark," she later wrote.

"There seemed to be even greater interest in the Emmett Till story than at other times, interest that came from way beyond Chicago."[30]

The Southern Poverty Law Center's (SPLC) decision to build a memorial to civil rights martyrs outside their headquarters in Montgomery, Alabama, reflected this historical moment of renewed public interest in the violence of the civil rights era. A nonprofit civil rights law firm founded in 1971 by Morris Dees and Joseph Levin, the SPLC pioneered the strategy of bankrupting hate groups by filing civil lawsuits against them when they committed acts of violence. In 1988, speaking about one of the organization's major legal victories at a NAACP meeting, Dees discovered that most of the younger members of the audience had never heard of the victims of Klan violence from the 1960s. The next day, Dees committed himself to building a monument to ensure that those who lost their lives during the civil rights movement would never be forgotten. He raised $650,000 for a memorial and commissioned young sculptor Maya Lin, famous for designing the Vietnam Veterans Memorial, to create it. The black granite memorial she constructed featured the names of forty "martyrs" of the civil rights movement, though the SPLC uncovered many more murders they might have included on the monument if they had been able to obtain more information about them. Six thousand people attended the dedication ceremony in 1989, including family members of thirty-nine of the forty victims. To Andrew Goodman's mother, the memorial was "poetry in granite." The martyrs' memorial wrote in stone the failures of the government to protect blacks and it represented one of the first efforts to document the extent of violence during the civil rights era. It also served as a crucial catalyst to bring further attention to these cases; when Jerry Mitchell began exploring cold civil rights murder cases, he used the research that the SPLC had done as his starting point.[31]

The increasing number of artistic works that took civil rights–era murders as their subject starting in the late 1980s further evidenced a renewed interest in civil rights crimes. Emmett Till's murder had inspired a great deal of artistic expression in the 1950s and 1960s, but had receded from public attention in the 1970s and early 1980s. But in the late 1980s and early 1990s, the murder again became a popular subject for artists, with over sixty novels, poems, or plays based on the Till case appearing since 1990.[32] Writers and filmmakers turned their attention to other crimes too, including the Birmingham church bombing,

The Civil Rights Martyrs Memorial, dedicated by the Southern Poverty Law Center outside its Montgomery, Alabama, office in 1989, reflected the growing public interest in civil rights–era murders in the late 1980s and 1990s. (© Philip Gould/Corbis)

the 1964 murders of Goodman, Chaney, and Schwerner, and a host of lesser-known murders. Many of these new works particularly sought to work through the relation of whites to these historic crimes. Lewis Nordan's 1993 novel *Wolf Whistle* focused on the response of working-class whites to an Emmett Till–like murder. Susan Carol McCarthy's 1991 novel *Lay That Trumpet in Our Hands* told the story of a white informer for the FBI in a case based on the bombing deaths of Harry and Harriette Moore. *Stick Wife*, a 1989 play by Darrah Cloud, imagined the position of the white wife of one of the Birmingham church bombers.

The impact of shifts in whites' racial attitudes could be seen not only in these efforts at memorialization or representation, but also in the new language that emerged in discussions of civil rights–era murders. By the 1990s, some advocates of reopening these cases began comparing the pursuit of civil rights murderers to that of Nazi war criminals, an analogy that portrayed civil rights murders, like the genocide of the Jews, as a special class of crimes that called into question the basic tenets of a democracy, or even of a civilized society. When asked about efforts to reopen the Emmett Till case in 1994, Bill Baxley equated the crimes "committed by the assassins of civil rights days" to those of "Nazi war criminals." Morris Dees of the Southern Poverty Law Center took the comparison further. These were not "simple murder cases," he argued. "It was a crime against a whole class of people, like the Holocaust. You should pursue these cases forever." The analogy with the hunt for Nazi war criminals underscored the validity of pursuing old men for crimes committed decades earlier.[33]

Given this comparison between civil rights murderers and Nazi war criminals, it is not surprising that some journalists saw new prosecutions in these cases as in the same class as the Nuremberg war crimes tribunals, the trials the victors conducted at the end of World War II to hold Nazi leaders accountable for a new class of "crimes against humanity."[34] Comparisons to Nuremberg were scant but powerful, for they implied by analogy that prosecuting cold civil rights cases would set new legal and democratic norms that established the illegitimacy and immorality of conduct that had been previously accepted. To the journal of the American Bar Association, a new prosecution in the Vernon Dahmer case would be a "Nuremberg-like trial," while prolific journalist Jerry Mitchell described civil rights trials as "the nation's Nurembergs."[35] The allusion to Nuremberg highlighted trials as a powerful affirmation of democratic norms of legality.

The changing political environment, which made it possible to portray efforts to bring civil rights–era murderers to court in the same light as the pursuit of the Nazi criminals, did not silence debate about the value of trying to put now-elderly men in jail for crimes they had allegedly committed decades earlier. When discussions of reopening the Beckwith case began in 1989, the Jackson newspaper reported that it could not find a single white person who favored the idea. Critical calls and letters flooded the attorney general's office arguing variously that the case was too old, that the defendant was too old, that a prosecution would cost too much money, and that it would open up old wounds. Pursuing prosecutions, such criticisms implied, not only represented a poor use of state resources, but would also have the negative consequence of fostering racial divisions. Reopening the investigation into Emmett Till's murder, a white woman argued in 2004, would just bring up "a lot of ill feelings and we have enough of that in the South as it is." A white man expressed his opposition in more vivid language. "Stirring up crap," he argued, "just makes it stink worse."[36]

But the influence of the shifts in attitudes and values that made civil rights–era murders a violation of the basic principle of equality before the law could be heard in the rejoinders to such arguments. Bobby DeLaughter posed his own questions in response to those who questioned whether it was worthwhile to reopen the Beckwith case. "We say that no man is above the law; but what if he is seventy years old?" Exactly "how much taxpayer money" was too much to spend in the pursuit of "justice and maintaining freedom?" And if pursuing justice would open an old wound, then wasn't that a wound that needed to reopened and cleansed? he asked. DeLaughter framed his support in terms of the importance of upholding the law and providing equal justice for all, no matter who the victim was or how much time had passed since the crime. An editorial in the *Arkansas Democrat-Gazette* explained that retrying Byron De La Beckwith was "as legitimate as Simon Wiesenthal's pursuit of aging Nazis." To not hold "home-grown practitioners of hatred" accountable in the same way we expected aged Nazis to be, another editorial declared, "would be to condone injustice."[37] Just as it was appropriate to track down old Nazis, elderly assassins in the civil rights South deserved their day in court.

As the new racial and political climate brought civil rights–era murders back onto the national stage, some white Southerners became more concerned about the consequences for the region if Southerners refused to address them. For decades, southern communities and political leaders had worked to silence discussion of these killings. Yet by the 1990s, it had become clear that the strategy was failing. A Mississippi county sheriff acknowledged as much when he was asked about efforts to reopen the investigation into Ben Chester White's 1966 murder. "That era that we like to try to forget, or put into the past," he admitted, "continues to haunt us to this day."[38] His language was telling; white Southerners, he acknowledged, had actively tried to put their violent history "into the past." But that history had not gone away, and as it began to resurface in the 1980s and '90s, it created a dynamic similar to that of the 1960s, when Southerners had complained that the media and other "outsiders" unfairly stigmatized the region as a backward place populated by racist thugs. It began to seem to some Southerners that ending Jim Crow and joining the rest of the nation in voicing support for the principles of racial equality would not be enough to allow the South to leave this past behind.

That, at least, was the message that some younger white Southerners took when Hollywood added its own entry to the bevy of new artistic works about civil rights murders that began to appear in the late 1980s and early 1990s. In 1988, theaters across the country were showing *Mississippi Burning*, a highly fictionalized account of the FBI investigation into the 1964 Goodman, Chaney, and Schwerner murders. While the movie proved a financial and critical success—it earned seven Academy Award nominations, including one for best picture—historians derided it for portraying the FBI agents who broke the case as heroes and blacks as passive, helpless victims of violence. To many white Southerners, especially those in Mississippi, it was the film's portrayal of them as a monolithic group of thugs and racists that particularly stung. During the federal trial in 1967, the local newspaper in Neshoba County had lambasted media descriptions of Philadelphia as a place where "a bunch of rednecks" stood "in tight little knots on the streets." In 1988, *Mississippi Burning* would resurrect and popularize this image, with scenes that featured not only gangs of "rednecks" on the streets, but also whites throwing black victims of violence out of their cars downtown in the middle of the day. It was, journalist Adam Nossiter would later write, "the simple, demoniacal picture of Mississippi most Americans had in 1964, reified for the screen a quarter century later."[39]

To a new generation of southern politicians who were eager to lead the South into a new era, the portrayal in *Mississippi Burning* made plain that many outside the South continued to see the region as they had in the 1960s. In Mississippi, the movie would be a wake-up call to a group of young and energetic reform-minded politicians who became known as the "Boys of Spring." Dick Molpus, the young secretary of state who was a native of Philadelphia, argued that the film put a burden on those who were part of a "new breed" to spread the word that the state "is a remarkably different place now than it was then." Mississippi's governor Ray Mabus agreed that the state needed to focus on improving its national image. "History is something that should be controlled and not controlling," he insisted in his 1988 inaugural address. "We in our generation can make the history of Mississippi." For Mabus and other like-minded politicians, *Mississippi Burning* presented a major public relations crisis that further demonstrated how important it was that Mississippians find a way to take control over a past that outsiders used to define them.[40]

In 1989, those who wanted to control history, not be controlled by it, assumed a different attitude towards the crime showcased in *Mississippi Burning*. In March, Governor Mabus threw his support behind the bus tour being organized by the Chaney, Goodman, and Schwerner families to commemorate the deaths of the slain activists. In May, the state approved a privately funded historical marker to commemorate the three men. And when the *Neshoba Democrat* editor who had not written anything about the murders in 1984 decided to organize a community commemoration ceremony for the twenty-fifth anniversary of the murders, Dick Molpus attended and became the first state official to apologize for the crime.[41]

Mississippi was not the only state to feel that it needed to find a new way to deal with a history that continued to stigmatize it. Even though Birmingham had sent one of the church bombers to jail in 1977, many leaders there still felt that the violence of the civil rights era tarnished the city's reputation. David Vann, who served as mayor in the late 1970s, argued that the city would never live down images of police using attack dogs against peaceful protestors or breaking up peaceful demonstrations with high-powered fire hoses unless they took the initiative to revisit their history. He began to pitch the idea of building a museum dedicated to the civil rights struggle as one way to help the city get past the stigma of being the site of iconic images of racial violence in the 1960s. As Vann saw it, a civil rights museum would both commemorate the past and help contain it. As he baldly asserted, the "best way to put your bad images to rest is to declare them history and put them in a museum."[42] Birmingham could not undo the racial violence that took place there, but it could do its part to frame that violence as a part of history that the city had moved beyond.

The desire to challenge negative portrayals of the region did not necessarily translate into a pressing concern to initiate new legal processes in old murder cases. For one thing, not everyone shared Dick Molpus's view that the region should act to improve its national reputation. When Molpus ran for governor in 1996, his opponent, Kirk Fordice, attacked him for publicly apologizing for the Freedom Summer murders. "I don't believe we need to run this state for *Mississippi Burning*," Fordice told the nearly all-white crowd at the Neshoba County Fair. "Never apologize! Never look back! Forward together."[43] He easily won the election. Many white Southerners would share Fordice's adamant opposition to changing their own behavior just to answer outside critics.

Even those who wanted to rehabilitate the South's reputation, moreover, did not necessarily agree that reopening old murder cases was the best way to do so. Focusing attention on old crimes, especially when there was no guarantee that a new trial would result in a conviction, could further damage the South's image. The prosecutor who had argued the case against Beckwith in 1964 thus warned Bobby DeLaughter that if he reopened the case, he better have the evidence to win, because if he lost it would deal a "damaging blow . . . to Mississippi's improving image." The lead investigator into Vernon Dahmer's murder in 1966 was more vigorous in his opposition when it looked like state authorities might reopen that case. The state of Mississippi had made "more progress than any other state in the union," he argued, and the more the case was discussed, "the more you bring it to the minds of people who don't remember it or who have gotten over it." It would be "ruinacious" to bring it back to court.[44]

Yet a sense that reopening these cases and holding new trials could help the region address and overcome the stigma of its racial history would prove a powerful motivator for at least some white political officials. Bobby DeLaughter came to understand the murder of Medgar Evers as an act that had unfairly tarnished the state. Evers's assassination, he wrote in his memoir, was not just a wrong dealt to the Evers family; "Mississippi's honor and reputation had been smeared by the assassin's bullet, as well." Even those who hadn't liked Evers should have been outraged by an act that delivered a "kick-in-the-balls blow" to the state's image, he insisted. When he began to think about the reopening as a way to bring "honor" to his home state, his commitment to the process increased.[45] When civil rights cases reached the courtroom, the arguments put forth by prosecutors would make clear that many shared DeLaughter's hope of using trials as a way to redeem the reputation of their home states.

At the same time as changes in the racial and political arena began to shift understandings of these crimes and to lead some whites to consider new legal action, activists working to get the legal cases of their loved ones reopened found themselves able to exert new pressure on state authorities because of African Americans' growing political power in the South. One of the most immediate and visible changes in the wake of the movement was the entry of blacks into the formal political system. After the passage of the 1965 Voting Rights Act, blacks began to win local, state, and even national political office, increasing their influence on the political stage. In Mississippi, for example, blacks accounted for over one-third of registered voters by the mid-1980s, and the state would have more elected black officials than any other in the nation by 1990, including the first southern black congressman elected since Reconstruction. In southern cities, too, blacks gained more political power, both because of shifts to more representative forms of government and because of white flight out of cities like Jackson to surrounding suburbs. By 1991, Jackson had become a majority-black city, and by 1993, blacks would dominate the city council.[46]

Although some critics charged that district attorneys who reopened cases were just trying to win black votes, there's little evidence that black voters were inclined to cast their ballots based on how a local DA handled a decades-old murder case. African Americans, like whites, were divided about the value and benefit of reopening these cases. Some younger African Americans didn't necessarily understand the political significance of the crimes. When Bryon De La Beckwith was finally charged again Myrlie Evers recalls wanting to go out and grab the young blacks whom she heard saying that it was a waste of time because Beckwith was so old. Older blacks, she argued, "had failed to communicate to our young people all that we had been through." She was dismayed that so few blacks from the community came to the courthouse to watch the trial.[47]

Those who had lived through the Jim Crow era had their own reasons to express reservations about revisiting the period. Seventy-four-year-old Mary Jackson of Leflore County remembered the Jim Crow era as a "dreadful" time with so much fear and prejudice, and wondered "what would be accomplished" by reopening the Till case: "We just want this story to die so people won't keep talking about it." For her, reopening the case threatened to upset the social order: "We don't need no more trouble," she explained. Other African Americans questioned the utility of pursuing trials in decades-old cases given other pressing needs in their communities. Thomas Foster, an African American from Ruleville, questioned whether the money being spent on Beckwith's trial was really worth it. "He's guilty as hell, but making him a priority doesn't do any good." He would have preferred the state to spend that money on a new factory.[48]

But for those for whom the pursuit of legal justice was important, the new electoral power of blacks ensured that their interests were accorded more respect by political authorities. The FBI reopened its investigation into the Birmingham church bombing case as a way to appease African Americans in that city. In 1993, after a Justice Department investigation that led to corruption charges against the city's first black mayor, the new FBI agent in charge of the Birmingham office began reaching out to local black leaders as a way to mend fences. When Rob Langford asked black leaders what he could do to try to repair their relationship with federal authorities, they asked him to see if anyone else could be prosecuted for the church bombing.[49] The FBI's move to reopen the case signaled its desire to maintain strong working ties with local blacks.

The growing number of black elected officials in the South, who could use their positions to move cases forward, created new opportunities for activists who were lobbying for legal attention to civil rights–era murders. Public pressure on authorities to reopen the Beckwith case intensified when one of the black members on the Jackson City Council convinced his colleagues to pass a resolution asking the DA's office to investigate Jerry Mitchell's charges of jury tampering. When Vernon Dahmer's family wanted to put pressure on state and federal authorities to move forward on the case, they turned to Bennie Thompson, a Mississippi congressman first elected to office in 1993. Thompson helped get the FBI to turn over forty thousand pages of records to Forrest County prosecutors. Black politicians like Thompson proved especially important in the 1990s before the idea of seeking new trials for civil rights crimes gained broader political support. When Thompson was asked about his role in the Dahmer case, he explained that he was "asked by this family for help, and it was clear from their request that no other federal office was going to help them."[50] Thompson assisted the Dahmers when few other national politicians would. In subsequent years, while black elected officials remained supportive of the process, they would not be the only ones willing to do so. While famed former civil rights activist John Lewis, now a Georgia congressman, sponsored the legislation to provide federal funds for civil rights cold case investigations in the House of Representatives in 2006, it would be two white senators, one Democrat and one Republican, who introduced the legislation in the Senate.

As much as the quest to reopen cases was fostered by shifts in political power, changing attitudes among whites, and the insistent demands of families, it would not have taken place or have generated as much momentum as it did without the work of journalists. Although Myrlie Evers committed decades of her life to bringing her husband's case back to court and Bobby DeLaughter prosecuted the case in court, when Byron De La Beckwith was finally led off to jail in 1994, the two words he supposedly repeated under his breath were, "Jerry Mitchell, Jerry Mitchell."[51] Beckwith's muttered mantra underscores the instrumental role the media played in generating momentum and support for reopening civil rights cold cases.[52] Convincing state authorities to begin new legal proceedings typically required both concerted political activism and coverage by the media. In their crusade for justice, many family members received assistance from journalists. The extensive media coverage of civil rights crimes signaled that revisiting these crimes was important and ensured that message would be communicated to a broad audience. That coverage also promoted particular frames for understanding the crimes that helped shape public opinion, and the investigations undertaken by journalists often proved the catalyst that led authorities to take action.

The new interest of journalists in civil rights murders stemmed from many of the same trends that led to a more conducive climate for reopenings. Jerry Mitchell, for example, began to investigate the state's racial history after attending a press screening of *Mississippi Burning* and realizing he knew very little about the civil rights movement. That movie spurred him to follow up on a rumor that some files of the Mississippi Sovereignty Commission had accidentally been left open in court records. His interest in those files led a source to begin providing him with many more, launching the process that would lead to Byron De La Beckwith's downfall.[53] At the same time, Mitchell's employer, the *Clarion-Ledger* of Jackson, had changed almost beyond recognition since the days of segregation. The *Clarion-Ledger* once actively colluded with state authorities to fight integration. But in the mid-1970s, the publisher began hiring more black staff, a process accelerated in 1982 when the national media firm the Gannett Corporation bought the paper. By the early 1990s, the paper had a black managing editor and a large number of black reporters. It had also begun some soul-searching, reporting in depth not just on the racial crimes of Mississippi's past, but also on the paper's own racist history.[54] Mitchell would begin focusing much of his reporting on Mississippi's racist past, gradually assuming what became a new kind of civil rights cold case beat.

Unrelated developments in the national media landscape also contributed to increased attention to the stories of civil rights murders, especially the seemingly boundless popularity of the format of the televised newsmagazine. Premiering in 1968, *60 Minutes* pioneered the new format, which featured lengthy in-depth reporting on each story. But the format really took off in the 1990s, when the four major broadcast networks routinely aired programs like Connie Chung's *20/20*, *Primetime Live*, and *Dateline NBC* up to ten hours a week.[55] The mainstream media has long treated "crime and justice as theater."[56] Newsmagazines would take that interest in crime as theater to a new level, presenting news as entertainment with character-driven stories akin to docudramas. The promotional tagline for NBC's newsmagazine, *Turning Point*, declared, "It feels like a movie, but it's real." Stories of unrepentant Klansmen and unsolved cold cases proved ripe for coverage by the newsmagazines' style of dramatic human-interest journalism, and many aired extended stories about civil rights-era murders. And although newsmagazines' confrontational style of coverage was derisively described as "Connie Chung looking for a Klansman" by one Mississippi newspaper journalist, TV journalists like Chung would uncover evidence that served as a catalyst to reopen more than one investigation.[57]

At the same time as the popularity of the newsmagazine format grew, the media began to show more interest in old unsolved criminal cases, or "cold cases." Three television shows popular in the 1990s and 2000s focused on investigative units that tackled such cases. The documentary-style series *Unsolved Mysteries*, which premiered on NBC in 1998 and is still running on the Lifetime channel, employed reenactments, special effects, and interviews with families and police to tell the stories of real unsolved crimes. The A&E network's *Cold Case Files*, which ran from 1999 until 2006, featured long-unsolved murders that were cracked through modern forensic science, criminal psychology, and newly cooperative witnesses. Most episodes ended with police arresting a killer while under the watchful gaze of the victim's spirit. *Cold Case*, launched by CBS in 2003, focused on a fictional Philadelphia cold case investigative unit. A cultural fascination with cold cases fostered the sense that reopening even decades-old cases was a viable project. These programs helped ensure, in the words of retired University of Georgia Law Professor Ron Carlson, that "the current mood is much more receptive to even old cases."[58] And all of the series featured at least one episode focused on a civil rights–era murder. *Unsolved Mysteries* reenacted the ambush that killed Oneal Moore in 1990. Vernon Dahmer's murder was the subject of a 2003 episode of *Cold Case Files*, while *Cold Case* featured two episodes during its seven-year run inspired by civil rights cold cases, the 1955 lynching of Emmett Till and the 1965 murder of Viola Liuzzo.[59]

This journalistic coverage played a vital role in bringing the past back into the present and making the crimes and their victims live again in ways that made them salient to the general public. Political theorist W. James Booth notes that "the past, at least in its public and political form, must be called into existence, put into words, or commemorated in stone, provided a vocabulary that will allow it to emerge." Media coverage has called this past back into existence in a way that, as Booth notes, "seeks to impose a duty on us." Just the telling of the story of the life of Ben Chester White or Charles Moore and Henry Dee kept their murders from "falling into the dustbins of history," as Dick Molpus expressed it, and implied that the victims were deserving of legal justice.[60]

Even more significantly, the media began to cover the crimes in a way that would help generate a sense of obligation to act by focusing on the suffering of the family members left behind. The attention given to relatives of those who had been murdered, the "secondary victims," was not unique to the coverage of civil rights murders. Indeed, the shift reflected the success of the 1980s victims' rights movement, which actively sought to focus the media on the pain of the grieving relatives of victims after a violent crime.[61] The vast numbers of media articles on civil rights cold cases from the 1990s and 2000s reflect this trend; articles nearly always featured the story of the widows who lost husbands, the now-grown children who lost their fathers, even grandchildren who never met their grandparents. A 2005 *Dateline* story on the efforts to reopen the case of Johnnie Mae Chappell's 1964 murder offers a typical example:

> About 41 years ago, Shelton Chappell's mother Johnnie Mae was killed by a single gunshot from a passing car. . . . Shelton was an infant when his mother died. A sad photo taken in the county morgue of his father looking down at his mother's body, is the only picture Shelton has of her. Growing up, he never knew the full story about who killed her or why—but was certain that he didn't want her to be forgotten.[62]

Lacking photos of Johnnie Mae Chappell, the piece instead showed her now-grown son standing near a gravesite. This new orientation could also be seen in documentary films like Spike Lee's 1997 *Four Little Girls*, which sought to make each of the four victims come alive as an individual by focusing on family members and friends recounting their memories of their murdered loved ones.[63]

Focusing on families enabled the media to give cold cases a human face, and made both the visual and rhetorical argument that the continued pain and grief of family members justified the efforts to revisit crimes committed long ago. This lens also served to take these cases out of a political context and to put them in a far more personal context; it made them less about a historically specific moment than the universal truth that families suffer when a loved one is killed. That lens offered a rationale for reopening that would resonate with the wider public. No parent or child, this coverage suggested, should have to endure the pain of knowing their loved one's killers remained free.

In their work, journalists not only helped humanize victims and their families, but as importantly, they undertook the investigations that proved crucial to prompting the reopening of many of these cold cases.[64] Cold cases by their nature are difficult to reopen. Witnesses may have died, memories may have faded, records and evidence may have been lost, if they were ever collected in the first place. Many civil rights–era murders were never explored as crimes at all; in others, state authorities did perfunctory, or even deliberately misleading, investigations. The FBI had examined a few of these murders at the time they were committed, but their files were not easily accessible. To prosecute these civil rights cases decades after they had taken place required extensive legwork and, often, the uncovering of new evidence that might convince a skeptical prosecutor that a case should be brought to court.

Yet the cases proved remarkably well suited to the skills of investigative journalists. Most civil rights murders are not cracked with new DNA evidence or scientific techniques—contrary to the popular *CSI* series, it is rarely new physical evidence that has proven central to reopening civil rights murder cases. Instead of forensic investigators studying blood patterns, DNA traces, or hair and fibers, civil rights–era cold cases require *historical* investigations that typically consist of hunting for lost transcripts or crime files, combing through old FBI records and newspapers, locating long-lost witnesses, and discovering new ones. These are cases cracked by a microfilm machine, not a centrifuge.[65] As such, journalists trained in finding obscure sources, securing and scouring government documents, and locating witnesses and conducting interviews were ideally positioned to do the investigative work required to enable a legal process to move forward. When Jerry Mitchell discovered information that undermined the alibi of one of the Birmingham church bombers or producers at *20/20* investigating the murder of Ben Chester White found lost trial transcripts, their research propelled the reopening process. State prosecutors and U.S. attorneys regularly turned to newsmagazine video outtakes, long-lost files found by reporters, and informants whose identity journalists had discovered as they considered whether to reopen old cases.[66]

Some in the media even came to see themselves as partners and advocates of family members seeking justice. Thomas Moore would likely not have succeeded in getting the case of the 1964 murders of Charles Moore and Henry Dee reopened if he hadn't found journalists who made his crusade their own. Moore began pressing authorities to reinvestigate the case of the murder of his brother and a friend in 1998, after the army veteran heard about the brutal murder of African American James Byrd in Texas. In some early reporting on the case, Jerry Mitchell and Harry Phillips of ABC found the FBI file about the crime that the local DA had been told did not exist and even discovered that the murders took place on federal land. But the case lost steam as reports emerged that the main suspect had died and as attention shifted to Neshoba County and the pending Freedom Summer murder trial.[67]

But then Moore joined forces with a print journalist and a documentary filmmaker who became passionate supporters of his cause. One of those advocates, Donna Ladd, had grown up in Mississippi in the 1960s and 1970s among, as she described them, "straight up Neshoba County rednecks." She had initially fled her home state for New York City, but she was moved to return to Mississippi when she decided that racism was not just a southern problem. In 2002, Ladd founded the alternative progressive newspaper the *Jackson Free Press*, named for the protest paper that had emerged out of the Mississippi civil rights movement in 1961, the *Mississippi Free Press*.[68] Ladd decided that her paper would cover the 2005 trial of Edgar Ray Killen by investigating other Mississippi civil rights–era cold cases that had not attracted such national attention, which led her to Charles Moore. The Dee/Moore case also caught the eye of David Ridgen, a Canadian filmmaker who learned of the murder in 2004 while preparing to make a documentary about the Killen trial. He convinced Moore to travel with him to Mississippi and to let him make a documentary about his quest for justice for his slain brother. Together, Moore, Ridgen, and a team from the *Jackson Free Press* would travel the back roads of Mississippi, searching for evidence and new information.[69] They discovered that the main suspect in the case, whom many journalists had reported dead, was in fact still alive. U.S. Attorney Dunn Lampton openly acknowledged the importance of their

Thomas Moore and Canadian filmmaker David Ridgen celebrate after the 2007 announcement at the Department of Justice that James Ford Seale would be tried in connection with the 1964 murder of Moore's brother, Charles, and his friend Henry Dee. The partnership between journalists and relatives of victims proved instrumental in the reopening of many civil rights–era murder cases. (© Kevin Lamarque/Reuters/Corbis)

efforts to his decision to reopen the case. "You don't come into an office and go back and start digging through all the old files to find something to do," he explained. "It's only when someone brings that to your attention."[70] Moore was able to bring him information that he could use to restart the legal process.

Keith Beauchamp, a young black documentary filmmaker, also brought authorities information that they could use. Beauchamp became fascinated with Emmett Till's story when he saw the photos of Till's corpse when he was just ten years old, and he eventually decided to turn that interest into a film. He dreamed of becoming a "black Steven Spielberg, because Spielberg made sure no one forgets his history." Beauchamp forged a close relationship with Mamie Till Mobley and regularly met with government authorities as he worked on a film that he always hoped would help get the case reopened. When he went to

Mississippi to do research, he knew he wasn't just doing interviews: "I was actually taking depositions." His documentary, *The Untold Story of Emmett Till*, garnered enormous public attention because of its contention that as many as seven other people had been involved in the murder besides the two acquitted of the crime in 1955. The Chicago City Council, the New York City Council, and several U.S. congressmen successfully urged the Justice Department to reopen an investigation based on Beauchamp's new evidence. The Mississippi district attorney cooperating with the federal officials on the case highlighted the importance of Beauchamp's film when she admitted that her office was starting by "following up on statements of people he has already located."[71] Beauchamp subsequently sought to use the docudrama form to galvanize the legal process in other cases, launching several cable series dedicated explicitly to showcasing unresolved civil rights murder cases with the hopes of encouraging witnesses to come forward so investigations could be reopened.[72]

Relatives of victims understood the vital role played by the media in generating momentum. As Myrlie Evers put it, the process of "dragging Mississippi to court" would not have been possible without "the forum through the media." Media coverage, of course, did not always lead authorities to bring new charges. The son of Johnnie Mae Chappell would lament in 2009 that his mother's case remained stalled even though "we've been on Oprah and Dateline."[73] But investigations and coverage by journalists played a crucial role in reopening many of the cases that would eventually result in new trials, including those of Medgar Evers, Vernon Dahmer, the Birmingham church bombing, and Ben Chester White.

By the mid-2000s, two trends emerged that reflected the impact of these changes in the racial, political, and media environment. More whites across the political spectrum came to express support for reopening these cases, including a growing number of political leaders who were not traditionally seen as allies of the black community. At the same time, activists and journalists, many of whom had no direct personal connections to these crimes, launched efforts to create an infrastructure that would enable a more systemic reckoning with the racial violence of the civil rights era. Together, these developments brought civil rights murders onto the national agenda, leading the federal government to take on the primary responsibility for investigating them on a scale that could not have been imagined even fifteen years earlier.

There is no question that white opposition to reopening civil rights cold cases has declined since the days of the Beckwith reopening. A 1994 poll in Mississippi found that only 45 percent of respondents felt it was fair to try Beckwith again, although only 11 percent thought he was innocent. While there are still vocal critics of reopening, attitudes have changed. In 2005, when authorities brought charges against Edgar Ray Killen for the 1964 Freedom Summer murders, a poll of five hundred residents of Neshoba County found that only 35 percent opposed the trial. By then, three-quarters of respondents felt the killings had led the rest of the country to have a negative image of Neshoba County. National polls found more support than local ones. Over 80 percent of the nearly seven thousand Americans polled in 2005 thought it was important to pursue Killen in order to "seek justice and bring closure to the families." Only 11 percent of respondents felt that doing so was a waste of money.[74]

The wording of the national poll question about the Killen trial suggests that framing the crimes in terms of the suffering of families played a powerful role in shaping public opinion. Indeed, the hundreds of comments about the process that have been published in newspapers, quoted on the radio, or posted on public forums suggest that many people have come to support pursuing legal justice because they understand it as so important for the victims' families. One man from Philadelphia, Mississippi expressed the increasingly common view that "when an injustice has occurred, regardless of when it happened, justice should be sought for the victims and their families." A man from Florence, Mississippi, concurred. The Goodman, Chaney, and Schwerner murder case should be reopened, he argued, because "each of the victims was someone's son or brother or friend and those loved ones have every right to expect justice be served." Focusing on the continuing suffering of families offered a universal argument for reopening cold cases, and for some, it became a way to convince skeptics. Barbara Marbury of Norfolk, Virginia, responded to a writer who had criticized the reopening of the Emmett Till case in 2004 by suggesting that if the critic had "lost a relative due to violent crime, even in a manner not as heinous as the manner in which Mr. Till was killed, he would expect justice." A white bookstore owner in Greenwood, Mississippi, told those who said the case should be left in the past, "What if that was your child?"[75] Times had changed since Bill Baxley complained that even the "good people" could not see the death of four black girls in the same way they would the murder of four white ones.

In the years since the first case was reopened, the argument that every individual deserves justice and the media's humanizing of the victims and their families shifted the climate for reopenings. Jerry Mitchell certainly noted a difference. When he first started writing about civil rights cold cases, critics constantly asked him, "What are you doing digging up the past?" But those cries had "really died down a lot" by 2003, he felt. There had been a marked shift in public opinion even between the first two trials in reopened cases, the 1994 Beckwith trial and the 1998 trial of Sam Bowers for Vernon Dahmer's murder. "There wasn't a lot of hue and cry" in 1998, he argued, and by 2003, he felt there was "very little." As public opposition lessened, the district attorneys and prosecutors who reopened cases suffered fewer political consequences for doing so. Bill Baxley maintains that his decision to reopen the Birmingham church bombing case contributed to the end of his electoral political career. Bobby DeLaughter too felt his decision to work on the Evers case would have political costs—as he put it, he knew from the start that having anything to do with the case was a "lose-lose situation from the very beginning politically," that his career would be hurt whether he won or lost. But within five years of arguing the case, DeLaughter achieved his ambition of being appointed a judge on the Hinds County Court. "Times do change, and life is good," he wrote in his 2001 memoir.[76] Subsequent prosecutors have not found that prosecuting cold civil rights cases harmed their careers.

Most dramatically, even conservative southern Republicans began to publicly express their support for the reopening process. In 1989, white members of Mississippi's congressional delegation refused to sign a resolution honoring Andrew Goodman, James Chaney, and Mickey Schwerner on the twenty-fifth anniversary of their deaths. In 1995, soon-to-be-governor Kirk Fordice attacked his opponent for issuing a public apology for the murders as the secretary of state. But less than ten years later, two leading state conservatives, Congressman Chip Pickering and Governor Haley Barbour, attended a major public commemoration ceremony in Philadelphia and joined community leaders in calling on authorities to reopen the case.

The open support of Mississippi politicians signaled to some the powerful changes in Mississippi politics that had taken place since the 1970s. *Jackson Free Press* editor Donna Ladd took Barbour's presence at the 2004 commemoration as evidence of a "chink," even if small, in the "armor" of the famed "Southern Strategy," or what critics have charged is the deliberate use of coded appeals to white racism by the Republican Party to win support among white Southerners. Ladd saw Barbour's presence on that stage as a sign that he was beginning to recognize that "racist crap" did not appeal to a growing number of Mississippians and that he now needed to make symbolic gestures towards racial tolerance and equality whether he agreed with those positions or not. Revisiting old civil rights cases, she claimed, had become "politically correct," something politicians felt they had to gesture towards whatever their personal feelings about the process. For Ladd, it was if the "earth moved."[77]

But while Barbour's change of heart shook Ladd's world, his willingness to publicly endorse efforts to reopen the Freedom Summer murders seemed to indicate less a rejection of the racial politics that he had been practicing for decades than a new understanding that supporting the legal process could serve his own political interests. Even as Barbour sat on the stage at the commemoration ceremony, he wore a Confederate flag lapel pin, a divisive symbol that many blacks associated with support for slavery and white supremacy. In the years after the 2004 ceremony, he praised the 1960s White Citizens' Council as an organization dedicated to civic peace and refused to distance himself from their successor organization, the Conservative Citizens' Council.[78] Barbour's support of new prosecutions seemed to reflect less a renunciation of his previous politics than a sense that reopenings might allow the state to escape its negative racial reputation once and for all. Barbour told the audience at the 2004 commemoration that it was "appropriate to remember this horrid evil 40 years past," but they should also "recognize and praise God for all the progress that has occurred since then especially here in Mississippi," which he described as "a wonderful state" in the "greatest and best country in the history of the world." By having a trial in the case, Barbour argued, the state could finally "reach closure and put that behind us." Around the same time that he came out in favor of a trial in the Freedom Summer case, Barbour announced plans to build the "National Civil Rights Museum in Mississippi."[79] Like the mayor in Birmingham, he seemed to have realized that one of the best ways to address a stigmatizing past was to declare it history and put it in a museum.

The broadening political support for reopening civil rights cases was evidenced not only by the willingness of white Republicans to endorse the process, but also by a growing number of activists and journalists who in the mid-2000s embarked on new efforts to build organizations and structures that could further the process in a more systematic way. For decades, efforts to reopen civil rights–era murder cases had been an ad hoc affair, usually the work of a family or a journalist working independently to generate pressure on state or federal authorities to release information and undertake investigations. Even when state authorities were the impetus for reopening a case, such as Alabama Attorney General Bill Baxley in the Birmingham church bombing, the effort remained largely the work of a few individuals operating on a case-by-case basis. But as journalists and activists watched families struggle to bring cases back to court, some decided that what was needed was an infrastructure that could provide organized assistance to families and enable a more methodical accounting of civil rights–era violence.[80]

The impulse to bring together those working in an ad hoc fashion on these cases into some kind of organization led a group of journalists to create the Civil Rights Cold Case Project in 2008. The Cold Case Project got its start when a reporter from the Alabama *Anniston Star* who was researching a civil rights murder there approached the Center for Investigative Reporting, a nonprofit organization that conducts and supports watchdog journalism. In response, the group's executive director gathered a group of journalists, including Jerry Mitchell and Canadian filmmaker David Ridgen, to discuss collaboration and funding of civil rights cold case reporting. They decided to create a partnership where journalists working on civil rights–era murders could share information and expertise with each other. The ultimate goal was to develop "a well-coordinated, multiplatform, long-term investigative project" fed by "interconnected storylines and resources" to tackle known cold cases and discover others that had not yet come to light. Although the Cold Case Project remains underfunded and only partially realized, it has provided some financial support for journalists working on cold case investigations and has established a website to further its goal of "bringing together the power of investigative reporting, narrative writing, documentary filmmaking and interactive multimedia production" to uncover the truth about unsolved civil rights murders.[81]

At the same time, academics at two different universities launched initiatives to galvanize and support efforts to reopen unresolved killings from the 1950s and 1960s. At Syracuse University School of Law, professors Janis McDonald and Paula Johnson founded the Cold Case Justice Initiative (CCJI) in 2007 after relatives of Frank Morris, who was murdered in 1964, contacted McDonald to ask for help investigating his death. Although McDonald had been doing historic research on Ferriday, Louisiana, she knew little about the 1964 crime. Horrified by what she learned, she helped launch the CCJI to teach law and journalism students how to scour documents, search for witnesses, and pressure authorities to conduct investigations into civil rights murders. Since 2007, McDonald and Johnson's students have spent summers in southern communities doing research, they have organized volunteers to comb through thousands of documents related to civil rights murders that had never been reviewed, and they have worked with state and federal officials on investigations.[82]

That same year, Professor Margaret Burnham of the Northeastern University School of Law decided to launch the Civil Rights and Restorative Justice Project (CRRJ) to serve as a clearinghouse and resource for scholars, activists, and policymakers who were researching civil rights–era violence. Burnham had helped organize Freedom Summer as a volunteer for the Student Nonviolent Coordinating Committee in 1964, and she had spent the 1970s working as a lawyer for the NAACP. Motivated by knowledge of all the African Americans who had been killed by the Klan while she had escaped harm, she created the CRRJ as a national center for ongoing efforts to study and address the pervasive racial terrorism in the post–World War II South. In 2007, the CRRJ brought together academics, activists, prosecutors, and families for a conference to share information and resources. The project has also created Case Watch, the most complete database of civil rights–era murders and each case's current legal status. In addition, Burnham and the CRRJ have trained more than forty Northeastern School of Law students, each of whom are responsible for gathering information and outlining what legislative or other remedies might be possible in the case of a particular crime.[83]

As journalists and scholars worked to create an infrastructure that would enable a more organized reckoning with civil rights–era violence, an unlikely African American activist from Kansas City began to press for the state to do the same. Alvin Sykes, a self-taught high school dropout, was born to a poor teen mother in Kansas City in 1956, and his childhood was marked by abuse and poverty. He began teaching himself law in the 1970s by reading books at the public library and sitting in at trials at the Kansas City courthouse. After working on federal school desegregation cases involving the city's schools, he shifted to victim advocacy in 1980, when a white defendant was acquitted in the murder of one of his friends. His work led to a federal trial after he uncovered a statute that gave the federal government jurisdiction on civil rights grounds.

In 2002, after reading an article about Mamie Till Mobley's efforts to get her son's murder case reopened, Sykes went to Chicago to meet her. Together with a friend who had worked for the Justice Department, they founded the Emmett Till Justice Campaign just a few days before she died. Sykes proved instrumental to the 2004 reopening of the Till case, working with state and federal authorities to convince them to dedicate resources to the case and connecting them with Keith Beauchamp so they could make use of the information he had uncovered while making his documentary.[84]

As Sykes learned about the many other unresolved murders from the civil rights era that had not received the attention the Till case had, he began to brainstorm ways to develop resources for pursuing legal justice for all of the murders of the era. As Sykes saw it, the country needed a "systematic approach to cleaning up past unsolved injustices." He came up with the idea of a new federal law, one that would create a dedicated civil rights cold case unit within the Justice Department and provide it with the money and resources needed to explore whether federal civil rights prosecutions were possible or to assist state authorities with investigations and prosecutions if there was no federal jurisdiction. By 2005, Sykes had convinced Missouri Senator Jim Talent to sponsor the "Unsolved Civil Rights Crime Act," which would be first introduced in both the Senate and the House that year.[85]

Sykes's idea caught on immediately. In response to the pending legislation, the FBI undertook the first systematic effort to document civil rights–era murders, canvassing its fifty-six field offices to compile a list of 108 unsolved hate crime murders from before 1969. Soon thereafter, the Justice Department announced its own Civil Rights–Era Cold Case Initiative, pledging to work with the NAACP, the Southern Poverty Law Center, and the Urban League to determine which of the 108 cases could be prosecuted.[86] In 2008, Congress joined the effort by acting on the legislation first introduced in 2005. The Emmett Till Unsolved Civil Rights Crime Act, now renamed in honor of the teenager slain in Mississippi, passed with unanimous consent in the Senate and with only two dissenting votes in the House. The new federal law authorized $10 million per year for ten years for a cold case unit within the Department of Justice tasked with investigating and assisting in prosecutions of pre-1970 racially charged murders. By 2012, the Department of Justice had reopened investigations into 112 cold cases involving 125 victims.[87] The project of revisiting civil rights–era murders had been formally embraced by the state.

Yet the federal government and the activists who created new organizations and lobbied the state to address civil rights–era violence explained their support for the process somewhat differently. Everyone could agree that these efforts were important for the sake of the families of victims and because all individuals deserved equal legal protection regardless of race. When FBI Director Robert Mueller explained in 2007 that action was necessary "because for the victims—and their parents, children, siblings, friends—the wounds were never closed," that certainly would have resonated with Janis McDonald and Paula Johnson of Syracuse University's Cold Case Initiative, who explained their own commitment to the cause in terms of the need to help bring resolution to suffering families and who brought nearly sixty relatives of civil rights–era murder victims together for a conference in 2010 because they "deserve justice as a matter of right."[88] Attorney General Alberto Gonzales's declaration that he supported the cold case initiative because there was "no statute of limitations on human dignity and justice" and Senator Christopher Dodd's claim that passing the Till Bill would "reaffirm" the nation's commitment to equal justice echoed Alvin Sykes's argument that it was vital that the United States send the message through the Till Bill that it would bring "to the bar of justice any and all perpetrators who may still be alive."[89]

But for activists committed to the project, a more systematic reckoning with the violence of the civil rights era was important not only as a way to assist families of victims. They hoped this new infrastructure would also play the vital role of highlighting societal and governmental complicity with these crimes when they occurred. Journalists came together in the Cold Case Project, project manager Hank Klibanoff explained, because civil rights murders belonged "to a genre of criminality that went beyond a few disconnected acts of violence." They hoped their in-depth reporting would expose not only the networks between the Klan, but also the extent to which police and politicians protected this "organized homegrown terrorism." Both the Cold Case Justice Initiative and the Civil Rights and Restorative Justice Project sought to hold accountable *all* the perpetrators involved in civil rights murders, "individual, governmental and corporate," as the CRRJ explained, or "individual, organizational, and institutional," in the language of the CCJI. The CRRJ was particularly focused on documenting the role states and the federal government had played in anti–civil rights violence and in redressing the "wrongs caused by government repression." Although Alvin Sykes was not so direct, he too saw pushing for a systematic reckoning with racial violence as part of an activist political project, one he described as linked to the goals of the civil rights movement. "Just like we had freedom riders, we have to have justice riders," Sykes charged, comparing his work on civil rights murders to the seminal challenge to segregation in 1961.[90]

The politicians who came to support the Till Bill expressed less interest in exposing the extent of government complicity with civil rights violence or holding the state accountable for it than in taking steps that would enable to country to say it had dealt with it and could move on. Prosecuting these cases, FBI Director Mueller explained in 2007, was important so that the United States would be able to close a "dark chapter in our nation's history."[91] At the House hearings on the Emmett Till Bill, Representative Jerrold Nadler recognized the wrongs that had been done during the civil rights era, but noted that the country had fully progressed beyond that history. Passing the Till Bill, he explained, offered a means of "cleansing our society of this great stain." In introducing the bill to the Senate, Christopher Dodd spoke of the need to hold "despicable criminals" accountable in an America that "stands for the principle of equal justice for all." He recognized that these crimes had hardly been investigated at the time—unlike the "much stronger efforts" of today—but did not take the step that activists did to link the failures of the justice system then to a broader understanding of complicity and governmental misconduct.[92] Perhaps not surprisingly, it would be less than a year before the activists who pushed for the Till Bill began to complain that the government was not doing enough to push these cases forward.

Many aspects of American politics and culture changed between the reopening of the Beckwith case and the passage of the Till Bill, but the different perspectives involved—activists pushing that bill as part of a larger political project and politicians supporting it as a way to achieve justice for individuals for the sake of grieving families—echoed the dynamics from the first meetings about the reopening of the Medgar Evers case. Before their first meeting in 1989, Bobby DeLaughter worried that Myrlie Evers would turn out to be some kind of activist intent on revenge. He was relieved to discover that instead of "demanding retribution against the racist who killed a civil rights martyr who happened to be her husband," she framed her "plea for justice" as a quest to hold accountable "the cowardly bushwhacker who had shot in the back her unarmed husband who happened to have been a civil rights leader."[93] The distinction for him seemed crucial: he could get on board with reopening the case of a killing of a man who happened to be a civil rights leader, but he seemed far more reluctant to reopen a murder investigation for a civil rights leader who happened to be a husband.

Myrlie Evers portrays that same meeting quite differently. She described bringing along Morris Dees of the Southern Poverty Law Center since she was so suspicious of state authorities. The woman who had long blamed her husband's murder and the failure to convict his assassin on the "white power structure in Mississippi" had few qualms bringing along the confrontational director of a leading civil rights legal organization. At one point in the meeting, Dees threatened to bring in his own investigators if the state failed to act. Myrlie Evers wanted justice for her husband, but she did not present herself just as a grieving widow.[94]

That Evers and DeLaughter became good friends—as Evers described it, though they came from "entirely different backgrounds," they were "able to shove everything to the side and focus on simple justice"—was testament to the ability of the legal process to appeal to people with different perspectives and motivations.[95] The momentum that came to characterize efforts to reopen civil rights–era murders in the years after that first meeting between Evers and DeLaughter reflects the ways in which the hard work of activists and changes in the political and media culture enabled a broader circle of people to view revisiting the racial violence of the era as necessary and, sometimes, even in their own or the state's interest. Dedicated family members and activists, in tandem with the media, helped make cold cases hot, creating a momentum for a legal reckoning that would reach the national level. But what that reckoning would look like, and whether it would serve to address the concerns of those who wanted not just to hold the men who had committed murder accountable, but also to explore the social and political forces that had enabled their reign of terror, could only be determined in the trials themselves.

4

Civil Rights Crimes in the Courtroom

At the heart of every case is a simple story.
—SheldonSinrich Trial Consultants

O N JANUARY 27, 1994, prosecutor Bobby DeLaughter stood up
in front of a jury to present his opening argument in the highly
anticipated case of *Mississippi v. Byron De La Beckwith*. In the same Hinds
County Courthouse where Beckwith's two earlier trials for murdering
Medgar Evers had ended in hung juries, DeLaughter laid before the jury
the way he wanted them to think about the case. The trial, he told the
jurors, was not about "trying to set an old wrong right." It was not about
"politics" or a "civil rights case that just incidentally involves a murder."
It was not about the "pluses and minuses of people's opinions" in the
1960s civil rights movement. This case, he told them, was about a man
who had been murdered by a bullet fired on June 12, 1963, a bullet,
he argued lyrically, that had been "aimed out of prejudice, propelled by
hatred, and fired by a coward from ambush at night."[1]

In just a few short sentences, DeLaughter mapped what would
become the terrain not only of the Beckwith prosecution, but also of
the many other civil rights trials that would be prosecuted in its wake.
These cases would be framed as murder trials, not civil rights cases. They
would focus on proving the culpability of an individual actor for a specific crime for the most part outside of a broader political or institutional
framework. DeLaughter would try this case on the same terms that had
led him to reopen it: it was about an unarmed man being gunned down

in front of his family, a crime that "every decent human being should be sickened by."[2] He would seek justice for Medgar Evers as a slain husband, not as a civil rights leader.

But even as DeLaughter insisted that the trial would not be about the politics of the civil rights movement, his arguments in the trial suggested that it would communicate some powerful political lessons. He would, over the course of the trial, make clear that he found Byron De La Beckwith and everything he believed abhorrent. Although he framed civil rights as incidental to the case, he would praise slain activist Medgar Evers for his efforts to end segregation in the South. DeLaughter would offer the jury a history lesson, constructing a past in which men like Beckwith were held almost solely responsible for the racial violence of the civil rights era. And he would tell jurors that convicting Beckwith would send a message to the world that Mississippi was nothing like the racist place portrayed in movies like *Mississippi Burning*.

All trials tell stories; indeed, the power of the legal process stems in part from its coupling of the legitimacy of the state with the influence of storytelling. The narratives that emerged from the civil rights courtroom reflected the conventions and rules inherent to any criminal trial, which require that arguments focus narrowly on the question of whether the defendant committed the crime at hand. Those conventions became even more important to uphold in the case of decades-old crimes that presented a host of practical and legal challenges. Legal rules made it difficult for trials to uncover the complexity of the racism of the Jim Crow era or the shared culpability for it.

The stories told in and by the trials were shaped too by the particular perspectives of prosecutors, many of whom saw new prosecutions as an opportunity to rehabilitate the reputations of communities or states stigmatized by unaddressed civil rights–era violence. Legal trials offer a powerful arena for performing and communicating societal values and norms. Following a predetermined set of rules, sponsored by the state, and staged as a public event, a trial is a civic ritual, a place where values can be affirmed, status relationships made clear, and beliefs about citizenship put into practice.[3] The symbolic space of the courtroom offered an ideal site to try to remake the South's reputation. In the courtroom, prosecutors could explain to a southern audience why it was so important to revisit these crimes, could suggest to a national audience how much the South had changed since the Jim Crow era, and could craft arguments about what convictions of old Klansmen meant.

As a result of both the inherent framing imposed by legal rules and the choices made by prosecutors, the trials of civil rights–era crimes all performed essentially the same civic ritual: they turned old Klan defendants into singular symbols of racism—defined narrowly as the hateful actions of individuals—and then symbolically renounced them, a framing that absolved the state and broader white community of responsibility for racial violence in the past and read the conviction of Klansmen as proof of racial progress in the present. Yet the experience in the courtroom suggested that the story of racial change since the civil rights era was decidedly more complex, even in relation to the trials' rather narrow depiction of racism in terms of individual attitudes. Cognizant of the many complications of trying politically and racially charged cases dealing with decades-old crimes, the prosecutors in contemporary trials undertook extensive jury research, including the use of professional trial consultants when possible. That research, which found that racial bias remained a potent, if often unspoken, force in the courtroom, shaped how prosecutors argued their cases and sought to appeal to juries. These contradictions help explain why Bobby DeLaughter would simultaneously praise Medgar Evers and the achievements of the civil rights movement while at the same time insisting that the case had nothing to do with civil rights.

Before any arguments could be made before a jury, cases first had to advance to trial. The path to a courtroom was rarely clear in these decades-old cold cases. Prosecuting murders that took place in the 1950s or 1960s posed serious practical, legal, ethical, and political challenges. Even the initial step of getting cases reopened took enormous effort. Once reopened, authorities had to assemble enough usable evidence and witnesses to build a case, an expensive proposition that required extensive resources. Prosecutors also had to convince judges that new trials would not violate any of the defendant's constitutional or due process rights. The odds against prosecutors, one legal expert familiar with these trials noted, were "hugely high"; convictions represented something of a "legal miracle."[4]

Most of the contemporary civil rights trials have taken place in state courts on state charges of murder or manslaughter. The trials of Byron

De La Beckwith for the murder of Medgar Evers, Sam Bowers for the murder of Vernon Dahmer, James "Doc" Caston, Charles E. Caston, and Hal Spivey Crimm in 1999 for the murder of Rainey Pool, and Edgar Ray Killen in 2005 for the killings of James Chaney, Andrew Goodman, and Mickey Schwerner were all prosecuted by the state of Mississippi. Tom Blanton and Bobby Frank Cherry, convicted of murder for the Birmingham church bombing in 2001 and 2002, respectively, were tried in Alabama courts.

Unlike in the 1950s and the 1960s, when southern state authorities resented federal interference in civil rights murders and federal authorities refused to work with state authorities they rightfully distrusted, the modern prosecutions have in many ways been a joint project of southern states and the federal government. In 1977, Alabama State Attorney General Bill Baxley found the FBI still reluctant to share information about the Birmingham church bombing with state authorities, but by the 1990s, state and federal officials developed active partnerships to prosecute civil rights murders. While it was the federal government that initiated a new investigation into the Birmingham church bombing in the 1990s, from the start the U.S. attorney for the northern district of Alabama began working with the local district attorney because he doubted there would be grounds for federal jurisdiction. The U.S. attorney, Doug Jones, had a strong personal interest in the church bombing case. Just nine years old at the time of the crime, he grew up in a segregated suburb just outside Birmingham. He began to focus on the racial strife around him when a judge mandated that the black and white high schools in towns be combined in order to ensure desegregation. As a leader in student politics, Jones undertook measures to make the transition work for both the black and white students, winning a local "Youth of the Year" award for his efforts to promote interracial cooperation. In law school, he idolized Bill Baxley, the young Alabama attorney general, and cut classes to watch Baxley prosecute Robert Chambliss for the Birmingham church bombing in 1977. He was "stunned" when he learned that the case had been reopened again and that he might have the opportunity to prosecute others for the same crime.

Jones knew that most federal cases in the 1960s had been brought under civil rights violations that carried a five-year statute of limitations. In the church bombing case, the federal government could claim jurisdiction only if it could prove that the explosives used in the church bombing had been taken across state lines. When Jones realized that he couldn't prove what kinds of explosives had even been used in the bombing, let alone whether they had crossed state lines, it became clear that the suspects could only be tried by the state of Alabama on charges of murder. But the Justice Department provided the funds for the state's investigation, and Jones asked the Alabama attorney general to allow him to prosecute on behalf of the state. It was, Jones claims, "kind of a joint deal."[5]

The two civil rights–era murders prosecuted on federal charges resulted not from an unwillingness of states to prosecute, as had been the case in the 1960s, but rather from judgments about jurisdiction. The federal government took the lead in prosecuting Ernest Avants for the murder of Ben Chester White since a Mississippi jury had acquitted Avants of the murder of 1966 and he could not be tried again by the state. The federal government had jurisdiction to prosecute Avants for murder because the killing had taken place on national land. James Ford Seale faced federal charges of kidnapping and conspiracy to kidnap because the government had evidence to show that Seale had abducted Henry Dee and Charles Moore and brought them across state lines—a federal offense—but could not conclusively prove that Seale had murdered the two teens. Although the state of Mississippi could have tried Seale on state charges of murder, the case seemed unlikely to succeed given the available evidence. But when Seale's federal conviction seemed in jeopardy of being overturned, state authorities began contemplating the possibility of bringing their own charges against him.[6] The few federal civil rights trials were not carried out over the objections of the states.

The hard work of assembling and arguing these cases fell primarily to local district attorneys or assistant DAs, like Bobby DeLaughter, Forrest County DA Bob Helfrich, who tried Sam Bowers and Charles Noble, or Neshoba County DA Mark Duncan, who was on the team trying Edgar Ray Killen. Mississippi State Attorney General Jim Hood also worked on the Killen case, suggesting the importance attached to these cases. In most trials, prosecutors faced dedicated and respected defense lawyers who saw it as their mission to secure a fair trial for the defendants. Sam Bowers and Edgar Ray Killen, however, hired lawyers who had been associated with the Klan, some of whom had actually defended them in earlier trials in the 1960s. But most of the defense lawyers were appointed by the state or federal government and were respected by their peers. James Seale's lawyer, Kathy Nester, was known for her strong record on civil rights litigation.

These defense attorneys worked hard to keep cases from ever going before a jury, and they had a great deal of potential ammunition for that fight. Before Byron De La Beckwith's trial, many doubted whether these decades-old murders could be addressed through the legal arena. Only three years before the state of Mississippi reinstated charges against Beckwith, Hinds County District Attorney Ed Peters dismissed the possibility that his office would ever be able to bring a new case against him. "There's no way under any stretch of law that case could be tried again," he told the press. "Anyone having taken the first class in law school ought to know that."[7] Defense lawyers would try to convince judges that civil rights–era violence could not be addressed fairly through the criminal justice system by raising objections that even first-year law students could recognize.

In cases where defendants had been tried in the 1960s, defense lawyers could argue that new trials violated the constitutional protections against double jeopardy. The Constitution bars any individual being twice "put in jeopardy of life and limb" for the same offense. Most defendants had not been tried before and the issue was therefore moot, but a few would try to use the double jeopardy protection to argue that it was unconstitutional to subject them to new trials. Legal rules do not bar retrying someone for the same crime if an earlier trial ended with a hung jury, but Byron De La Beckwith still made the case that a new trial would violate his constitutional rights. His lawyers insisted that when the state dismissed charges against him in 1969, it had effectively acquitted him of the crime and thus a third trial was prohibited. A Mississippi Supreme Court ruling would disabuse them of the notion that the dismissal of charges was the same as an acquittal. Ernest Avants, who was acquitted of Ben Chester White's murder in a state court, could not face state murder charges again for the same crime, but a federal trial for the same murder was permissible since the Supreme Court has held that the state and federal government are "different sovereigns" who can each try an individual for the same offense.[8]

Defense lawyers had a far stronger case that new trials violated another constitutionally guaranteed right, namely the Sixth Amendment's provision that in "criminal prosecutions, the accused shall enjoy the right to a . . . speedy trial." Could any trial held thirty years after the original crime be considered "speedy"? A higher court would need to resolve this issue in relation to the Beckwith case before other prosecutors would feel confident moving forward with any of the other cases. As Mississippi Attorney General Mike Moore explained in 1992, reviving any other civil rights–era murder cases "would depend a great deal on what decisions the courts make in the Beckwith case."[9]

While common sense suggests that any trial held more than three decades after the original crime cannot fairly be construed as "speedy," the law's definition of "speedy" stemmed from procedure and precedent that was considerably more complicated than the term implies. The U.S. Supreme Court maintains that the right to speedy trial begins when a person is arrested and lasts until they are convicted, acquitted, or charges against them are formally dropped. Since most of the defendants in these cases had never been arrested or charged, or, if tried during the civil rights era, had not experienced a lengthy gap between their indictment and their original trial, judges would rule that they had little basis to claim a speedy trial violation. Beckwith's lawyers, however, could make a strong argument that he had been denied a speedy trial because he had been under indictment for five years after his two mistrials, from 1964 until the state formally dismissed charges against him in 1969. The Mississippi Supreme Court was sharply divided on the issue, but a slim majority ruled that Beckwith could not claim a speedy trial violation because he had boasted at the time that he had "the power and connections" to keep out of jail and thus had been complicit in preventing another trial at the time. While Beckwith's lawyers railed that the ruling was the "most egregious" speedy trial violation in the state's history, the U.S. Supreme Court refused to hear their appeal.[10] If a new trial for Beckwith did not violate his Sixth Amendment rights to a speedy trial, then there was little chance any of the other cases would. While other lawyers would sometimes try to make the "speedy trial" argument, the Beckwith case set a legal precedent that ensured that similar cases could move forward.

Yet even if new trials didn't place defendants in double jeopardy or violate their right to a speedy trial, defense attorneys could argue with some merit that new trials violated their defendants' due process rights to a fair trial. Defense lawyers suggested that these trials were inherently unfair because they took place so many years after the original crimes had occurred. The fear that a long lapse between a crime and prosecution might make it difficult for defendants to receive a fair trial has deep legal roots, expressed most clearly by statutes of limitations that lay out the maximum amount of time that can pass between a crime and its prosecution. Although most of these men were charged with murder, for which there is no statute of limitations, defense lawyers argued that no new trial could be fair because the long passage of time had hurt defendants' ability to mount a credible defense in court. To meet that charge, they had to pass a two-part legal test: they had first to prove to the judge that the long passage of time had prejudiced the defense and they then had to show that the delay had taken place for "improper" reasons.

Defendants had a great deal of ammunition to support the claim that their cases had been hurt by the long passage of time. Kathy Nester, the public defender assigned to James Seale in his trial for the murder of Charles Moore and Henry Dee, spoke for many when she urged the judge to dismiss charges because so many witnesses had died or were not available to testify. "Every time we went down a road," she told the judge, "it ended in a grave." Counsel complained that their clients could not receive a fair trial because trial transcripts were missing, because the defendants had hazy memories and could not aid in their own defense, or because physical evidence had been destroyed. They insisted that introducing the testimony of witnesses from previous trial transcripts was problematic because old testimony might have been collected in ways considered inadmissible under contemporary legal standards and because defense lawyers could not subject a transcript to the kind of cross-examination they did with live witnesses. Byron De La Beckwith's lawyers, for example, would try to keep testimony from his first 1964 trial out of the courtroom because his lawyers at the time had not had access to police reports that they would have had under modern discovery rules.[11]

But to get cases thrown out of court, defense teams also had to prove that state or federal authorities had improperly delayed the case in order to gain some kind of advantage in court. In pretrial hearings in nearly every case, they thus argued that prosecutors had purposefully waited to try these cases until they were more confident they could secure a conviction, either because of changes in racial attitudes or because key witnesses had died or memories might have faded.[12] Some prosecutors found this charge laughable; as the lead prosecutor in the Rainey Pool trial told the judge, it suggested that he had been sitting in high school praying that state authorities wouldn't move forward with a case in the 1960s.[13] The charge of intentional delay to gain strategic advantage would be a hard one to make in court since the record clearly showed that state authorities had typically sought to impede investigations or stonewall trials, not that they had hesitated to hold trials in the 1960s because they wanted to ensure that legal justice could be achieved in the future. In the scenario put forth by defense teams, the long delay in bringing murderers from the civil rights era to trial suggested not the presence of racism in the workings of the American justice system, but the fervent desire of those in the legal system to make sure that the alleged murderers would ultimately be convicted. Delay became evidence of the keen desire for justice, not the lack of it. Even in pretrial hearings the kind of story these trials would ultimately tell about the civil rights era began to be shaped by the need to frame arguments legible to the legal process.

The objections voiced by defense attorneys were clearly strategic, but some legal observers raised the vexing question that lay at their core: could murders from the civil rights era be addressed through the legal process without violating the rights of individual defendants? As Mississippi prepared to try Byron De La Beckwith for a third time, Georgetown University Law Center Professor Paul Rothstein questioned whether Beckwith could get a fair trial given that "people die, memories fade, and documents disappear." Although he abhorred the miscarriages of justice that had taken place at the time these crimes were committed, he thought it might be best to simply let "court proceedings go." Putting these men on trial after so much time had passed, he lamented, "pits a civil libertarian against himself." A dean at University of Mississippi School of Law expressed similar misgivings when Ernest Avants faced charges in 2003 for a crime committed in 1966. How, he wondered, could one fairly prove or disprove something that "happened before Neil Armstrong walked on the moon?" Even some trial supporters argued that convictions might only be possible if legal rules were set aside. James Seale, one observer insisted, was certainly guilty but he had not heard enough relevant admissible evidence to justify a guilty verdict. "Should we ignore the rules to correct a past injustice?" he pondered.[14]

None of these legal, ethical, or political concerns ultimately prevented trials from moving forward. In many pretrial hearings, state and federal judges ruled that civil rights trials were legally permissible. And when defendants appealed their convictions on a wide range of due process grounds, they uniformly lost. The nearest an appeal came to succeeding was in the case of James Ford Seale, who charged after his conviction that the federal government had not had jurisdiction to try him in the first place. The federal government tried Seale under a 1932 statute known as the "Lindbergh Law"—passed after famed aviator Charles Lindbergh's infant son was abducted and killed—which made transporting a kidnapped victim across state lines a federal offense. That law, which originally had no statute of limitations, had been amended by Congress in 1972 to have a five-year statute of limitations. At issue in Seale's appeal was whether that 1972 amendment should apply retroactively, which would mean that he could no longer be charged with a crime that took place in 1966. After a complicated legal battle—during which Seale's conviction was temporarily vacated—the Fifth Circuit Court of Appeals allowed the initial verdict to stand.[15]

The repeated rulings by trial judges and appeals courts that civil rights–era cases could be addressed fairly in contemporary trials did not satisfy all critics. Some of those sympathetic to the defendants charged that contemporary prosecutions forfeited the rights of the accused for the purpose of making a political point.[16] The state, Byron De La Beckwith's lawyers charged in appealing his conviction, had "sacrificed the petitioner's constitutional rights to atone for Mississippi's past sins."[17] White nationalist lawyer Richard Barrett complained that the 2003 Avants trial had been a "kangaroo court" where the jury was more interested in affirmative action than justice, while he described the outcome of the 2001 trial of Tom Blanton for the murder of four girls killed in the Birmingham church bombing as foreordained before any evidence was even presented: "There would have been the same result if the Indians had put Custer on trial."[18]

Concerns about whether trials violated defendants' rights or were influenced by politics compelled prosecutors to be especially vigilant about focusing on the narrow question of individual culpability and avoiding any actions that could be construed as overstepping legal rules. As prosecutor Mark Duncan emphasized in comments to the media before Edgar Ray Killen's 2005 trial, his only job "was to hold a man accountable for his role in these killings." Pursuing a "social cause" was "not the role or purpose of bringing any prosecution."[19] The symbolic nature of these cases shaped the stories and strategies that emerged in the courtroom, encouraging prosecutors like Duncan to stay focused on what would turn out to be a very small piece of the much larger puzzle of civil rights–era violence.

Once judges ruled that trials could go forward, both sides had to face another vexing challenge: they had to empanel a group of jurors who would be sympathetic to their case. In the trials held in the 1950s and 1960s, finding a jury willing to judge the evidence on its merits proved exceptionally difficult. Voting restrictions ensured that jury pools were almost always all white, and defense lawyers could assume with some confidence that the jury might be swayed by appeals to white pride and white supremacy. Choosing a jury in the modern trials presented a very different challenge. With the changes in voting laws, all of the contemporary juries would include blacks and women, making it important for prosecution and defense teams to find strategies that could appeal to a broad range of people who might have different perspectives on the civil rights struggle. Picking a jury in these civil rights trials often took as long as the actual presentation of the case. Both sides knew that, as Bobby DeLaughter put it, "twelve strangers would make the critical decision."[20]

The process of selecting a jury was especially complicated in the case of decades-old, racially motivated crimes. As Birmingham church bombing prosecutor Doug Jones noted, there were "so many more issues that permeated the case that could influence a juror: the age of the defendants, the age of the case, the historical significance of the case, the racial overtones, the life experiences of each juror living in the South, then and now."[21] At least some potential jurors were likely to see efforts to put now-elderly men in jail as a waste of time and money, views that might be held by blacks as well as whites. Prosecutors knew that in order to get potential jurors to see the now frail and old defendants as dangerous killers, they would need to focus intensely on their racist attitudes and membership in the Klan. But prosecutors also worried that jurors might have hidden racial biases that could influence how they felt about the evidence or the crime. The jury selection process illuminated the complicated racial terrain of the "colorblind" post–civil rights era. Although public expressions of racism had become unacceptable, prosecutors feared that potential jurors might privately have critical views of the civil rights movement or negative attitudes about blacks that could create problems in the courtroom. The need to convince jurors who might still harbor some racist views to convict elderly men of racially motivated murders led to what many defense attorneys would come to see as the fundamental contradiction at the heart of the prosecutorial strategy: that prosecutors spent a great deal of time proving that the defendants were racists even as they claimed the trials were not about politics, race, or civil rights.[22]

The Beckwith prosecution would blaze the trail in establishing the procedures for selecting a jury that would become common in nearly every civil rights trial. Bobby DeLaughter and his team decided to undertake extensive research into jurors' attitudes, research that would be conducted by professional jury consultants trained in psychology, sociology, and communications. DeLaughter did not initially think he needed the help of jury consultants to choose a jury for the Beckwith trial. Jury selection, he felt, boiled down to "common sense and gut feeling," and he trusted the instincts of his team. And like most state prosecutors, DeLaughter had never had the opportunity to use consultants who could provide insight into juror psychology or preexisting biases.[23] But he changed his mind after several jury experts excited about the possibility of being part of the trial volunteered their time.

The Beckwith trial set the pattern for most of the major civil rights cases, and one of the consultants on that case—Andrew Sheldon of Sheldon Associates, now SheldonSinrich—would offer pro bono or at-expense assistance for the prosecutions in most of these trials, including both Birmingham church bombing trials, the prosecution of Sam Bowers for the killing of Vernon Dahmer, the Seale trial, and the Killen trial. Sheldon was not the only jury consultant who worked on civil rights cases, but he and his firm proved the most important. Sheldon had been raised in Miami, Florida, by parents who taught him everyone was equally worthy. Born in 1942, he grew up in the segregated South and attended Emory University, where he admits that he did not pay enough attention to racial injustices. But he came to see the miscarriages of justice in the 1950s and 1960s as examples of the failure of the legal system that had left blacks rightfully mistrustful of the law and was committed to ensuring that "American justice is 'for all.'" He saw his pro bono work as an "ethical injunction" to spend at least 10 percent of his time working for the public good.[24]

Sheldon's team crafted an extensive questionnaire that potential jurors were asked to fill out in most of these trials. The team also conducted focus groups to see what kinds of evidence and arguments might work best in the courtroom, and they conducted community-attitudes surveys when appropriate to get a better sense of what local issues might contribute to how potential jurors would respond to a case. Defense teams occasionally conducted their own limited jury research, but they did not have the luxury of jury consultants eager to do pro bono work for them. Defense lawyers spent most of their time instead contesting the tools the prosecution was using to try to select a jury or trying to use the tools of the prosecution team to serve their own ends.

The jury selection process offered a way for each side to determine what challenges they would face in the courtroom and to lay the groundwork for the strategies they thought would help their cause. Prosecutors signaled early on their hope that trials could help to change the national image of the South by asking potential jurors what they thought about the movie *Mississippi Burning*, the film that served as a lightning rod for concerns that white Mississippians continued to be stereotyped as as rednecks and racists in national popular culture. For the prosecution, questions about *Mississippi Burning* worked to remind jurors that civil rights murders had stigmatized the state and its residents and to suggest that trials and convictions might be a way for Mississippians to finally do something about it. They looked for jurors who thought, as some admitted they did, that the crimes had given the state a "black eye."[25] Defense lawyers instead asked questions that portrayed the contemporary prosecutions as symbolic attempts to blame all white Southerners for crimes that had taken place long ago. When Beckwith's lawyer asked jurors if they had heard that "Mississippi is on trial in this case" he hoped that they might harbor resentments against what they saw as an unfair portrayal of the state, which would make them less likely to convict.[26] But if in the 1950s and '60s portraying civil rights murder trials as a referendum on the state or the southern way of life helped convince juries to acquit, by the 1990s, both sides seemed to recognize that portraying trials as a way to address the damage done to the South's reputation by unpunished racial violence would make juries more sympathetic to the prosecution. As Kathy Nester, the lead defense attorney in the James Seale trial, later admitted, she should have known the verdict would be guilty as soon as prosecutors began asking jurors what they thought of *Mississippi Burning*.[27]

Jurors also faced numerous questions about their racial attitudes. They were asked about their views of the Ku Klux Klan, whether they had ever belonged to an organization committed to white supremacy, and whether they would be offended by the use of racist language, especially the word "nigger." Occasionally, such questions came from defense lawyers who thought they might be able to keep blacks off the jury by getting them to admit that they could not judge a racist defendant fairly.[28] But prosecutors proved far more eager to pose questions like these as a way to begin portraying the defendants as outspoken racists or as Klansmen, which as Bobby DeLaughter saw it, would help keep jurors from identifying with the men on trial.[29] Prosecutors needed to get potential jurors to begin thinking of the defendants as something other than old men in prison jumpsuits, and they believed that highlighting the vicious racism of the defendants was the best way to do so.

Most defense attorneys saw these questions about the Klan and overt racism as a dangerous harbinger of a courtroom strategy to make the trial a referendum on the racial attitudes of the defendants rather than the evidence at hand. They sought to convince judges that questioning jurors about the Klan and racist language was a device to prejudice the jury against the defendants before the trial even began. When Charles Noble went on trial for the murder of Vernon Dahmer in 1999, defense attorneys fought to keep the prosecution from asking jurors the same kinds of questions they had when they prosecuted Sam Bowers for the same crime a year earlier. Their "improper voir dire" in Bowers's trial was "highly prejudicial" and "may very well inflame other potential jurors," Noble's lawyers charged.[30] Defense lawyers for James Seale objected strenuously to the prosecutor's motion to use

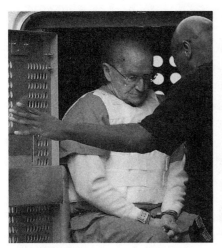 

The visual image of elderly defendants—like James Ford Seale, shown here on his way to the courtroom for the second day of his 2007 trial for the murder of Charles Moore and Henry Dee, or Edgar Ray Killen, who sometimes arrived at the courthouse in Neshoba County in a wheelchair—concerned prosecutors, who needed jurors to imagine these now-old men as dangerous and violent. (Left: © Rogelio V. Solis/AP/Corbis; right: © Kyle Carter/Reuters/Corbis)

what had by 2007 become the standard juror questionnaire in the case on the grounds that it was "laced with prejudice and bias." They feared that the questionnaire would send the message to jurors that the case was totally about "race, racial beliefs, and racial prejudices" rather than a criminal case about a specific criminal charge. The prosecution, they charged, wasn't just playing the race card; they were "putting the whole deck in play."[31]

Both efforts by prosecutors to make jurors aware of the racist attitudes of the defendants and defense lawyers' concern that potential jurors would be offended by their clients' extreme, outspoken racist views highlight the racial environment that had developed in the wake of Jim Crow. By the 1990s, overt expressions of racism had become socially unacceptable. When the trial judge in the Beckwith case told one of Beckwith's lawyers that he couldn't just excuse every juror who said they would be offended if they learned that Beckwith used racial epithets—he had to "assume they are going to be offended"—it

highlighted the extent to which the rules had changed since the days of
the open racism of the Jim Crow era.[32]

But being offended by overt racism of the kind practiced by the Klan,
jury consultants knew, did not mean that potential jurors might not harbor racial attitudes that could influence their views of a racially charged
case. The trick for prosecutors, then, was twofold: they had to get people
to admit what they really thought about race in an environment where
everyone was supposed to be colorblind, and they had to craft strategies that allowed them to highlight the now socially unacceptable racist
attitudes of the defendants without offending jurors who might resent
some of the racial changes that had taken place since the civil rights era.

Andrew Sheldon's Atlanta-based trial consulting group had a background in racially charged cases that made them particularly well suited
to advise prosecutors in these trials. They were experts in helping prosecutors understand the racial issues that could affect their cases and in
crafting strategies that would reduce the power of racial biases to influence the outcome in the courtroom. Attorneys could not simply trust
jurors when they denied holding any racist beliefs, they advised. "Racism and racial bias is something only the most flamboyant racist will
admit in court," a SheldonSinrich advice column explained. As their
team discovered when they did anonymous phone surveys with five
hundred potential jurors in Birmingham in the period before Tom Blanton's trial, many people had "attitudes and opinions which would not
be considered politically correct," things they might reveal during an
anonymous phone survey but would not admit to during voir dire questioning. Prosecutors had to find questions that could reveal racial bias
without offending a potential juror.[33]

To get at attitudes that potential jurors might not be willing to admit
in public, Sheldon developed a series of more indirect questions designed
to uncover racial bias. Jurors were asked whether their children went
to public or private school and what they thought of the Martin Luther
King Jr. holiday, questions that might allow prosecutors to discover
a potential juror's attitudes about integration of the schools or about
the changes that had resulted from the civil rights movement. Questions about what bumper stickers jurors had on their cars or whether
they had any tattoos might reveal whether someone was partial to the
racially coded symbol of the Confederate flag.[34]

But Sheldon found the most useful questions to be those that focused on how jurors understood the status of race relations today. What, for example, did a potential juror see as the cause of racial tensions today? And did they think that the problems of racial discrimination had mostly been solved? Jurors who said that they thought race was no longer a problem raised an immediate red flag. Such people were typically "in some degree of denial," Sheldon argued, which might make them unwilling to judge the evidence about racial discrimination fairly.[35] Sheldon's concern about whites who claimed that racial problems had been solved highlights that even as overt racism became less acceptable, refusing to acknowledge race could work as another form of racism.[36]

Concerns about the unacknowledged or hidden racial biases that might be lurking among jurors shaped the strategies that prosecutors used in the courtroom. Andrew Sheldon advised prosecutors in every case he worked on to focus on the suffering, pain, and loss that resulted from the murders rather than the political aspects of the case. Although prosecutors had diligently sought to uncover any latent racial biases among the jurors, he admitted that some people on the jury might still have "some segregationist tendencies." Prosecutors framed their arguments keeping that in mind, knowing that the safest approach was to highlight the loss of the victims and the continued suffering of their families. Thus the murder of Medgar Evers would be portrayed as the murder of a father coming home to his family at night rather than as a terrorist act or political assassination. As Hinds County District Attorney Ed Peters noted, if prosecutors could successfully focus on the "single issue" or "whether or not a person in a cowardly way shot a person in the back from ambush at night with his family just a few yards away," it wouldn't matter if some jurors harbored racial prejudices.[37] Similarly, Sheldon suggested that prosecutors in the Birmingham church bombing cases describe the crime first and foremost as an attack on four girls and on a house of worship rather than as a civil rights struggle. He urged Doug Jones to incorporate the powerful phrase "a mother's heart never stops crying" into his closing argument. When a witness in the Dahmer trial testified that he had heard "a man's voice in distress" after the house was set afire, Sheldon immediately decided that should be the hook for the closing argument in that case.[38] Even as prosecutors would make every effort to highlight the racist attitudes of the defendants, they would simultaneously try to convince jurors not to think of these crimes primarily as civil rights murders.

After the conviction of Byron De La Beckwith, a reporter for CNN offered a summary of what would be the central symbolic tension in all of these trials: while both sides insisted that the case should be "treated strictly as a murder trial—one man killing another back in 1963," there was no way to escape the fact that the trial was "wrapped in" politics, in race, and in Mississippi's history.[39] Picking a jury proved so time-consuming precisely because everyone knew these trials were about more than whether a particular defendant should be held legally responsible for a crime that had taken place long ago. Trials that have historical or political significance inevitably address "something larger than law," one legal scholar notes. They communicate messages that go beyond the basic issue of individual accountability.[40] Contemporary civil rights trials by necessity focused on the actions of a particular defendant and a specific crime, but they were always about much more. The messages that emerged from the courtroom—messages shaped by legal realities as well as prosecutorial choices—offered arguments about the nature of the changes in the South since the 1960s, who bore responsibility for the racial violence of the civil rights era, and the meanings and significance of the legal process. And the site of the courtroom conveyed a gravitas and legitimacy to whatever took place there, giving the messages these trials would communicate a particular kind of power.

Even as they focused on the narrow legal question of the guilt or innocence of individual men, the trials crafted a narrative about how much the South had changed since the era of legal segregation, and especially about the ways in which whites had adjusted to and accepted the demise of the Jim Crow system. In 1991, a journalist imagining how changes in Mississippi's racial climate would make Byron De La Beckwith's upcoming trial different from his earlier ones came up with a lengthy list: the courthouse had rid itself of whites-only restrooms, blacks could sit anywhere they wanted instead of being restricted to a segregated area, the press would not refer to Myrlie Evers as "that Evers woman," and prosecutors in the 1990s would not have to ask potential jurors, as prosecutor William Waller did in 1964, if they thought "killing a nigger was a crime."[41] Three years before the trial even started, it was clear that civil rights trials would function to showcase how far the South had come since the days of Jim Crow.

The civil rights courtroom could not help but highlight the contrast between the old southern order and the new one that had replaced it. The courtroom, prosecutor Jack Lacy noted during the Ernest Avants trial, became like a "time machine where the past and present have collided."[42] Trials brought some of the practices of civil rights–era criminal justice back to life. Some of the character witnesses for the defendants brought old racist canards out into the open. Witnesses in two different trials, for example, testified that the Klan was a peaceful and benevolent organization, known, one said, for bringing fruit baskets to people in need. Past could also collide with present when defense witnesses presented the same testimony that they had in earlier trials. But now prosecutors were on hand to subject defense witnesses to withering cross-examinations of a kind that they had not encountered before. Hinds County District Attorney Ed Peters tore apart the testimony of James Holley, a police officer who had sworn in Byron De La Beckwith's 1964 trials that he had seen Beckwith ninety miles away from Jackson on the night of Medgar Evers's murder. Peters got Holley to admit that he hadn't reported that he had seen Beckwith far from the crime scene until he was asked to do so at the trial, even though Beckwith had spent months in jail before the trial began. Why, he asked Holley, had he let his friend Beckwith sit in jail for eight months if he knew where he was at the time of the crime? Trials exposed the kinds of lies that people had been willing to tell to help defendants. No wonder that Andrew Sheldon described the civil rights trials he witnessed as "surreal."[43]

Yet even as the courtroom brought aspects of the Jim Crow era back to life, it also communicated how far the South had come since those days. That message sometimes emerged rather subtly from the ways that attorneys assumed that the region's racist past was absolutely foreign to modern-day jurors. When Doug Jones told the jury in Tom Blanton's trial that "as much as we find it hard to believe today," there had been separate lunch counters, restrooms, and water fountains for black people and whites in Birmingham in 1963, he suggested that the distance between the Jim Crow South and the modern-day South was vast. The claims by prosecutors, reiterated in many trials, that the overt racist language common in the 1960s had become so offensive that jurors might find it hard to even hear these cases further reinforced that sense of separation from the past. The "n" word, prosecutor Bob Helfrich told potential jurors in the Bowers trial, "was used then, and it's going to be used now." Could jurors still be fair no matter "how offensive that might be to you?" U.S. Attorney Paige Fitzgerald cautioned jurors in her opening argument in the 2003 trial of Ernest Avants that they would "see and hear words that we don't hear very much anymore. You're going to hear 'negro,' 'colored,' 'darky.' You're going to hear another word too. You know the one."[44] The use of such hateful, profane names had no place in the modern South, these arguments made clear.

The ways in which attorneys, especially prosecutors, talked about the victims who had been civil rights activists in the courtroom also crafted a narrative about change. Trials provided a forum for white Southerners to demonstrate that they had embraced the principle of formal legal equality and had accepted the civil rights movement as a positive force that had helped the nation live up to its democratic potential. At Byron De La Beckwith's first trial in January 1964, prosecutor William Waller strove mightily to keep any discussion of Medgar Evers's political work or activism out of the trial. When the defense asked Myrlie Evers whether her husband had been the head of the NAACP in Mississippi, whether he was active in the integration movement, or whether he had tried to integrate the University of Mississippi, Waller objected again and again, knowing that such associations could lead white jurors to feel that his murder had been justified. But in 1994, Bobby DeLaughter readily acknowledged and applauded Evers's political activities. Evers, he told prospective jurors, was a leader in the NAACP who was "trying to get some changes made" when he was killed, trying to integrate schools, win the right to vote, achieve equal access to department stores and restrooms. He was assassinated, DeLaughter argued, for wanting himself and his family "to be accepted as human beings with some dignity."[45]

Evers was not the only figure who would inspire such recasting. Prosecuting attorney Bob Helfrich described slain activist Vernon Dahmer as "a man's man" who believed in hard work and the American dream. No longer would activists who had come south to work in the movement be "outside agitators" with Communist leanings; now they were young people devoted to helping the community. Andrew Goodman, James Chaney, and Mickey Schwerner, prosecutor and Mississippi Attorney

General Jim Hood argued, had been doing "God's work" in Mississippi. They were "freedom fighters," just like American troops in Iraq, Hood told the jury during his closing arguments. When prosecutor Mark Duncan asked potential jurors in that same trial if they could treat Andrew Goodman, Mickey Schwerner, and James Chaney "like they were from here and were our neighbors," it encapsulated the message that white Southerners had accepted the goals of political and legal equality that civil rights activists had died to achieve.[46]

Indeed, trials served to demonstrate that criticizing the civil rights movement had become disrespectful in the modern South. Defense lawyers in contemporary trials repeatedly felt they had to emphasize that, regardless of their role as advocates for the suspects, they saw the crimes as tragedies, they had great respect for the victims and their families, and they supported the goals of the movement. Even as he asked jurors to acquit Tom Blanton, defense attorney John Robbins insisted that the four girls killed in the Birmingham church bombing had not died in vain. Because of the changes caused by their deaths, "we're better as a community. We're better as a nation," he reassured them. In the few instances where defense lawyers offered the kinds of arguments about movement activists that had been common in earlier trials, it did not help their case. When an attorney at Beckwith's 1994 trial made even a mild attempt to stigmatize Medgar Evers by asking a police witness whether he had ever fingerprinted Evers for a crime, one observer in the courtroom noted "you could actually hear the bodies stiffen in the courtroom, along with the outraged inhalation of breath." Travis Buckley, the former Klan lawyer defending Sam Bowers in the Dahmer murder, seemed almost a comic figure as he considered asking the pathologist testifying about Vernon Dahmer's autopsy if he was a Cuban immigrant; in his closing argument, he ventured an analogy comparing the government's persecution of Sam Bowers to Hitler's persecution of the Jews. Andy Sheldon, taking notes as a jury consultant, described Buckley's defense as a "travesty" that the Dahmer family should not have to sit through.[47] Just as the racist language of the defendants was now unacceptable, the defense strategies of the 1950s and 1960s had no place in the modern courtroom.

Civil trials told a clear story: the South had progressed because it had moved far away from the Jim Crow era, embraced the goals of the civil rights movement, and now treated blacks with respect. No matter that the image of progress presented masked the possibility that racism might still operate in subtle or institutional ways or that even the arduous jury-selection process highlighted the complexity of the changes in the racial order in the years since the 1960s. Modern civil rights trials implied that racial progress could be measured by how far the South had moved beyond the trappings of the segregated caste system.[48] Like the popular renditions of the civil rights movement that focused on Martin Luther King Jr.'s calls for interracial brotherhood in his "I Have a Dream" speech rather than on his more radical critiques of poverty or institutionalized inequality, prosecutors explained the goals of the movement primarily in terms of interracial friendship and better interpersonal relations, a strategy that made sense when seeking to appeal to a multiracial group of jurors who might differ in their political views. Thus prosecutor Doug Jones told jurors in Bobby Frank Cherry's trial that what the movement had sought was best epitomized by a picture of eleven-year-old bombing victim Denise McNair holding "her best friend—her white Chatty Cathy doll." In 1963, that image of interracial friendship had been "the hope of a race of people," but by 2002, it had become "the hope of us all."[49] Everyone, that is, except the defendants who were on trial. They would become symbolic of everything that had been wrong with the past.

If the trials' depiction of the crimes and victims promoted a narrative about the positive racial change that held up whites' acceptance of integration and interracial friendship as the ultimate proof of racial equality, the discussion in the courtroom about the defendants reinforced an understanding of racism as overt racial hatred expressed by individuals. Prosecutors in civil rights trials sought every way they could to expose the racist beliefs of the defendants and to highlight their ties to the Ku Klux Klan. Given that the defendants were now elderly men, some of whom were in wheelchairs or on oxygen during the trials, they needed to recreate the men they had been: they had to make them intimidating again. Defense teams fought to keep evidence of defendants' racial attitudes out of the courtroom; they would insist that such evidence had nothing to do with whether the men on trial had committed the crimes at hand. But the struggle nearly always favored the prosecutors, and the result was the same in every trial:

the intense focus on the racial views of the defendants served to turn these men into the very embodiment of racism—defined as individual hatred manifested in violent speech and actions.

Defense attorneys would have preferred to keep evidence about their clients' racial attitudes out of the courtroom altogether. They wanted to keep trials focused solely on the question of whether the evidence showed that their clients had committed the crimes in question. Defense lawyers knew that the direct evidence in these cases was old and some of it—such as testimony read in from old trial transcripts—might not carry that much weight with jurors. They had a better chance to win an acquittal or mistrial if they kept jurors focused narrowly on that evidence. They also knew that some jurors might be reluctant to convict an old man for a crime committed so long ago.

Their goal was to keep the story simple. They fought to keep prosecutors from bringing in what was described as "hate crime evidence," which would show that defendants had been motivated by racial hatred. To them, such information had, in legal terms, "no probative value." In layman's terms, it meant that defense lawyers feared guilt by association. If jurors knew about their clients' racial attitudes or history in the Klan, they might simply assume that they had committed the crime in question. As Byron De La Beckwith's lawyers complained, the prosecution was asking the jury to "infer" that Beckwith murdered Evers because he had "allegedly made derogatory statements about African-Americans." Lawyers for the men accused of murdering Rainey Pool asked the judge to dismiss the case before the trial because the prosecutor had said that Pool's body would not have been so mishandled if he had been a white man. That was a "racial type of statement" that was "extremely damaging" and prejudicial to the defendants, they insisted. And James Seale's lawyers lodged a continuing objection to any and all testimony about Seale's racial beliefs. As Seale's lawyer Kathy Nester reminded the court, "The Klan is not on trial here. James Ford Seale is on trial for kidnapping."[50] The more they could keep the story focused narrowly on the actions of one man, the better their chance of winning an acquittal.

But prosecutors always won the battle to make the racial attitudes of the defendants a central aspect of the trial. They could fairly claim, as they did in every case, that information about the racial views of the defendants was necessary to show motive. After all, in most of these cases, the alleged killers didn't even know their victims. How to explain to a jury *why* the crimes had been committed or *why* these particular victims had been targeted without any evidence about what the defendants believed or what was happening at the time? Prosecutors at Tom Blanton's 2000 trial thus insisted over defense objections that they must be allowed to introduce evidence that Blanton had belonged to the Klan in order to show his hatred of blacks and willingness to resort to violence. The team prosecuting Beckwith successfully argued that evidence of his violent animosity towards blacks, the NAACP, and civil rights was relevant to establish his motive for the killing. During the trial, they introduced letters that Beckwith had written in which he called the NAACP cancerous and said it should be eliminated, joked about Medgar Evers greeting Kennedy in hell after Kennedy's assassination, and called blacks "boll weevils" and "beasts of the field." Beckwith's lawyers would later appeal his conviction to the Supreme Court on the grounds that the "sole purpose" of this kind of evidence was "inflaming and prejudicing the jury against the defendant."[51]

Prosecutors sorely needed this kind of evidence. As Doug Jones wrote about the 2002 Birmingham church bombing trial, "To the courtroom spectator, Bobby Frank Cherry appeared to be anybody's grandfather: a seventy-one-year-old man more comfortable wearing overalls in the garden than wearing a suit sitting in a courtroom." One of his goals, "beginning with opening arguments," was to show jurors what Cherry was like "as a 33-year-old man in 1963." To get jurors to distance themselves from defendants, prosecutors used what Bobby DeLaughter called a "'we're not like him' strategy." They fought to show that these men had belonged to the Klan or had shared the Klan's white supremacist views. They presented evidence, when they were allowed, about the defendants' history of engaging in racial violence. And they made sure that jurors knew how the defendants had talked about blacks, highlighting again how unacceptable overt expressions of racism had become. In the 2003 trial of Ernest Avants, federal prosecutor Paige Fitzgerald fought hard to convince the judge that she should be able to show the jury a clip from *20/20* where Avants used "what we refer to as the N word." Fitzgerald argued the tape was vital because it was so "powerful to hear him speaking the words." She would ask a witness in the James Seale trial testifying about Seale's racial views "to use the words that he used, not necessarily the words that you would use."[52] In Tom Blanton's trial, prosecutors reminded the jury that when Blanton told one witness that he wanted to kill black people, he didn't use the word black. "He had names for black people," the prosecutor reminded jurors, " . . . hateful names. Profane names."[53] Emphasizing the way these men spoke became a way to remind jurors, again and again, that the elderly men in wheelchairs were not doting grandfathers.

Defense lawyers worked hard to prevent the trials from becoming a referendum on the Klan and the overt racism it represented. Defense counsel felt the need to repeatedly remind jurors that simply being a racist or a Klansman did not make one a murderer. The state was asking them to convict the defendant "because of his opinions," defense lawyers in the Beckwith case charged. Tom Blanton's lawyer admitted that the state had proved that his client "had a big mouth and racist tendencies." As one James Seale's lawyers put it, racism may not be right, "but it is not a crime."[54]

But even if not a crime, being openly racist was certainly a handicap in court. The evidence showcasing the defendants' racist language and attitudes, both sides understood, would make defendants unsympathetic figures. Defense teams conceded that juries would find the defendants unappealing. In case after case, they reminded jurors that, as Jim Kitchens told the jury in the Beckwith case, it didn't matter whether they liked Beckwith or wanted to take him home. "Forget you don't like him," he implored them. Tom Blanton's lawyer readily conceded in opening arguments that Blanton was "as annoying as hell" and that jurors weren't going to like him.[55] As a result, not one of the defense teams in these trials chose to put the defendant on the stand to testify on his own behalf. Some of the men charged had testified in earlier trials, like Beckwith and Avants, but defense lawyers saw it as too risky to allow them to speak in the contemporary trials. They refused to do so even if it meant losing the ability to present important alibis. The defendants had become too "repulsive" to the jury to be heard.[56]

The sheer volume and repetition of the evidence about the racial views of the defendants helped turn them into symbols of the racial horrors of the segregated system. Cases that might have offered more sympathetic defendants, or that might have raised complex and painful questions about the workings of racism or the broader story of white supremacy in the Jim Crow era, have not to date come to trial. Some of the crimes of the civil rights era raised the possibility of charges being brought against defendants who might have been more challenging for a prosecutor to stigmatize. One of the chief suspects in the reopened Emmett Till case, for example, was Carolyn Bryant, the white woman who claimed Till whistled at her and who allegedly identified Till for her husband. There was even talk that a black man who had certainly been coerced by his white boss to restrain Till and to clean up his blood might be charged in the crime.[57] If there had been a jury trial in the case of James Bonard Fowler, an Alabama state trooper who shot and killed civil rights activist Jimmie Lee Jackson while on duty during a 1965 protest in Marion, Alabama, it might have raised interesting questions about the role of state authorities in the racial violence of the Jim Crow South. But Fowler chose to plead guilty to manslaughter and serve a sentence of six months rather than face a trial in 2010, and insisted despite his plea that he had acted in self-defense and had done nothing wrong.[58] Defendants like these might have been harder to turn into living embodiments of Jim Crow–era racism.

There has been no such ambiguity about the men who have actually been brought to trial. They tended to be relatively poor outsiders, men on the margins of their communities. Men like Killen, Beckwith, Cherry, and Avants had not undergone any kind of transformation in the wake of the destruction of the world they had known in the 1960s. Most still believed in black biological inferiority and supported racial segregation, and they had failed to temper their outspoken racism or to present it in a coded or more muted style. As one reporter at the start of the Beckwith trial noted, unlike most people in Mississippi, Beckwith "somehow has managed to maintain a kind of Berlin Wall between his language and the reality all around him." These defendants could be readily portrayed as not just racist but, as Bobby DeLaughter said of Byron De La Beckwith, "the quintessence of evil." As Bobby Frank Cherry's lawyer complained, his client was easy to prosecute because he was so easily portrayed as "the human equivalent of a cockroach."[59]

And the trials affirmed that this evil was quickly passing into the past. When Edgar Ray Killen appeared in court using oxygen tanks, or Ernest Avants was seen using a listening device so he could hear the courtroom testimony, it served as a form of visual evidence that the

Byron De La Beckwith, like nearly all the other defendants in contemporary civil rights–era trials, had not tempered his racial views in the years since the 1960s. Beckwith is shown here standing in front of the Confederate flag out-side his home in 1990. (AP Photo/Jeff Guenther)

racism they had embodied was near death, with one foot in the grave. Bobby Frank Cherry, whose trial date was delayed after lawyers temporarily convinced the judge he was not fit to stand trial, was described by his lawyers as a "feeble old man suffering from dementia." James Seale, suffering from tumors and emphysema, seemed to one observer of the trial that he could die at any moment, while Byron De La Beckwith appeared so frail and feeble that reporter Adam Nossiter described him as "a spectral disengaged presence at his own trial."[60] The "specters" at these trials were not only the ghosts of victims, but also the ghosts of a racial era that was rapidly passing into oblivion.

Journalists watching the many trials offered metaphors and analogies to communicate to their readers just how out of place these defendants seemed in modern America. Beckwith, one reported, "appeared as almost a relic of a long-lost era," while Edgar Ray Killen embodied "an archetype on the verge of extinction." Richard Cohen of the *Washington Post* compared Killen to "addled Japanese soldiers" found on Pacific islands still fighting World War II forty years after the war had ended. He seemed, Cohen wrote, "a human abandoned by time itself." When Beckwith talked, "it was like listening to someone who's been locked away in a time capsule for the last three decades," a report on National Public Radio claimed. "You have to look long and hard to find Mississippians today who express agreement with Beckwith's racist rantings."[61] The country and the state had changed, but these men had not.

Prosecutors, in short, did not have to work hard to portray these defendants as a "walking time capsule" or as "antiquarian curiosities" who embodied everything that was hateful from the southern past and who would soon be extinct.[62] James Chaney's brother, Ben, charged that the desire to present that very image explained why only Edgar Ray Killen was tried for his brother's murder, instead of some of the wealthier, more respectable suspects who could have been charged too. "A lot of people in the South would like to get rid of these old diehard racists or these racists who are unrepenting, and say that everything had changed," he argued. The Klan, he recognized, was now a "lightning rod" that was very easy to dismiss. By the 1990s and 2000s, the defendants in these trials had become "embarrassing relics of a shameful past," easy to portray as the outmoded practitioners of a racism that was very narrowly defined.[63]

While there was little doubt that the defendants in these trials were unrepentant and hateful, the civil rights trials portrayed their racist attitudes outside of any political context of the 1950s and 1960s. Lacking that broader context, it became easy for trials to suggest that the defendants bore full responsibility for the violence of the era. The trials would raise few questions about the role or responsibility of government actors or the broader white community in the racial violence of the civil rights era. Instead, they offered their own skewed version of a "great man" theory of history, where a handful of evil men became the driving agents of Jim Crow racial violence.[64]

A criminal legal trial offers at best a blunt instrument for exploring any accountability for wrongdoing that extends beyond that of the individual defendant. The focus in criminal law on individual intent— its "individualistic bias"—made it difficult for trials to admit or recognize that the institutions and workings of the broader community or the state had played a role in fostering and even enabling the racial violence of the era.[65] Although relatives of victims and activists would have liked to see state authorities held accountable for their role in condoning or promoting the racial terror campaign of the Klan, as the Mississippi attorney general gently told Andrew Goodman's brother, David, a criminal court could not try the state. Doug Jones recognized that the actions of police and politicians in Birmingham in the 1960s had "empowered the Klan," but that wasn't something that he could bring into the courtroom. As he explained, he had "no evidence that anybody in the city or the county was actively involved" in the bombing. He could not talk about how Alabama Governor George Wallace or Birmingham Police Commissioner Bull Conner had created an environment that led the Klan to bomb churches. As a result, journalist Diane McWhorter observed as she watched the church bombing trials, the trial presented no evidence of how "the Klansmen were acting on the authority of the official culture."[66]

Prosecutors did sometimes recognize that the state had neglected to take these murders seriously at the time they were committed. "Law enforcement did not do their duty," Jim Hood admitted in the closing arguments of the Killen trial. It "probably was the State's fault" that nothing was done about Rainey Pool's killing for thirty years, the lead prosecutor in that case noted.[67] But the role of the state, when addressed at all, was presented in terms of a failure to act to contain violence, rather than in terms of actively enabling or engaging in violence.

In the rare instances when the state's role in repressing civil rights protests or working with Klansmen came into the courtroom, lawyers making the charge would invariably minimize it through their rhetorical choices. When, during Beckwith's trial, defense lawyer Jim Kitchens asked a police officer who was testifying whether he had ever arrested civil rights leader Medgar Evers, he told the judge that the question was important to show that Beckwith was not alone in opposing integration: "Even the Jackson Police Department was upholding segregation laws," he explained. That *even*, however, minimized the role the Jackson police historically played in repressing racial protest and implied that the Jackson police would have preferred not having to enforce such laws. When federal prosecutors had to show that the Klan had worked with law enforcement in Franklin County in order to prove the charge of conspiracy in the 2007 James Seale trial, they went out of their way to suggest such collusion was extraordinary. Although the prosecutor presented evidence that the local sheriff was part of the conspiracy involved in the kidnapping of Charles Moore and Henry Dee, he expressed disbelief that such a thing could happen. "Now, this is just unbelievable. Right?" It was "just about as unbelievable a story as I can come up with."[68] The police may have been involved in this instance, but courtroom arguments suggested that such involvement was very rare.

Given the history of the Jim Crow era, what was truly unbelievable was the space the legal process could provide for an almost complete rewriting of the state response to civil rights violence. In their decision upholding Byron De La Beckwith's conviction, the Mississippi Supreme Court took the occasion to applaud the legal and law enforcement communities of the state "for their energetic, patient, and longsuffering efforts, beginning only minutes after the shooting of Medgar Evers, to squeeze some justice" out of the harm caused by the murder.[69] In one paragraph that will remain on permanent record in court files, the Mississippi State Supreme Court remade the state's history, making the police and legal authorities into eager justice seekers rather than representatives of the forces arrayed against legal justice at the time.

But the difficulties of exploring the government's complicity in the racial violence of the civil rights era served as only one of the forces responsible for the "great man" version of history that emerged from the courtroom. Rules governing the admissibility of evidence also shaped the historical narrative in ways that put the defendants at the center of the story of violence in the civil rights South. Legal scholars recognize that criminal trials cannot effectively communicate the complexity of the past. Trial records do not, and in many ways cannot, seek "a full historical account" that goes beyond the actions of particular individuals. The histories offered in trials tend to be "partial, and preoccupied with the either/or simplifications of the adversary process."[70] Defense lawyers, in fact, fought to keep historical evidence out of the courtroom altogether. Just as they saw evidence about the defendants' racial attitudes as immaterial to the question of whether the men on trial had committed the crimes with which they were charged, they saw information about the historical context in which these crimes took place as irrelevant and not directly related to the actions of the individuals on trial. To Tom Blanton's lawyers, for example, the civil rights protests taking place in Birmingham at the time of the 1963 church bombing were "peripheral stuff" that should not be considered by the jury.[71] Few judges were so draconian as to forbid historical context altogether, but they did limit the extent to which it could be brought into the courtroom and they would forbid evidence that did not pertain to the defendant's acts in relation to the crime in question.

Civil rights trials reflected these constraints by shaping histories of civil rights violence that focused narrowly on a specific crime and placed the actions of the defendants at the center of the narrative. Bobby DeLaughter, for example, framed the murder of Medgar Evers as a collision course between two men: he opened by telling the jury of Evers's quest to integrate the University of Mississippi, which made him "the focal point of everything this defendant hated." DeLaughter portrayed the struggle against civil rights in Mississippi as the fight of one man. As he told jurors in his opening statement, Byron De La Beckwith had been on a "one-man mission to purge society of anyone and everything that was for integration."[72]

The two Birmingham church bombing trials offer perhaps the best example of the ways in which the format influenced the historical narrative that emerged from the courtroom. In both trials, Doug Jones explained that he "took jurors on a journey back through history." He told jurors about court-ordered school integration in Birmingham in 1963 and about the children's marches that started at Sixteenth Street Baptist Church, where black children became key figures in the ongoing civil rights protests there led by Martin Luther King Jr. and Fred Shuttlesworth. This information, he maintained, was vital to show why men like Thomas Blanton and Bobby Frank Cherry had targeted young people at the Sixteenth Street Baptist Church. Yet while the jury learned something of the history of Birmingham in the 1960s, they did not learn much about the broader context of segregationist opposition to the civil rights protests there. The bombing, the jury learned, was the work of men like Tom Blanton and Bobby Cherry, who saw "their segregated way of life dissolving in front of them" and "decided to meet and talk and do those kinds of things that those kind of men do during that time."[73] Such language implied that it was primarily, or only, Klansmen hiding under a bridge who had opposed the civil rights struggle.

Jones knew that this was a truncated version of history. In public presentations on the trial, Jones talks about the ways in which the racial and political climate in Birmingham helped enable the bombing. But he recognized that he could never "tell the story" of the bombings with as much complexity as he wanted to in the courtroom. Even being able to bring in evidence about school integration and the children's marches was a "liberal interpretation of the rules," and he knew the judge would "keep a tight leash on us." Besides being limited by what the judge would allow, Jones feared that if he tried to talk about the community complicity at the time, it might have led the judge to order the trial moved to another venue and could have given jurors an excuse to acquit. Why convict this one man if so many people were at fault?[74] As a result, even though Jones had a very different understanding of the crime, the trial for the most part portrayed the Birmingham church bombing as the mission of a very few men, acting alone outside of the broader social context.

The portrayal in the courtroom of Klansmen as the embodiment of Jim Crow racism who were solely responsible for the racial violence of the era not only simplified the historical record, but also served to affirm the innocence of the state and the broader community in civil rights crimes. As defense lawyers argued, the narrative put forth by prosecutors suggested that their clients were "the only racists back then" or "the only segregationists back then."[75] Defense lawyers occasionally tried to remind jurors that, as defense counsel Jim Kitchens told jurors in the Beckwith trial, "Just about every white person in this state was for segregation" in the 1960s.[76] But the fact that lawyers had to remind jurors that their client was "not the only segregationist" speaks volumes about the success of prosecutors in pinning responsibility for the racism of the Jim Crow era on just a few men.

Trials more commonly presented history in ways that excused the government or community of any complicity in upholding the segregated order. In trials, witnesses could rewrite their own past to deny their culpability for Jim Crow. The editor of the *Franklin Advocate*, for example, testified that James Seale had complained that the paper was running too many articles supporting integration in 1964. In fact a page-by-page analysis of the 1964 *Advocate* found that the paper featured instead anti-integration editorials and ran "pro-white" propaganda, both in its editorial content and in its advertising.[77]

The message that white Southerners more generally bore no responsibility for the actions of the Klan would be communicated too when prosecutors made the claim that defendants in these cases did not represent the attitudes or actions of the community at the time. Even before the Bowers trial started, prosecutor Bob Helfrich told reporters that "it was a very small minority of people" who felt like the Klan. He took the case, he later explained, because "the Klan didn't represent Mississippi then, now or any time."[78] In the courtroom prosecutors instead emphasized the vast distance between the men who now stood as the embodiment of racism and other white Southerners in ways that denied the possibility of any larger community complicity. When Bobby DeLaughter told the jury in his impassioned closing argument in the 1994 Beckwith trial that this wasn't a case about "black versus white" but one about "society, civilized society versus the vile, society versus the reprehensible, society versus the shocking," he left little ambiguity that Beckwith stood apart from the broader community. Edgar Ray Killen's crimes, prosecutors in that case insisted, were no reflection on the white community. Despite what jurors may have heard about the racial situation in Philadelphia and Neshoba County during the trial, fellow defense attorney Mark Duncan insisted that the crimes of forty years ago were "the actions of a few and not the actions of a whole." The result, as the prosecutor in the 1999 trial of three men charged with the 1970 murder of Rainey Pool explained, was that while the whole state had paid a price for ignoring racially motivated murders, a jury could now put "the debt on who it belongs to."[79] The costs had been shared, but the debt would be paid by a limited few. White Mississippi may not have been on trial, but prosecutors made clear that it could be acquitted by a conviction.

In 2005, commentators on Court TV, a cable station devoted to legal issues that was televising the Edgar Ray Killen trial live, questioned who was really on trial—Killen or the state and its way of life. Was this a trial, they mused, or an exorcism? In truth, the Killen trial, like the other contemporary prosecutions of civil rights–era murders, was both a trial *and* an exorcism. Prosecuting Killen and others like him served as a way to "exorcise" the Klan and the overt, violent racism it represented from the history and present of the white South. Legal responses to historic injustices, legal scholar Robert Gordon argues, often scapegoat a few "bad agents . . . for wrongs that derived from the routine functioning of an entire social system." Criminal trials can thus serve "as ritual acts of exorcism of the monstrous, abnormal elements of a system with which, at the time, almost everyone in one way or another went along."[80] Contemporary civil rights trials performed this kind of ritual, offering a public renunciation of the Klan and overt racism as a way to remake the image of the South.

Although they held just a few men responsible for the racial violence of the era, the prosecutors in most contemporary civil rights trials insisted that convicting those men would send a powerful message that states like Mississippi and Alabama had rejected the racism of the past and that the criminal justice system was no longer infected with politics or biased by bigotry. While the prosecutors leading these cases did not all share the same political beliefs or party affiliations, many of them came to these cases with a common understanding that these cases offered a chance, as Mark Duncan explained, "to say something good about where I live" or, as Doug Jones argued, a chance to show that Alabama was no longer "hiding under a rock" and running from the past. To Forrest County District Attorney Bob Helfrich, the trial of Sam Bowers had the potential to "cleanse" the "sore in Mississippi's past" left by his crimes.[81] These prosecutors saw in trials an opportunity to tell a positive story about their communities and their states.

Even in his first arguments before a grand jury seeking an indictment against Byron De La Beckwith in 1990, Bobby DeLaughter was not shy about the potential for a conviction to remake his state's image. The shooting of Medgar Evers, "this one cowardly act by one individual," he told the grand jury, "probably did as much to hurt this state and the way our state is viewed across the nation and possibly even the world than any other single act." It would be a mistake to give up a chance to "correct that wrong," he warned. As he saw it, what happened in cases like those of Beckwith and Bowers had given a "tremendous black eye to everybody in Mississippi" and these trials offered a way to undo some of that damage. DeLaughter was so worried about how it would look if the state tried Beckwith again and lost that he took the unusual step of presenting the grand jury not just the state's evidence, but also what he thought would be the main elements of Beckwith's defense. He wanted to see Beckwith indicted only if he could be confident a jury would convict him; an acquittal or even a hung jury in 1994 would be a "defeat for Mississippi."[82]

In making the case that a conviction offered a way to undo the damage left by these crimes, prosecutors were not urging jurors to ignore facts. They were not asking jurors to decide the case based on ideology rather than evidence, or to set aside the norms of legal justice just to make a political point. Rather, they offered to the jurors a frame for understanding the significance and symbolic import of a guilty verdict that they had shown these defendants richly deserved. A legal trial can legitimately be used to make a dramatic statement or teach a symbolic lesson as long as it adheres to what legal theorist Mark Osiel describes as the "primary limit that liberalism imposes on storytelling in criminal trials," which is the "principle of personal culpability."[83] Trials cannot hold a defendant responsible for the wrongs of others. But they can suggest what holding a defendant responsible for his own wrongs means. In these cases, prosecutors sought to define what these trials meant.

Some prosecutors made this argument quite explicit in the courtroom. As Mark Duncan told the media before the Killen trial, people in Philadelphia and Neshoba County hated what the killers "had done to the reputation of their home" but had been powerless to do anything about it. In his closing arguments to the jury in trial, he made clear exactly what was at stake in their decision. For forty-one years, he told them, Edgar Ray Killen and his friends had "written the history of Neshoba County." The jury, he argued, could "either change the history Edgar Ray Killen and the Klan wrote for us or you can confirm it."[84] By convicting Killen, jurors could cleanse the stain left on their communities and white Southerners' reputations by these crimes and the failure to prosecute when they occurred.

Even when prosecutors were not as direct as Duncan in calling on jurors to rewrite the history of the South, the closing arguments of defense lawyers in nearly every case showed how freighted the trials had become with this symbolic meaning. Again and again, defense teams insisted to jurors that a criminal trial could not and should not serve as a forum to remake the state's reputation or to undo the harm of the past. The Birmingham church bombing trial could not remove Birmingham's "tarnished image" or make "everybody in Birmingham feel good about themselves" so that "the rays of sunshine will shine down on this state and city and everything will be all better," Tom Blanton's lawyer told the jury. Convicting James Seale, his lawyer argued, would not, as the prosecution had implied, bring "justice for this state, whose reputation has been harmed by the government's failure to prosecute this case when they should have." Or as Mitch Moran would put it in his closing arguments to the Killen jury, "Folks, we can't change history."[85]

Perhaps the trials could not change history, but they could craft a story about how it should be understood. Despite the pleas of defense lawyers that civil rights trials should not be symbolic spaces to remake the reputation of the community or of the South, these trials communicated important symbolic messages. In the ritualized space of the courtroom, prosecutions made clear that white Southerners had come to accept the goals of the civil rights movement, had embraced the tenets of formal legal equality, and had eschewed overt racism. But trials also placed the responsibility for the racial violence of the past on the shoulders of a few old men in ways that minimized, if not completely erased, any community or governmental culpability for these crimes. The trials sent the message that putting a few old Klansmen in jail would repair the racial wrongs of the civil rights era. These cases offered both a narrow vision of the workings of racism in the Jim Crow South and an easy solution to whatever legacies of that racism remained.

In the aftermath of the Beckwith trial, journalist Adam Nossiter noted a lingering sense of dissatisfaction with the outcome. Beckwith, he felt, "resembled nothing so much as those Nazi war criminals that have proven unsatisfactory, small and pathetic, when brought to judgment. . . . All of these men, like Beckwith, seemed smaller than their world-altering crimes." James Seale, too, seemed too small, too insignificant to bear the symbolic weight he was being asked to bear: "The acts of which he is accused seem almost too powerful for him," noted trial observer Harry Maclean.[86] That lingering sense that convicting these aged, extremist defendants seemed somehow a bit too small reflected the ways in which the courtroom narrowed and simplified a broad story of the workings of a white supremacist society and state into one about the crimes of a few men. As individually responsible as they were—and there is no question that they bore great individual responsibility for the deaths for which they were held accountable—holding them accountable did not require anyone else to accept responsibility for condoning the Klan or creating an environment that fostered racial terrorism. When an elderly woman approached Rita Schwerner Bender during Edgar Ray Killen's trial and informed her that "good people" in Neshoba County would never have allowed the murder to happen if they had known what was going on, Bender felt a palpable denial of community responsibility, one that the stories told at and by these trials, it seemed, had done nothing to change.[87]

And not only did these trials tell stories; stories would also be told about them, in the media, in made-for-television movies and feature films, in books, and on the radio. In his opening argument in the trial of Tom Blanton for the Birmingham church bombing, prosecutor Doug Jones warned the jury not to expect as neat a story as they would likely find on a television show. "This is not a T.V. movie," he warned them.[88] But the media would find that trials in fact were much like TV movies. The media would fit what happened in the courtroom into popular modes of representing the civil rights struggle, racial politics, and the South, and they would offer their own rendition of what putting these elderly defendants in jail meant for the South and the nation.

5

Civil Rights Trials and Narratives of Redemption

There is no public narrative more potent today—or throughout American history—than the one about redemption.

—Michiko Kakutani, 2001

IN JANUARY 2002, just three months before Bobby Frank Cherry's trial in the Birmingham church bombing, the FX cable channel premiered a new original movie that focused on one aspect of the long journey to bring Cherry to justice. *Sins of the Father* told the story of Tom Cherry, Bobby Cherry's adult son; the dramatic tension at the heart of the film was whether Tom would decide that telling authorities what he knew about the bombing was more important than protecting his father. Over the course of the film, Tom moves from being so eager to win his father's approval that he moves to Texas to be near him to finally coming to see his father as a living incarnation of the worst racism of the Jim Crow era. In the climactic scene near the end of the movie, Tom symbolically renounces the racism embodied by his father by testifying before the grand jury considering new charges in the Birmingham church bombing. The film ends with his father's arrest.[1]

Sins of the Father reflected many of the tropes common to media portrayals of civil rights–era murder trials. It featured a white male hero, who would become the key agent for racial change by rejecting his racist upbringing. Blacks became secondary characters in the story, either vulnerable innocent victims—a point emphasized by the film's portrayal of the four girls killed in the bombing as only eight- or nine-year-olds rather than as the fourteen-year-olds most of them actually were—or wise guides who gently lead whites to change their racial views.[2] And even though Tom Cherry told prosecutors nothing that they saw as helpful to building a case against his father—indeed, the prosecutor in the church bombing case and Cherry's own daughter doubted that he had told the full truth about what he knew—his symbolic renunciation of the "sins" of his father became in the film the sign of a new South, one no longer set apart from the rest of the nation.[3]

The fact that there was a TV movie about efforts to bring Bobby Frank Cherry to trial highlights the media's fascination with contemporary civil rights trials. They have attracted immense attention from all kinds of media since Mississippi first brought Byron De La Beckwith back into the courtroom in 1994. Just three newspapers—the *New York Times*, the *Washington Post*, and *USA Today*—ran a collective ninety-five articles on the Beckwith trial, which would also become the subject of a major Hollywood film within two years of Beckwith's conviction. At least one hundred newspaper editorials about civil rights trials were published between Beckwith's trial in 1994 and that of James Seale in 2007. Trials have been featured on countless television news programs and radio talk shows, in popular magazines like *Glamour* and *People*, and have spawned memoirs written by prosecutors and witnesses. No fewer than 221 journalists from sixty different organizations registered for media passes to cover the 2005 trial of Edgar Ray Killen, a trial which cable channel Court TV broadcast live in its entirety.[4]

Civil rights trials proved of great interest to the media in part because of their inherent theatricality. The basic story lines of the courtroom, with its clear adversaries and its promise of a dramatic resolution, fit well within news-making conventions.[5] In civil rights trials, those basic story lines would resonate with common literary and cinematic representations of American race relations and the American South. In many ways, the trials were "ready-made for Hollywood," even, as one photographer suggested of the Beckwith prosecution, "better than anything anyone could conjure up on television."[6]

The political context of the 1990s also heightened media interest in the contemporary prosecutions. Civil rights trials clearly struck a responsive chord with an American public concerned about the state of American race relations. In 1995, a Gallup poll found that 68 percent

The media center in Philadelphia set up for the Edgar Ray Killen trial was indicative of the intense attention journalists paid to civil rights trials. Here journalists watch on many different monitors as Rita Schwerner Bender, widow of slain activist Mickey Schwerner, testifies. (AP Photo/*Neshoba Democrat*, Kyle Carter)

of Americans believed that black-white relations would always be a problem for the country.[7] The first trials took place around the same time as President Bill Clinton's 1997 One America Initiative, designed to foster dialogue about America's continued racial divide. The enormous attention all kinds of media outlets paid to the contemporary civil rights prosecutions—and the common arguments they made about their importance—suggests that the trials provided commentators and journalists a beacon of hope, a sign of racial progress at a time when racial divisions seemed stubbornly entrenched.

Given the desire to read trials as evidence of racial progress and the fit between trials and popular literary conventions, a remarkably consistent narrative emerged from the many articles, reports, and popular cultural representations of them. Trials, the dominant narrative held, promised redemption. Through trials, southern white men could redeem a masculine identity tarnished by its association with hateful Klansmen and assume their position as leaders of the post–civil rights South by making clear they had rejected the racism of their past. The South, a region that had stood for so long outside of national norms, could show that it had atoned for its racial sins. The southern justice system could prove that it now offered fair and equal treatment to blacks and whites. The trial narrative simultaneously contained racism, both in the South and in the bodies of hateful men, and portrayed civil rights prosecutions as a way to overcome it. It thus excused the larger nation for any racial sins while suggesting that prosecutions could free Southerners and the region from the burden of their history of racial violence.

In 1994, in the wake of a Mississippi jury's conviction of Byron De La Beckwith for the 1963 murder of Medgar Evers, newspapers around the country searched for ways to describe the importance of the trial and the guilty verdict. Beckwith's conviction was a "moral victory," the *Washington Post* declared, suggesting that the forces of good had finally overcome the forces of evil. To the editors of the *Memphis Commercial Appeal*, Beckwith's conviction meant that "the scales of justice finally are balanced." While Beckwith's earlier trials had "served the cause of racial prejudice," the contemporary trial "served the cause of justice." The *New Orleans Times-Picayune* suggested that although justice had been long delayed, the verdict offered stark evidence of how much Mississippi had changed since the 1960s. The *Atlanta Constitution* proved even more enthusiastic; to it, the trial meant "an evil ghost has been exorcised, an ugly chapter has been closed, and Mississippi's changes for the better have been confirmed." Although the paper noted that Beckwith might still appeal his conviction, that race remained an issue in daily life in Mississippi, and that many other civil rights murders had yet to be called to account, it still maintained that "the verdict provides Mississippi a measure of redemption in one of its most infamous cases."[8]

The coverage of the Beckwith trial helped establish the way that the media interpreted the significance of civil rights prosecutions as they continued over the subsequent decades. While media coverage did not fully determine the meanings invested in these trials, it played a powerful role in explaining their significance, both for Americans and in American history.[9] Newspapers and other media reports almost uniformly agreed that prosecutions must go forward because they held great personal meaning for the family members of victims who had waited so long for justice. Yet the media also signaled that the importance of these cases went well beyond the needs of the victims' families. These were symbolic cases that, as the *Atlanta Constitution* said of the Killen trial, were "important not only for the surviving families" but "for the rest of us, too—those who never knew Chaney, Goodman or Schwerner, those who've never been in Philadelphia, Miss., those too young to remember Freedom Summer."[10] What the significance of these trials was for those who had not known the victims, lived in affected communities, or even been born at the time of the crime would be communicated through the rhetoric the media employed in its trial coverage.

That the media seemed to settle on redemption as the best way to understand these trials should not be surprising. Stories of redemption have traditionally held powerful sway in American culture and politics.[11] The belief that a person—or a society—can atone for one's sin and become pure has great appeal in this predominantly Judeo-Christian society. Rooted in a nation born of revolution, American culture places great store in the belief that people and communities can remake themselves, shedding the ties of the past in order to create new, better lives for themselves, whether that is portrayed in a classic Horatio Alger "rags-to-riches" tale, embodied in the addict overcoming his addiction through a twelve-step program, or reflected in the narrative of America rupturing its ties to Europe and birthing itself anew through the American Revolution. Redemption is so potent a narrative in American literature, Pulitzer Prize–winning literary critic Michiko Kakutani suggests, both because Americans desperately want to believe that people can change and because the comforting "cycle of sin-and-redemption" can offer a sense of closure.[12]

Few aspects of American society contradicted this cultural investment in rebirth and redemption more than the arena of race relations, where even the groundbreaking civil rights laws of the 1960s had not enabled the country to remake itself fully. Indeed, thirty-odd years after the passage of legislation that was supposed to end racial inequalities, rates of black poverty and unemployment remained far higher than those for whites, and the wealth gap between blacks and whites remained vast. Blacks were being imprisoned in ever-increasing numbers as a result of a punitive war on drugs. And despite the *Brown* decision, it had become clear by the mid-1990s that efforts at school integration had not eliminated educational disparities between black and white students or even ended racial segregation in classrooms. The "ship" of integration, Gary Orfield of the Harvard Project on School Desegregation lamented in 1993, seemed to be "floating backward toward the shoals of racial segregation."[13]

The continuation of the racial divide despite the passage of seminal civil rights legislation led to a heated debate in the 1990s between those who attributed the racial gap to poverty, structural and institutionalized racism, and residential segregation and those who instead blamed it on misguided government programs and deficient black cultural practices. Controversy erupted over books by Charles Murray and Dinesh D'Souza that explained continuing inequalities by pointing to low black IQ scores or African American cultural dysfunction. In the political arena, battles waged over efforts to dismantle affirmative action and other government programs designed to aid African Americans on the grounds that they were a form of "reverse discrimination." President Clinton, recognizing these continuing racial tensions, announced his Presidential Initiative on Race in 1997, launching a year-long conversation to help bridge racial divides and to foster constructive dialogue on race relations. Clinton's initiative reflected the depth of concern in the country about the root causes of racial inequalities, about tensions between blacks and whites, and about the country's seeming inability to solve racial problems despite the end of legal segregation.

Civil rights trials offered an antidote to these depressing stories of racial stagnation and controversy. For the media, they could become a ray of hope and a way to demonstrate that there had been meaningful changes since the 1960s. As an editorial in the *Pittsburgh Post-Gazette* explained, "In a country still struggling with race relations and defensive about its racist past, Americans can measure progress by their willingness to address the wrongs of the past, no matter how long it takes."[14] Kenneth Lavon Johnson, a Mississippi native who became an attorney in the Civil Rights Division of the Justice Department, recognized the ways in which the trials offered a narrative of redemption and atonement. Southerners, he argued, "grow up with the notions that there is no end to the power of storytelling or the desire for redemption." The prosecutions of Beckwith, Bowers, and Killen might not cure all "deep-rooted attitudes about race," Johnson noted, "but a story always needs a final chapter."[15] Before the election of Barack Obama as America's first black president—an act that has also been taken as evidence that America has finally overcome its original racial sins—civil rights trials could be interpreted as that "final chapter," offering the country some closure on its racial history.[16] In the trial narrative, they came to do so through the reiteration of four key themes: that whites were positive agents of racial change, that racism was a matter of individual attitudes that could be overcome when people changed their hearts, that racism was primarily confined to the South, and that by holding trials, southern whites could atone for their history.

In 2002, shortly after the conviction of Bobby Frank Cherry for the Birmingham church bombing, the ABC news program *Nightline* featured jury consultant Andy Sheldon and journalist Jerry Mitchell, both white, in a program about the reopening and prosecution of civil rights–era murders. It was these "unlikely advocates," reporter John Donovan noted, who were responsible for exposing and helping to prosecute Cherry. White racists had once smirked at the law, knowing that the system would protect them, but in Cherry's 2002 trial, the prosecutors who had argued the case had all been white. The jury that convicted Cherry included nine whites. And the Cherry trial was no anomaly: "Across the South," *Nightline* noted, "a generation of white men, all sons of the South, all born into a segregated world, have felt compelled to take on these old cases."[17]

Nightline was especially interested in the question of why white men like Sheldon and Mitchell, both of whom admitted that they had been largely unaware of or uninterested in the civil rights struggle in the 1960s, had become part of this quest for racial justice. Sheldon, a college student in the 1960s, ruefully acknowledged that he had not spoken out against the racism he saw around him at the time; Mitchell, a bit younger, remembered not saying anything when classmates teased a black girl and admitted that he likely would not have taken a stand against segregation if he had been older. But both men had evolved, moving from professional interest in these cases to outrage as they learned about the history of white violence and legal intransigence. In these "two conversations, two white men talking about conscience," *Nightline* traced what it described as a "metamorphosis" in white racial attitudes, a dramatic change that had resulted in justice.

Nightline may have been a news program, but its fascination with white southern men who became positive agents of racial change followed a genre common in Hollywood, offering what historian Mark Golub has deemed "Hollywood redemption history."[18] In these antiracist narratives, the lead actor is a white figure—typically a man—who fights against oppression, and the central tension in the story revolves around his salvation or racial awakening. Civil rights trials offered a seemingly real-life example of a genre that included such well-known films as *Glory, Amistad, Dances with Wolves, Schindler's List, Mississippi Burning*, and—of course—the film made about the Beckwith trial, *Ghosts of Mississippi*, which focused on white prosecutor Bobby DeLaughter as the lead character. *Nightline* explicitly recognized that Hollywood's decision to focus on white characters like Bobby DeLaughter "took black pain and turned it into a story about white conscience." But, in this case, the program noted, fact echoed fiction: "The fact is DeLaughter is white and he did get the conviction." The trials, in short, proved ripe fodder for portrayals of heroic white men standing up for racial justice that the media found both familiar and comfortable.

The white male journalists, FBI agents, and prosecutors who investigated and tried these cases in court were hailed as heroes and earned recognition, honors, and awards in ways that portrayed them as the lead actors in the continuing struggle for racial justice. Journalist Jerry Mitchell, for example, has won at least twenty national awards for his reporting, including a MacArthur genius grant and the prestigious John Chancellor Award for Excellence in Journalism, becoming the youngest recipient of a prize designed to honor cumulative professional achievements. Hailed as "an American hero" and as "the South's Simon Weisenthal," a reference to the famous Nazi hunter, he has been profiled on radio, television, and in the *New York Times* and *USA Today*.[19] The two FBI agents assigned to the reopened Birmingham church bombing case have won acclaim as well, being named 2002 Federal Employees of the Year and awarded the Partnership for Public Service's inaugural Service to America Medal in 2002.[20]

The most extensive notice has been reserved for the prosecutors in these cases, especially the native white Southerners who have argued the cases in court, like Bobby DeLaughter, Doug Jones, and Mark Duncan. The lead prosecutors have been described as heroes by the media, recognized for their hard work to secure justice, and featured in articles and on news programs. Bobby DeLaughter was profiled in *The American Lawyer*, praised as "a gutsy young prosecutor" in newspaper editorials, and turned into the lead character in a Hollywood feature film. Birmingham church bombing prosecutor Doug Jones won awards for his work on the case, including the 2002 FBI Director's Community Leadership Award and the SCLC's Drum Major for Justice Award in 2003, while Killen trial prosecutors Mike Moore and Mark Duncan became celebrated figures in media coverage of that case. A feature on Mark Duncan in the *Clarion-Ledger* contrasted Duncan's "modest," "plain-spoken and unassuming" manner with the fact that he was "a man who is now making history."[21]

The trials offered vivid images of upstanding, moral, courageous native white "sons of the South" prosecuting defendants who became the embodiment of violent racist hatred during the trials and in the media. Civil rights dramas in film and television typically portray the racial struggle as one between whites, with the wrong being committed by a southern "cracker"—an archetypal figure in popular culture "representing intolerance, racism, and senseless violence"—and the corrective action performed by his "alter-ego . . . the man of law, the redeemed southern white man." The defendants neatly fit the common representation of the deviant "cracker" as typically poor, irrational, violent, racist white men. Trials brought to life a familiar story of lone rednecks being brought to justice by upstanding white men of the law; they offered real-life examples of white male authority figures eradicating the southern racist. With primarily white male journalists, investigators, and especially prosecutors as the heroes of the trial narrative, the main "plot" became a battle between the archaic, hateful rendition of white masculinity represented by the elderly Klansmen on oxygen tanks, and the rehabilitated, vibrant, and nonracist identity of the young lawyers who were prosecuting them.[22] The heroic prosecutor became the southern avenger fighting "man to man," with blacks and women playing supporting characters at best.

For the press, the role of native "sons of the South" in reopening and trying these cases served as proof of the enormous changes that had taken place since the civil rights era. Neshoba County District Attorney Mark Duncan was "a symbol of what has changed in Mississippi since the civil rights movement," according to the *St. Louis Post-Dispatch*. The *St. Petersburg Times* read the fact that "most of the prosecutors and investigators revisiting these unfinished atrocities are white" as a sign of a biracial commitment to justice and of "the long-awaited arrival of a New South," while the Jackson *Clarion-Ledger* held up the "dogged work of the local prosecutors and the attorney general's office" as proof that Mississippi was "not the same state it was thirty years ago."[23]

While white prosecutors and journalists have played an instrumental role in the trial process, the many references in articles to the new generation of energetic and devoted white men who represented the transformation of the South threatened to erase the struggle and efforts of blacks and civil rights activists from the historical record. The heroes in the trials became journalists like Jerry Mitchell or prosecutors trying the cases, not the activists who had been murdered, who came off more as passive martyrs of the movement. Moreover, the coverage could easily portray, in the words of the *Atlanta Journal and Constitution*, "prosecutors of Southern origins" as taking "the lead in righting old wrongs" in a way that obscured the long struggle it had taken relatives and activists to get cases reopened in the first place.[24] By making white men into heroes, the trial narrative downplayed black activism both during the civil rights era and later in the efforts to bring civil rights murders back into court.

This coverage troubled many of the journalists and prosecutors who were being celebrated. Indeed, Jerry Mitchell, Doug Jones, and others protested that the real heroes were those who had fought for change or the families or activists who had long pushed for justice. But the popular redemption narrative proved hard to shake. Even as Don Simonton, a graduate student whose research was used in prosecuting Ernest Avants for the murder of Ben Chester White, protested in a *Natchez Democrat* profile that he hadn't "done anything heroic," the paper countered, "Some of us disagree." Similarly, one of the FBI agents lauded for investigating the Birmingham church bombing found it "a little embarrassing sometimes." He "really didn't do anything heroic," he insisted. This focus on heroic whites at least offered some consolation to critics of the trials. Judge W. O. "Chet" Dillard, a native Mississippian who insisted the Beckwith trial was an unconstitutional form of reverse racism driven by political concerns, was comforted by the fact that the trial could not be described as a "victory for the blacks" since it was white jurors, white witnesses, and white prosecutors who had convicted Beckwith.[25]

The emphasis on white prosecutors who took on evil Klansmen reinforced another theme of the trial narrative: that racism was a problem of individual attitudes and thus could be vanquished when racist whites came to see the error of their ways. That formulation, however, belies a more structural understanding of racism and white privilege. Portrayals of racism as primarily the result of personal prejudice downplay, or even obscure, that racial disparities are also a product of economic and structural inequalities. But the media finds it difficult to talk about race in the absence of clearly identified "racists." Coverage of race relations in the South rarely appear without the image of the racist southern "redneck" in part because institutional racism cannot easily be dramatized within existing literary narrative frameworks. The civil rights trial narrative, like most common media representations of race, failed to interrogate or represent institutional racism, focusing instead on deviant individuals as the purveyors of racial hatred.[26] Only the rare article or editorial on the trials acknowledged the state-sponsored terrorism or community complicity that had fostered racial violence; only seven of one hundred editorials on the various civil rights trials made any mention of broader state or community complicity. The trial narrative instead portrayed racism as the purview of a handful of hateful, usually lower-class men, echoing the ways that the arguments in the courtroom ignored the larger community and political institutions that had enabled and encouraged those who used violence to uphold white supremacy.

In the trial narrative the most important mark of racial progress would be demonstrable changes in the attitudes of whites. Media coverage implied that civil rights murders were important precisely because they had spurred a change among whites. For example, newspaper editorials on the Cherry and Blanton trials variously described the 1963 Birmingham church bombing as the event that "galvanized a horrified nation behind the civil rights movement," the "single point at which America's collective heart and mind began to change on matters of race and rights," and a time when "America searched its soul and changed forever," portrayals that uncritically equated "America" with white Americans.[27] Such characterizations overstated and simplified the impact of these crimes; the nation did not simply come together in support of racial equality after the bombing. Even in its wake, opposition to desegregation in the South remained intense. These murders did not forestall the need for further black struggle to win basic political rights, like the right to vote. These descriptions gauged the success of the civil rights movement in terms of how it had changed the hearts and minds of whites, not in relation to the economic status of or educational opportunities for blacks.

The importance of changing hearts and minds would be communicated even more powerfully through the media's focus on those whites who, like Tom Cherry in *Sins of the Father*, renounced their own racist upbringing and agreed to testify against their white relatives. The trial narrative explicitly framed the story of civil rights trials as one where whites were redeemed by testifying against those whites who remained unrepentant. Bob Stringer, who had worked for Sam Bowers when he was a teenager, became a media favorite when, looking to make amends as part of a twelve-step program for a gambling addiction, he approached the Dahmer family and agreed to testify against Sam Bowers. Stringer, one TV special argued, became "an unlikely hero" because "his courage to confront his past provided the impetus for prosecutors to take another look at the case." A *People* magazine article celebrated Stringer's transformation from a "living reminder of the old Mississippi" to someone who had "the satisfaction of helping deliver justice, however long delayed." Billy Roy Pitts and Charles Marcus Edwards, somewhat less sympathetic figures since they had participated in the 1960s crimes, also became the subject of widespread media attention when they testified in the respective cases against Sam Bowers and James Seale. A *Nightline* story on Pitts was framed as "the conscience of a Klansman and the search for redemption." Pitts's story, *Nightline* explained, demonstrated "how the South has changed in the last third of a century."[28] Like the white prosecutors, these white informants came to stand in for racial progress more generally.

In these media representations, testifying in civil rights trials became a sign of personal liberation, a way that whites could free themselves from the racism of their upbringing. A memoir by Peggy Morgan, a white woman raised in an abusive family in the civil rights–era South, suggests the symbolic importance accorded the trials. *Her Mother's Witness* spent only a few pages on the event that likely made Morgan's book publishable: she testified at Byron De La Beckwith's 1994 trial that she heard him admit to killing Medgar Evers during a shared car ride. While the book focused on how Morgan, unlike her mother, had the strength to escape from an abusive marriage to a racist man, her testimony at the

Beckwith trial opened the book and the entirety of her trial testimony was reprinted at the end. Testifying against Beckwith became symbolic of Morgan's transformation from a scared victim to a strong woman. Morgan's act became even more freighted with symbolism because she claimed that her mother knew something about Emmett Till's murder that she never found the courage to divulge. By testifying against Beckwith, Morgan "finally found her freedom," a review in the *Memphis Commercial Appeal* noted, thereby turning what was in many ways a bleak picture of abuse into "an ultimately uplifting story of one woman who found the courage to help right a wrong."[29]

These stories of individuals remaking themselves, renouncing their families and their upbringing, and finding the courage to testify provided powerfully compelling subjects for the media. They offered hopeful, emotionally wrenching examples of the potential of individuals to break free from a cycle of hatred passed down from generation to generation. A *Glamour* magazine feature on Teresa Stacy, Bobby Frank Cherry's granddaughter, proved typical of the coverage. Stacy, the article argued, finally achieved her long quest "to cleanse herself of her family's racist legacy" when she told the FBI what she knew about her grandfather's involvement in the Birmingham church bombing. The day of her grand jury testimony was the day she "cut herself loose from the racism she had absorbed as a child."[30]

Moreover, given that none of the defendants in these trials ever repented and apologized, the apologies of family members or former Klansmen who were testifying offered the only chance for the media to document any kind of reconciliation between the victims' families and whites who had renounced their previous racist beliefs. The image of Bob Stringer embracing Vernon Dahmer Jr. after Sam Bowers's conviction served as powerful evidence that whites could ask for, and black families could grant, forgiveness. For journalist Jerry Mitchell, seeing Billy Roy Pitts apologize to Ellie Dahmer became one of the most powerful emotional moments of all the trials. "Isn't that what we're supposed to be about?" he wondered.[31]

Yet these stories of individual courage, of rejecting racism and of being granted forgiveness, again made whites the heroes of these trials and their struggle to overcome their racist upbringing the main measure of racial justice. In this individualistic model of racial change and progress, racism became essentially a psychological problem with a therapeutic solution. Obscuring the ways in which race structured political institutions and economic realities, the trial narrative implied that changing hearts and minds was the most important and effective way to combat whatever lingering issues of racism remained in American society. The *Glamour* magazine article about Teresa Stacy neatly encapsulated the takeaway message of the trial coverage. "Racism," the article explained, "has given way to a desire to see justice done."[32] If racism was nothing more than attitudes, then surely the rejection of hatred by people like Stacy meant it had been laid to rest.

Even as the trial narrative framed racism as a problem of personal beliefs, it also safely contained it in the South. Like longtime media and cultural representations of American race relations, coverage of civil rights trials implied that racism was primarily a southern problem and that the South was an outlier to national norms of racial equality and tolerance. The South has long served as the negative reference point for the rest of the nation to construct its own, more positive identity. From its founding, the nation's sense of itself as a place committed to democracy and freedom has been constructed on the basis of comparisons between the North and South. Portraying the South as a place uniquely beset by racism and burdened by its history allowed Americans outside the South to see themselves as virtuous and free of racial problems. National vices such as slavery, racial oppression, and racial violence become the legacy of the South alone and uncharacteristic of the "real" America. Southern writers, although unwilling to excuse the North its racial failings, have often promoted their own version of southern distinctiveness stemming from what they perceive as a unique connection between Southerners and the land, the traumatic experience of losing the Civil War, and the region's history of plantation slavery.[33]

The trial narrative as promoted in both southern and nonsouthern media outlets reflected the tendency to depict the South as a monolithic region uniquely burdened by its past, especially through the use of the metaphor of unaddressed racial murders as "ghosts" that continued to haunt the South. Journalist Maryanne Vollers chose to call her 1995 book on the Beckwith trial *Ghosts of Mississippi;* its subtitle, *The Haunting of the New South,* made even clearer how Vollers saw the murder and the racial violence of the civil rights era as a "lingering nightmare" that still troubled the South, despite efforts of new leaders to "shake off the past." The South's past continued to impinge upon its present, this metaphor made clear, and it was one that would be employed repeatedly in discussion of the trials. Rob Reiner would borrow the book's title for his feature film about the Beckwith trial. When Alabama held trials for the Birmingham church bombing, the *Birmingham News* described it as an effort "to lay to rest ghosts from the past." In the South, in an oft-quoted aphorism of one of its most celebrated authors, the past was "never dead."[34] The region, these depictions implied, continued to be tied to its history in a way that the rest of the nation was not.

The trial narrative consequently demanded that the South scrutinize its own history and practices, while the rest of the nation could envision itself as free of racism and luxuriate in its innocence. Much of the trial coverage reinforced the sense that the rest of the United States could and should be judging Southerners as they sought to deal with their unique and particular problems. Making clear that the North would be keeping an eye on the South as it undertook the trial process, a *San Francisco Chronicle* editorial praised the indictments in the Birmingham church bombing as the result of an "indefatigable four-year effort by federal investigators" and noted that although the Alabama justice system had come a long way, "Americans will be watching and demanding a dose of justice." Americans and Alabamans here seemed mutually exclusive. Other coverage too painted the South as an anomaly in a nation committed to justice. The killing of Ben Chester White would have "been a cut-and-dried, sure thing of a case in enlightened places," the *Chicago Defender* remarked, but it "wasn't to end up with a just conclusion in the 1960s' Deep South." Although an article about Edgar Ray Killen's 2005 trial in the *Ottawa Citizen* carried the headline "The U.S. Confronts Its Shameful Past," the content made clear that this shameful past was the burden of the South. "America will face its old southern demons once again," the article concluded.[35] America as a whole might be seeking to reckon with its demons, but those demons were definitely southern.

Nor did the discussion of the actions of the federal government during the civil rights era do much to suggest that anyone outside the South should be considered responsible for racial violence. Although the federal government had done little to address state failures to protect civil rights activists or to challenge state participation in racial violence, it would not be called to task in any meaningful way by the media. Indeed, the actions of the federal government were largely invisible in the trial narrative except in relation to a single crime: the 1963 Birmingham church bombing. During Tom Blanton's trial, the media repeatedly criticized the FBI's failure to bring charges against the bombers in the 1960s, Hoover's decision to close the investigation in 1965, and the failure of the FBI to share evidence about Blanton with Bill Baxley when he reopened the investigation into the bombing in 1977. The *Birmingham News* described the role of the FBI as "perhaps the most disconcerting element" in the "lengthy drama" of achieving justice in the case, while the *Times Picayune* felt that the thirty-eight-year delay in bringing charges against Blanton in the case "doesn't reflect as poorly on the people of Alabama as it does on the FBI."[36]

Yet this criticism of the FBI did not engender any kind of in-depth consideration of the larger national politics of race or the racial policies of the federal government in the civil rights era. Instead, it very quickly localized, not just on the single incident of the church bombing, but on the single figure of J. Edgar Hoover, whose antipathy to the civil rights movement was well known. Pointing to Hoover's 1965 decision to end the investigation into the bombing without pressing charges, the *Washington Post* asked why his name remained on the FBI building in Washington, D.C. It was a "disgrace," the paper charged, that "the name of the man responsible for blocking prosecution in the most inhumane act of racial violence in the '60s is emblazoned at the entrance of the FBI building." *USA Today* too called for Hoover's name to be "stripped off the FBI headquarters' building and stored in the same deep recesses where he hid the evidence against the Birmingham church bombers."[37] The trial narrative thus reduced federal failings to the actions of a lone individual.

Even these limited criticisms of the FBI tended to be outweighed or offset in the trial narrative by other representations. The television movie *Sins of the Father*, for example, depicted Hoover as unsympathetic to civil rights protestors and showed him quashing the Birmingham church bombing investigation, but one of the film's heroes was an FBI agent who investigated the church bombing in 1963, remained obsessed with the case, and was portrayed as the key figure in eventually bringing Bobby Frank Cherry into court. And even Hoover's reluctance to press charges could be given a positive spin. As one editorial explained, Hoover must have known he could not secure a conviction in Alabama in the 1960s in front of an all-white jury. If Tommy Blanton had been put on trial and acquitted in the 1960s, he could not be tried again. "So maybe," one editorial after Blanton's conviction explained, "J. Edgar Hoover was, in the very long run, right."[38] Inaction became proof of Hoover's foresight, not of his racial views or the failures of the federal government.

Overall, the trial narrative characterized the federal government in terms more positive than negative. In one particularly rosy assessment, the *Huffington Post* praised the government both for its actions in the 1960s and for its commitment to reopening cases in the 2000s. "During the darkest days of the civil rights struggle, when all-white juries acquitted obvious perpetrators or Southern state officials flat refused to prosecute racial killings, families could still turn to the federal government for some modicum of justice," the article reassured readers. When, decades later, southern prosecutors began reopening some of those old cases, "the Department of Justice again stepped forward."[39] The trial narrative for the most part echoed this approach and ignored the history of federal inaction in response to the racial violence of the era.

Yet even as the media coverage tended to portray the South as responsible for racism and uniquely burdened by its history of racial violence, it celebrated trials for the work they could do in helping the South to make itself anew and to shed the burden of its divisive and painful past. In vivid language that suggested prosecutions had the potential to heal the South's wounds, to cleanse the stain of racial history, and to exorcise the ghosts of racial violence, the trial narrative offered a complex, but nevertheless powerful, affirmation of the legal process as both meaningful justice and a form of racial redemption.

The metaphors of cleansing, healing, and exorcising common in the media coverage of civil trials invested prosecutions with enormous symbolic power. Trials, media representations argued, would cleanse the stain or blemish left by historic racial violence. As a *New Orleans Times-Picayune* article explained, the Bowers trial represented "a kind of cleansing for Mississippi, a way the state can atone for the silence of its past." The Birmingham church bombing trials would be viewed through the same lens. The *New York Times*, whose editorials were typically more circumspect about these trials than other papers, still described Bobby Frank Cherry's 2002 trial as a "process" that would enable Birmingham "to cleanse itself of a stain on its history." Trials could not only cleanse the past, but also heal wounds left behind by the original crimes. The Bowers trial, the *Times-Picayune* explained, symbolized "the healing of old wounds." To the *San Antonio Express-News*, the conviction of Bobby Frank Cherry meant that "the city of Birmingham can heal the wounds left from the violent days of the civil rights movement."[40]

Given the ways in which the crimes were viewed as "ghosts" still haunting the South, many reporters also invoked the term "exorcism" to explain the role trials could play in finally laying these specters to rest. The Killen trial was, for the *Baltimore Sun*, "an important step toward exorcising past ghosts," while to *Clarion-Ledger* columnist Sid Salter, it represented an effort to "make a once-and-for-all political and moral exorcism of the 1964 acts of Klan terrorism in Neshoba County."[41] The choice to describe trials as a form of exorcism freighted a legal ritual with powerful religious symbolism. Trials, this metaphor suggested, were rituals that would drive the demons of the South's racial past away. They would purify the region, casting off its painful history.

These depictions of trials as healing, purifying, and cleansing inevitably led the media to describe trials as a form of atonement for and redemption from the sin of racial violence. Jack Davis, an expert in southern history who was frequently sought out by journalists for his views of the trials, referred to them simply as "atonement trials." Trials as a form of atonement would be regularly invoked by journalists; a headline about Ernest Avants's trial read "Miss. Doggedly Persists in Atoning," offering a mental image of a state insistently seeking redemption from its past sins. Articles described the case against Killen as "a trial that marked Mississippi's latest attempt to atone for its past," and his conviction as "the latest in about two dozen 'atonement trials' over the past 15 years." The portrayal of trials as a way to atone for the history of racism was further reinforced by descriptions of trials as "part of a cathartic process," as providing "the nation a chance to expiate the sins of American apartheid," in the words of a London newspaper, or as a way for the South to "gain some redemption for itself."[42]

Much of the trial coverage suggested that prosecutions and convictions would enable the South to shed the historical baggage it had carried for so long. As the *Times-Picayune* wrote of the Bowers trial, it had come to "symbolize the shedding of the past." The *St. Petersburg Times*

The editorial cartoon that ran in the *Clarion-Ledger* of Jackson on June 23, 2005, two days after Edgar Ray Killen's conviction, encapsulated the trial narrative's claims that "justice" had replaced racism in the South. (By permission of Marshall Ramsey and Creators Syndicate, Inc.)

heralded the reopenings and trials as evidence not only of a new biracial commitment to justice, but as a sign of the "long-awaited arrival of the New South" that people had been looking for ever since "General Lee handed over his sword at Appomattox." Maybe, the paper hoped, "the New South is finally coming to pass." Emotional editorials hailed the arrival of a new day when the South would no longer be stained by its past. A 2001 editorial in the *Pittsburgh Post-Gazette* praising Alabama for finally bringing Tom Blanton to trial offers a particularly poetic example. Once, "racial hatred covered the South like early morning dew." But with Klansman like Blanton facing trial, "there's a promise of a new morning."[43] The *Post-Gazette* article reflected what became one of the most powerful messages to emerge from coverage of the trials: that they represented meaningful change, a form of justice, and even a rebirth for a region that had long been mired in racial hatred.

No single example better encapsulates the media framing of trials as redemptive than the film produced in Hollywood about the 1994 Beckwith trial.[44] The making of *Ghosts of Mississippi* demonstrates that the trials attracted media attention in part because they already fit within familiar literary and fictional frames. But it also highlights how representations of the trials were shaped to emphasize the theme of the redemption of the South.

After witnessing Byron De La Beckwith's 1994 trial, Mississippi-born writer Willie Morris, whose work was celebrated for its reflections on his native South, sensed almost immediately that it would make a good movie. Less than three weeks after a Mississippi jury delivered its guilty verdict, he wrote to Hollywood producer Fred Zollo—the same man who had made the film *Mississippi Burning*—to sell him on a movie about Beckwith's prosecution. The trial process offered "a profoundly moving and dramatic story which I think envelops what movie-goers like to see," Morris wrote. Surely, there was a hero figure in white prosecutor Bobby DeLaughter, with Myrlie Evers deserving top billing as a heroine in the story. The long quest for justice, the search for evidence, the visuals that could emphasize how much time had passed since the original crime—all would prove dynamic on the screen. And, then, of course, there was the figure of Beckwith himself: "surely an Oscar here," Morris predicted.[45]

Zollo quickly decided to make the film. He approached Rob Reiner, already well known for directing such films as *The Princess Bride*, *When Harry Met Sally*, *A Few Good Men*, and *The American President*, to take on the project. Soon a screenwriter arrived in Jackson to interview Bobby DeLaughter and crews arrived to scout physical locations. Within two years, the movie, *Ghosts of Mississippi*, would be ready for release. The film dramatized the story of the reopening, investigation, and prosecution of the Beckwith case; its cast of characters included Bobby DeLaughter, Myrlie Evers, Jerry Mitchell, Hinds County District Attorney Ed Peters, case investigators Benny Bennett and Charlie Crisco, and, of course, Byron De La Beckwith. Committed to getting the story right, director Reiner gave Myrlie Evers veto power over the script and sought to recreate the setting as much as possible, including restoring the Evers home to exactly as it had been in 1963 for shooting the assassination scene and using the same Hinds County courtroom where the trial took place in the movie. Although not a commercial success, the film attracted widespread media commentary and—as Willie Morris predicted—an Oscar nomination for James Woods, the actor who portrayed Beckwith.

Hollywood proved so eager to make a film of the Beckwith trial in large part because of the many parallels between the trial and existing cinematic tropes. As early as 1992, even before the trial took place, Hollywood producers had begun considering the story for a feature or television movie. It offered, as one producer saw it, a great story of a "young lawyer driven to right an old wrong." It was the presence of that young, white lawyer as a ready-made leading man that made the story attractive to Rob Reiner. Reiner had long wanted to make a film about American race relations, but he didn't feel that he, as a privileged white man, had the right to tell the story of a black subject such as Martin Luther King Jr. or Medgar Evers. But here "was a white person who walked into a civil rights case and had to face his own feelings of racism." Reiner felt that he could "tell the story through this guy," that "because he was white," it offered him a "way into the subject."[46] And he emphasized that he didn't need to make up the figure of DeLaughter; he really had spearheaded the prosecution.

Myrlie Evers was disappointed by the decision to focus the film on Bobby DeLaughter. She had been trying for years to get a film made about her husband's life in the hope that a movie that told his story would help cement his reputation as a national civil rights leader. While she admired Bobby DeLaughter and appreciated his efforts in prosecuting the case, as Evers saw it, there never would have been justice or a trial if her husband had not fought to change Mississippi. Although she gave her approval to *Ghosts* once she realized that the movie would be made whether she was part of the process or not, Rob Reiner recognized that the film he felt comfortable making was not the film that Myrlie Evers wanted to see. "I can't make the movie the way you want me to make it," Reiner told her.[47] The project was attractive to him only because it offered the possibility of telling a civil rights story with a bona fide white hero.

Ghosts of Mississippi reflected the typical media conventions for portraying the civil rights struggle. With Bobby DeLaughter as the main character, Myrlie Evers became a bit player in her own story. The film minimized her thirty-year struggle that helped create the climate that forced the state to reopen the investigation. DeLaughter became the active agent, pushing the investigation, standing up to those who opposed reopening the case, and suffering for his principled stand. Myrlie Evers, in contrast, was more often portrayed as waiting—waiting for the DA to act, waiting for DeLaughter's weekly phone calls and updates, and waiting for a jury verdict. Justice came to her, courtesy of Bobby DeLaughter. She was portrayed, one reviewer charged, as "a resigned bystander, waiting for a few good white men to come along and save the day."[48]

On screen, Evers was reduced almost to a caricature of the noble, but passive, black woman. Evers had urged Whoopi Goldberg, the actress who would play her, to "show some anger, some spunk." There was "a fire that burns in this Mississippi woman," she told Goldberg; that fire had led her to aggressively and tenaciously pursue legal justice for her husband. But there was little Goldberg could do to convey that fire or anger. The movie cut several scenes from the original script that had delved deeper into Myrlie Evers's life and had made her a more active presence. Evers came off as "a plaster saint" acted with "stoic nobility" by Goldberg, who seemed, one reviewer felt, to think she was playing Mother Teresa.[49] Even that was more screen time than Medgar Evers received; the movie cut several planned flashbacks to his life and reduced his struggle to a montage of old news clips that played as the opening credits rolled.

The creators of *Ghosts of Mississippi* also tweaked the story so that it would fit even more squarely within the redemption narrative that made the struggle of the white lead character the main drama of the story. Although it opened with the stark claim that "this is a true story," *Ghosts* took a great deal of dramatic license in exaggerating the racism DeLaughter encountered as he worked on the case. One scene depicted DeLaughter's parents disparaging blacks and trying to convince him not to reopen the Beckwith case as they eat lunch together at an elite country club. In reality, Bobby DeLaughter's parents supported his work on the case. In another scene, his mother-in-law tries to stop him from finding and taking the murder weapon, which is now among her late husband's gun collection. In reality, she invited him to look for the weapon at her home. One dramatic—but completely fictional—scene shows DeLaughter leaving work to find a giant swastika painted on his car. And the movie implies that his decision to take the case led

DeLaughter's wife, Dixie (her real name), to leave him, a simplification of the causes of their failed marriage. As a result, the movie really was, as one reviewer noted, "a story of the price a white Southerner pays for defending a 'black' cause."[50]

Ghosts emphasized not only how DeLaughter suffered in his pursuit of justice, but also his personal growth as he became more committed to the struggle against racism. That growth was made almost comically explicit in two contrasting scenes. In one early scene, after his young daughter is scared by a nightmare, DeLaughter comforts her by singing "Dixie," which, he tells her, is the favorite song of every ghost in Mississippi. Later in the film, when she is scared again, he suggests that they sing "Old McDonald" instead. "Maybe 'Dixie's' not the right song," he tells her. "Maybe that's why this ghost keeps coming back." Over the course of the movie, DeLaughter has thus moved from a man who had no understanding of the powerful presence of white supremacy ("Dixie") in southern history to one who recognizes that the history of white racism still haunts the South.

The trials offered a version of racism that proved very easy to slot into the typical Hollywood narrative, where racism was a matter of bigoted attitudes (on the part of the white elite) and violent acts on the part of a few evil "crackers." DeLaughter's family came to represent the respectable racism of those who did not understand the need to deal with the region's history of violence. But James Woods, playing Byron De La Beckwith, understood that his character had to embody the evils of the entire system of segregation that Medgar Evers had been fighting. Although one reviewer found Woods's performance as a "wicked but lively old cracker" "shockingly off base," most others praised the performance for its energy and power. "James Woods' every gesture, every nuance as Beckwith, was a body punch, a terrible reminder of a past that cannot be ignored," one reviewer argued. Woods proved so effective at capturing Beckwith's essence that he took Myrlie Evers's breath away the first time she saw him in full costume.[51]

Beckwith, of course, offered an easy target for Woods; like other defendants in these cases, he was unrepentant, prone to public display of his white supremacist views, and willing to threaten those who crossed him. He was easily made, both during the trial and in the trial narrative, to stand in for the totality of Mississippi's racist history. As the review in the *St. Petersburg Times* noted, the portrayal in the film quickly divided "the good guys from the bad guys" in a way that ignored the complexity of racism, "as if the only expressions of intolerance were the outrageous rants of people like De La Beckwith." And neither the film's representations of the more "genteel" country-club racism of DeLaughter's parents nor its representations of the evil, violent racism of Beckwith offered any way to explore racism as anything beyond attitude, as something systemic that might persist even when Beckwith had gone to jail and DeLaughter had achieved heroic status. *Time* magazine reviewer Richard Corliss astutely grasped the film's portrayal of racism when he compared it to one of "those fact-based disease-of-the-week dramas," with the virus here being the racism that a principled stand by DeLaughter could cure.[52]

Together, all these elements ensured that the film told the story of Mississippi's progress from a state that had allowed someone like Beckwith to go free to one where he would be pursued, exorcised, and jailed. Although elements of the film continued to stigmatize the South—as one reviewer noted, in emphasizing the resistance DeLaughter faced Reiner in some ways presented "the South of the 1990s as one of repression"—it more powerfully offered a story of the redemption of the white South through the courageous stand of one man of conscience. The Beckwith trial, *Ghosts* producer Fred Zollo insisted, was "an example of a state cleansing its past." The film, he explained, dramatized an "incredible 31-year journey from this horrible act of violence to redemption." And making explicit the ways in which the evolution of the characters symbolized larger racial changes, Zollo noted that the journey was "not only for the individuals involved, but for the state of Mississippi and the country."[53]

Bobby DeLaughter too saw the redemptive narrative as the movie's main point. The movie, DeLaughter argued, may have taken some liberties but it got the larger story right: that "the system can work." And most importantly, the movie made clear that the verdict was "a giant step for Mississippi" that had "slammed the door on an age far too long in the making." One critical review of the film summed up the entire thrust of the trial narrative. *Ghosts of Mississippi*, the reviewer suggested, didn't show Medgar Evers's struggle or his successes. "It only celebrates the fact that his murderer was finally convicted, as if that deed were a measure of how much progress has been made against racism."[54] Indeed, in the trial narrative, it was.

Films like *Ghosts of Mississippi*, along with the larger media narrative about the civil rights trials, offered a form of ritualized forgiveness, promising southern whites absolution through the process of reckoning with their history. Following the conventions of many Hollywood films about race, they featured courageous white actors standing up against racial hatred, a structure that encouraged viewers to assume a position of innocence that distanced them from any responsibility for the wrongs the trials documented. Those who committed the harm, moreover, were depicted as so horrific (the "human equivalent of a cockroach," as Bobby Frank Cherry's lawyer complained) that it became impossible for anyone to identify with them. Those watching the trials might be able to imagine themselves playing the role of the person battling racism, but not that of the racist defendant.[55] And ending with a ready-made cathartic moment of closure in the form of a guilty verdict contained the harm of the past and suggested it had been remedied.

The trial narrative in the media did not require any consideration of personal, community, or corporate responsibility for historic wrongs. Instead it suggested that putting a few men in jail equaled justice. Justice might take a while, media coverage admitted, but it would always triumph in the United States. As the *Pittsburgh Post-Gazette* concluded from the indictments of Blanton and Cherry, "Justice often tarries, but it is rarely denied." To the *Natchez Democrat*, the Seale trial was proof that "justice never sleeps; justice never gives up; and justice can never come too late."[56]

Whatever flaws the nation might have, the trial narrative offered reassurance that ultimately, the United States was free of bias and the system worked. The indictments of Tom Blanton and Bobby Frank Cherry were hailed as proof that "the system came through for the four little children—even if justice has been long delayed." The arrest of James Seale was "a gratifying reminder" to the *Chattanooga Times Free Press* that "the rule of law in this country eventually triumphs over evil," while to a writer in *National Minority Politics*, the Beckwith conviction meant that "the United States has come as close to the promise of liberty and justice for all as any nation in history."[57] For many in the media, the trials affirmed their faith in the ultimate rule of law in the United States.

And since justice had been served by the trials, the narrative offered the nation its ultimate absolution. The South had finally reckoned with the burden of its history, and thus, there could be closure, an end to the nation's long struggle with race. As countless articles and editorials about the trials expressed it, trials "closed a chapter" on a painful era in southern history, "brought to a close" a notorious episode, "closed the books," or symbolized that "this evil chapter in history is closed."[58] Closure as a psychological concept implies achieving a satisfying resolution to an emotional trauma, but arguing that the trials "closed a chapter" or "closed the books"—an accounting term—suggested that prosecuting a few unresolved racial murders was all that was necessary for the region or the nation to make up for the racism of the civil rights era. This was a relatively painless redemption, one that did not require white Americans to fully confront, let alone admit, the nature of, the legacies of, or their responsibility for racial violence.

At the 1963 March on Washington, when Martin Luther King Jr. told the audience of his dream of a world where blacks and whites would be truly equal, where they could finally hold hands and thank God that they were "free at last," he linked it to an expansive and radical agenda of changes required to free Americans from the burden of racial oppression. The conviction of civil rights murderers like Byron De La Beckwith would be met with similar rhetoric but without King's substance. "Mississippi is now free at last," University of Mississippi historian David Sansing declared in response to the guilty verdict in the Beckwith case, a cry echoed eleven years later on the pages of the *Neshoba Democrat* when Edgar Ray Killen was convicted. The people of Neshoba County, the *Democrat* celebrated, were "free at last, free at last, thank God Almighty we are free at last."[59] The narratives of redemption that dominated media coverage and popular representations of civil rights trials allowed, and even encouraged, the jailing of Klansmen for crimes committed decades earlier to be the actions that freed whites, the South, and the nation from the bonds of their racial history. And it was a powerful narrative indeed that enabled the convictions of a few elderly men to be read as a sign that racial problems were a thing of the past.

The framing of trials as a form of atonement, a shedding of history, and a rebirth for a region long plagued by racial violence proved remarkably consistent and resilient because it was so seductive. How wonderful if history and its legacies could so easily be put right. Yet that narrative has not gone uncontested. Activists, trial advocates, and some residents of the communities that have held trials have criticized the claim that the contemporary trials alone can solve the problems of race or free Americans from the burden of history. Even as the trial narrative provided fodder for suggesting that whites, southern communities, and the region were now "free at last," others pointed to these crimes and the histories they uncovered as evidence of the continuing responsibility of Southerners, and the American nation, to attend to the history of race and racial violence. The legal process and the trials themselves became a site of struggle.

6

From Legal Justice to Social Justice

If you don't tell it like it was, it can never be as it ought to be.
—Fred Shuttlesworth, Birmingham civil rights leader

JUST DAYS AFTER the jury found Edgar Ray Killen guilty for the 1964 Freedom Summer murders, Mickey Schwerner's widow, Rita Schwerner Bender, wrote an open letter to Mississippi Governor Haley Barbour. Chastising Barbour for his declaration that the verdict "closed the books on the crimes of the civil rights years," she accused him of continuing to encourage racism in symbolic ways—wearing a Confederate flag lapel pin and resisting efforts to remove the Confederate symbol from the state flag, for example, or attending functions of the successor group of the White Citizens' Council, the Council of Conservative Citizens. Real justice, Bender wrote, could come only when the wrongs of the past were acknowledged and when people today, especially leaders like Barbour, took responsibility for them and for undoing the harm they had caused. The murders of her husband and his companions were just one of many examples of racial violence used to uphold the racial order. "Until individuals and their government understand why they do have responsibility," Bender insisted, "they cannot ensure racial justice and equality."[1]

Bender had long fought for state authorities to prosecute the perpetrators of her husband's murder. She had written repeatedly to then Neshoba County District Attorney Ken Turner in the wake of the 1989 release of *Mississippi Burning*, urging him to bring indictments in the case. When State Attorney General Michael Moore told her that he was having trouble getting the FBI files related to the case, she angrily responded that he should just pick up the phone and call United States Attorney General Janet Reno. When Moore's office told her that they had no authority to work on the case, the trained lawyer went to the law library, researched Mississippi law, and wrote a position paper documenting the constitutional authority of the Attorney General's office to bring charges. Bender wanted to see legal justice in this case.[2]

But for Bender, as for many of the other activists who became involved with prosecutions, the real goal in revisiting the past was not just putting a few old men in jail. It was getting people to confront America's history of racism and racial violence and to understand why it mattered in the present day. For her, contemporary trials offered an opportunity to begin a conversation about the history of white supremacy in the United States that could potentially reframe people's understandings of the past to encourage them to act in the present. She worried that the trial narrative promoted in the media and embraced by politicians like Barbour— one that described trials as an act of "closure"—threatened to rob the legal process of whatever political potential it might have. "Please don't squander this moment by proclaiming that the past does not inform the present and the future," she implored the Mississippi governor.

Rita Schwerner Bender was not alone in criticizing the notion that trials alone could address the wrongs of the past or in hoping to link the legal process to an activist political project to promote new ways of understanding U.S. history. Indeed, in the same years as the trial phenomenon gained momentum in southern states, activists in communities across the South launched efforts to encourage the larger public to consider the significance and legacies of the white supremacy of the Jim Crow era and of the racial violence used to maintain it. The 1990s and 2000s witnessed the creation of a host of new organizations that embraced the premise that their communities and the country could begin to address their present-day problems only if they began to understand their past in a new way. These local groups ranged widely in focus and orientation, but they shared a commitment to the belief that, as Donna Ladd, the editor of the alternative *Jackson Free Press*, put it, communities that had experienced racial violence needed "to look backward in order to move forward."[3]

The relationship between the prosecution of civil rights–era murders and this broader movement was complex. Most of those involved in the grassroots movement that linked reframing understandings of the past to the cause of racial equity in the present had few illusions that a legal trial on its own would foster the kind of understanding of history that they thought was necessary to serve the cause of racial equality and social justice. A trial, Rita Bender explained, could offer only "a little bit of justice." Yet she and many other activists believed that the legal process had the potential to serve the cause of social justice, to help create a world where the "inequities of the past" no longer dictated "the possibilities of the future."[4] Those committed to fostering a deeper understanding of how America's past informed its present would fight to define the meanings of civil rights trials as they sought to dislodge the powerful narratives that portrayed them as the act that freed the South, and the nation, from the burden of its history.

Nowhere was the struggle to define the meaning of the contemporary trials more openly and fiercely contested than in Philadelphia, Mississippi when Edgar Ray Killen was prosecuted in 2005 for the 1964 Freedom Summer murders. In the 1960s, the triple murders of Goodman, Chaney, and Schwerner—and the refusal of the white community to acknowledge or condemn the crime—had stigmatized Philadelphia as a mean, secretive town with a hatred of outsiders bordering on the pathological, a representation popularized again in the 1989 film *Mississippi Burning*. In the decades after 1990, as other civil rights–era murders became the subject of new legal investigations and trials, the failure of state authorities to bring charges in the Freedom Summer murder case, despite years of prodding by local activists and relatives of the slain men, only exacerbated the perception that Philadelphia and Neshoba County were uniquely retrograde in their continued intransigence on racial issues, and indeed in their isolation from the rest of the South.

By the early 2000s, the relatives and local activists who had long pressured authorities to bring new charges in the crime began to despair that there would ever be new prosecutions. Ben Chaney, brother of the murdered James Chaney, accused Mississippi Attorney General Mike Moore of "waiting for all these perpetrators to die off so he doesn't have to prosecute them." Rita Bender complained that the state had dragged its feet so long that it now seemed like "geologic time." Activists and civil rights veterans at the 2002 annual commemoration ceremonies orga- nized by the Mount Zion Memorial Committee and held in the black community harshly criticized the state's inaction. "Everybody knows who these murderers are," neighboring Kemper County NAACP Presi- dent George Roberts charged, and he called on Mississippi authorities to "prosecute these terrorists."[5]

That Mississippi authorities reopened the case and indicted Edgar Ray Killen two years later reflected less this long struggle for legal justice by activists than the emergence of a community group that decided the state finally had to take action in the case if Neshoba County ever hoped to improve its image. In 2004, a multiracial group of local residents came together to prod the community to finally reckon with the 1964 crime. Calling itself the Philadelphia Coalition, the group decided to pursue three key projects: to organize a major community-wide commemoration of the fortieth anniversary of the murders, to lobby the state to name a portion of Mississippi Highway 19 after the activists, and to call for legal authorities to seek indictments in the case. The fissures that ensued—both between longtime activists like Ben Chaney and the Coalition and between mem- bers of the Coalition who had different long-term goals for the group— offer a vivid example of the political struggle that trials could engender.

The idea for the Philadelphia Coalition emerged out of a 2004 conver- sation between Leroy Clemons, the African American chairman of the Neshoba County NAACP, and Jim Prince, the white editor of the *Neshoba Democrat.* Clemons, who had been born in Philadelphia in 1962, grew up learning little about the murders in school, but he had long been aware of how the event affected other people's perception of his hometown. When he told people from outside Mississippi where he was from, "they would always look at you with such disdain as if you'd cussed them." As he grew older and learned more about the murders, he became upset that there was no community-wide commemoration of them. There was a small annual ceremony organized by John Steele, who had been with his family at Mount Zion Methodist Church the night the Klan burned it down to try to stop Mickey Schwerner from using at as a meeting site. But that commemoration, Clemons felt, attracted primarily civil rights veterans who continued to see the state as they had in 1964 and who thus portrayed Neshoba County negatively. Although Clemons had faced his own share of discrimination in Philadelphia, he felt the criticisms of movement veterans did not fairly represent the community he lived in and did not acknowledge how much Philadelphia had changed since the civil rights era.[6] He ran into Jim Prince, a former school classmate, at the Philadelphia City Hall and the two began talking about the need for Philadelphia to "tell its own story" for the fortieth anniversary of the murders. They soon decided to gather a group of people to organize a community-wide memorial service in honor of the slain men.

The founding members of the Philadelphia Coalition included many of the key leaders in Philadelphia and in Neshoba County. The initial meetings brought together Stanley Dearman, who had been editor of the *Neshoba Democrat* until 2000 and had been one of the earliest community members to advocate reopening the case; Rayburn Waddell, the white mayor of Philadelphia; David Vowell, a white businessman, and president of the Community Development Partnership, the county's economic development association; and James Young, the black president of the city's Board of Supervisors. But as the Coalition grew to thirty members, it attracted a wide range of local people with diverse relationships to the 1964 crime. Members included Jewel McDonald, a local black woman whose mother was among those beaten at the Mount Zion church in June 1964; Deborah Posey, a white woman who had once been married to a brother of one of the Klansmen convicted in 1967; and representatives from the Choctaw Indian tribe, which had a large reservation near Philadelphia.

The members of the group found that they initially disagreed on many aspects of how to proceed. When some black participants suggested that the Coalition should organize a march, the whites in the room blanched; for them, marches meant riots and violence. Black and Native Americans, meanwhile, reacted negatively to the suggestion of some whites that the group should issue a resolution, which they saw as a meaningless gesture unlikely to result in any real change. Coalition members learned to talk to each other with the help of Susan Glisson, the director of the William Winter Institute for Racial Reconciliation at the University of Mississippi, who facilitated meetings and served as the "glue" that helped keep the group together.[7]

Coalition members could at least agree that they shared a common goal of wanting to rehabilitate the image of Neshoba County. A concern about image transcended race; both black and white members of Coalition felt the stigma of being from a place widely viewed as "a community of silence and cowardice and hate." For blacks, this stereotypical picture of Philadelphia implied a passivity, a willingness to accept racism that they found degrading. Whites instead felt the sting of being presumed to be racist and retrograde, no matter what their personal views. "You feel like a social leper" when outsiders discover you're from Philadelphia, Leroy Clemons complained in 2004, a feeling certainly shared by one young white Coalition member who learned to her dismay that her college classmates viewed her hometown primarily as a "place where people got away with murder."[8] Coalition cochairs Clemons and Prince both described refuting negative stereotypes as one of the group's primary goals—as Leroy Clemons told the County Board of Supervisors, the Coalition was "about changing the image of our city and our county"—and they recognized that changing Philadelphia's image would require more than just telling the outside media how much the city had changed. As another anniversary of the crime approached, just telling people "how good we are—absent redemption or atonement—would be a terrible mistake," an editorial in the *Neshoba Democrat* warned.[9] The community, members of the Philadelphia Coalition insisted, needed to publicly demonstrate its desire to atone for its past sins by organizing a commemoration for the fortieth anniversary of the murders and calling on authorities to seek justice in the case.

The Coalition planned its 2004 commemoration to showcase how much the community had changed since the days when the murders were ignored or denied. Previously, the memorial ceremonies had only taken place in black community spaces. The 2004 commemoration was instead to be held at the Neshoba County Coliseum, a much larger space that was not associated with the black community. Furthermore, in addition to an impressive roster of former civil rights activists and Freedom Summer participants, the 2004 commemoration would include speeches from leading political figures from Neshoba County and the state of Mississippi, most notably Governor Haley Barbour and Representative Chip Pickering, both conservative Republicans.

But these efforts to broaden the constituency for the commemoration and to bring it into the center of the white community did not sit well with longtime activists like John Steele and Ben Chaney, who had

Leroy Clemons (left) and Jim Prince (right), founders and cochairs of the Philadelphia Coalition, read a resolution calling on Mississippi authorities to reopen the 1964 Goodman, Chaney, and Schwerner murder case. (AP Photo/*Neshoba Democrat*, Steven G. Watson)

been planning to stage a large ceremony at the church that would draw in movement veterans from across the country. Although the Coalition invited them to be part of the planning process, Steele and Chaney felt that most of the plans had already been made without their input and they objected strongly to the decision to invite Barbour and Pickering—whom they viewed as panderers to white racists—to speak at the ceremony.[10] Most fundamentally, they worried that the Philadelphia Coalition really represented a white power structure seeking to co-opt the event with the help of a few "negroes to do their bidding," as Ben Chaney put it, in order to sell a simplistic story of racial progress while ignoring the continuing racial problems in the state. Their criticisms only became more heated when a Neshoba County grand jury charged only one of the nine living suspects in the case. Chaney, Steele, and ally John Gibson, a white man who had begun working with John Steele in 2001 to bring attention to the failure to prosecute anyone for the 1964 crime, accused authorities of specifically targeting Edgar Ray Killen because he was poor and vulnerable, while protecting wealthier suspects like Olen Burrage, a successful businessman in Neshoba County. Since the 2005 trial, the refrain "Why Only Killen?" has been their drumbeat, repeated in documentary films, press releases, and their own annual commemoration ceremonies.[11] To these critics, the work of the Philadelphia Coalition and the Killen trial highlighted not the state's positive transformation but the same old story of entrenched and systemic Mississippi racism.

Their charges had some merit. In some ways, the work of the Philadelphia Coalition offers a vivid illustration of how civil rights trials could be used to serve the interests of elites who sought to use a prosecution to tell a story of progress while doing little to address historic or contemporary racial realities. The leading figures in the Coalition did hope to tell a story of positive change, and it quickly became clear that cochairs Clemons and Prince thought they needed to contain Steele and Chaney in order to do so. In a revealing editorial in the *Neshoba Democrat*, Jim Prince charged that local community leaders needed to plan the fortieth anniversary commemoration because, if they once again remained silent, "we can expect others to set the tone." The result would be "another series of national headlines that read: Nothing's changed in Mississippi or Neshoba County." As planning progressed, Clemons and Prince began describing Steele and Chaney, both of whom were natives of the area and had deep family connections to the event, as "outsiders" who did not reflect the real Neshoba County. In a meeting with the county board of supervisors, Prince and Clemons stressed the need for local residents to organize the commemoration. In the past, Clemons argued, "we've had these guys coming in from California, from New York" who portrayed Neshoba County as it was forty years ago. But now the community was wresting control from those who wanted to tar them as racists. "We are going to paint our own picture from here on out and let the world see how Neshoba County really is," Clemons stressed.[12]

That picture, at least for Jim Prince, was of a Neshoba County that had never condoned the terrible acts of a handful of evil Klansmen. Editorials in the *Neshoba Democrat* characterized the murders as "a single heinous act committed by a handful of extremists." Contacted constantly for interviews in the media frenzy before the trial, Prince explained that he always told reporters the same basic story: the crime of 1964 was "despicable," the majority of people in Neshoba County had been appalled by it, and they resented having to live with negative images about their community ever since. A trial, he argued, would excise "an old evil that a majority of the people here never condoned in the first place."[13] Here Prince neatly encapsulated one of the main narratives that emerged from the courtroom and had been popularized in the media.

Some members of the Coalition seemed intent on framing Neshoba's history as a narrative of redemption because they thought doing so might serve the cause of economic development. Jim Prince suggested that a community-wide commemoration and prosecution could lead to favorable national press coverage that would spur business investment and even attract tourists interested in sites associated with the civil rights movement. Prince was particularly interested in creating some kind of civil rights tourist trade that could appeal to the many out-of-town visitors who came to the area to visit nearby Indian casinos. A 2002 *Neshoba Democrat* article emphasized the economic advantages that linking the resorts with civil rights tourism could bring to the county. A civil rights tour "is a gold mine waiting to happen," the sales manager at one of the casinos claimed. Prince argued that supporting the Coalition was "an economic development issue" and unashamedly told other whites that if they could not support the call for justice because it was the right thing to do, then they needed to "do it 'cause it's good for business."[14] Tellingly, at the same May 2004 press conference where the Philadelphia Coalition issued its call for justice in the murders, county officials announced a major civil rights tourism initiative. At the Coalition's 2004 commemoration ceremony, audience members were provided with funeral fans touting Philadelphia/Neshoba County tourism.[15]

Six months after Edgar Ray Killen's conviction, Ben Chaney charged that the trial was "a farce," an effort by the existing power structure to scapegoat one unrepentant man in order to obscure the complicity of the state government in the crime when it took place.[16] To him, John Steele, and John Gibson, the lone prosecution of Edgar Ray Killen was proof that the legal process had been co-opted by those who wanted to promote a celebratory and sanitized version of history that denied the truth about racism in the past and ignored the reality of it in the present.

Ben Chaney and Rita Schwerner Bender at a news conference in Philadelphia, Mississippi, shortly after a jury found Edgar Ray Killen guilty. Although both sought legal justice in the case, they each questioned what kind of justice the trial offered. (Reuters/Corbis)

Yet while some members of the Philadelphia Coalition may have wanted to showcase a trial as the act that proved Philadelphia had overcome its racist history and closed the door on the past, others in the Coalition saw their work very differently. Even as critics like Chaney and Steele attacked the work of the Coalition, a political struggle was going on inside the group over how the 1964 crime should be portrayed and whether the group's mission should extend beyond calling for justice in the case. Even very early on, the Coalition adopted a more complicated position about the crime than was reflected by Jim Prince in the pages of the local newspaper. The public resolution the Coalition issued urging authorities to reopen the case noted that "some of our own citizens, including local and state law enforcement officers" helped plan and commit the murders, and criticized the "shameful involvement and interference of state government" in thwarting justice. Such language was notably absent from a similar resolution made by the Philadelphia City Council in the wake of the Coalition's call for justice. The Coalition proved more willing to raise questions about government misconduct and community responsibility for the crime than local authorities were. After hearing both resolutions read at the fortieth anniversary commemoration ceremony, one former Freedom Summer volunteer noted how the city's version "took the meat out of it." The Coalition's version, at least, had some meat.[17]

As the group pursued its work, moreover, some members began to push for it to embrace an agenda that went beyond legal justice in the case. Two months before the trial began, Jim Prince was already warning of "cracks in the coalition" between those he characterized as moderates or conservatives and those he considered "white liberals" who were pushing the Coalition towards what he saw as divisive political activism. He clashed particularly with Fenton DeWeese, a lifelong resident of Neshoba County from a prominent white family who insisted that the Coalition must do more than seek justice in one case. "If we don't do more than what we've done, we've failed," he told Coalition members at the group's celebration after they issued their call for justice in 2004. A committed Democrat from a family that had taken a stand against the Klan as early as the 1920s, DeWeese argued that the Philadelphia Coalition should become an activist group to fight for educational initiatives and political reform. Other members of the Coalition also supported broadening the group's agenda beyond pursuing prosecutions in the Freedom Summer murders. While cochair Leroy Clemons agreed with Jim Prince that the Philadelphia Coalition should not be an "advocacy organization," he saw the Coalition's ultimate goals as fostering greater community cohesion and educating young people about what had happened in Philadelphia. In his view, uncovering the "whole truth" about what went on in Neshoba County was more important than a conviction.[18]

Those who hoped to use the Killen trial to launch a deeper conversation about the region's past won this debate. They arranged for the Coalition, in conjunction with the University of Mississippi's William Winter Institute for Racial Reconciliation, to sponsor a summit on civil rights education in Philadelphia, bringing together teachers from across the region for workshops about teaching the movement by using first-hand accounts of the era. The summit, Donna Ladd reported in the *Jackson Free Press*, showed planners believed that "public atonement for past racial crimes must be combined with sustained education about America's racial history" if Americans were to "properly address and begin to eradicate racism in our country."[19] Jim Prince publicly expressed his opposition to the education summit, which he characterized as "sensitivity training" partially funded by a grant from the United Nations. And worse, although the event had not originally been planned to coincide with the trial, because of delays in the court proceedings the summit began only a day after the verdict was handed down. "Wise timing?" Prince wrote in his paper. "Hardly. The U.N.? We are heading into some tenuous days," he warned. Prince soon lost the battle for control of the Coalition; he left the organization—or was forced out—shortly after the trial, and Clemons became the sole chair of the group.[20]

In the years since the Killen trial, the Philadelphia Coalition called on state authorities to pursue further investigations into the Neshoba case and has voiced support for the federal legislation to assist civil rights–era murder cold case investigations. It continued to work on educational initiatives, helping to develop age-appropriate civil rights curricula and successfully lobbying for a 2008 Mississippi law that mandated the teaching of civil rights history in the public schools. It also pushed for a far more serious reckoning with the history of violence in the community and throughout the state than the Killen trial had enabled. A 2008 Coalition resolution insisted that white residents of Mississippi needed to come to terms with their role in these killings and that if further prosecutions proved impossible, the Coalition would call on state and federal authorities to release all records about racial crimes so that the citizens of Mississippi could "begin an honest investigation into our history." Only by "creating a truth process to tell the story" would the people of Mississippi undertake an "honest appraisal" of the past that could "insure justice" and "nurture reconciliation."[21]

The members of the Philadelphia Coalition who saw prosecutions as just a first step towards an in-depth and honest appraisal of the region's history of racial violence were not alone. Even as the lawyers made their arguments about Edgar Ray Killen in a Philadelphia courtroom, some in the audience were making plans to carry that project further by engaging activists throughout the South in a conversation about how the region could best confront its history and why it was so important to do so. Sitting next to each other at the trial, William Winter Institute Director Susan Glisson and trial consultant Andrew Sheldon came up with the idea for a conference to bring together community groups from across the South to build a regional alliance to confront the region's history of racial terror. The resulting 2006 meeting, held at the University of Mississippi, gathered representatives from twenty-four different groups that were working on the local level to heal communities scarred by histories of racial violence. Meeting for what was described as a "regional summit on racial violence and reconciliation," the conference reflected a growing interest in, and momentum for, addressing the legacies of the brutality of the Jim Crow period in the post–civil rights era South.[22]

The histories of the various groups meeting on the campus of the University of Mississippi, an institution that had once proudly embraced its role in protecting the segregated way of life, reflected the diverse factors driving interest in the region's history of racism and violence.[23] The same impulse to try to bring Americans together across racial lines by promoting positive cross-racial dialogue that had inspired President Clinton's 1997 One America Initiative on race gave rise to some of the groups gathered at Ole Miss almost ten years later. The William Winter Institute had its origins in that national conversation on race. In 1997, the University of Mississippi hosted the only forum in the Deep South during the One America Initiative. The conversation went so well that the university decided to "formalize the dialogue process" by creating the William Winter Institute in 1998 "to promote racial reconciliation and civic renewal." By 2006, under the energetic leadership of Executive Director Susan Glisson, the Winter Institute had developed a wide range of initiatives to help address the material inequities that resulted from racism in Mississippi, to preserve and commemorate the region's civil rights history, and to foster reconciliation and dialogue in communities divided by race.[24]

The passage of time and the maturation of a generation whose members had been children in the 1940s, '50s, and '60s and who were seeking to come to terms with their personal histories also contributed to this momentum to revisit the past. When a man came forward in 1992 to describe a quadruple lynching in Georgia that he had witnessed as a child in 1946, the subsequent coverage in the local papers led concerned residents and activists to form the Moore's Ford Memorial Committee. The Moore's Ford group sought to educate the community about the lynching, to commemorate the victims, and to explore the possibility of pursuing legal charges in the case. A woman who was twelve when Lemuel Penn was murdered near Athens, Georgia, in 1964 helped found another of the community organizations represented at the conference. Her main goal was "to keep Lemuel Penn's name alive because it was forgotten." The state, she felt, wanted to erase this history rather than acknowledge it, but local whites needed to hear how terrorized blacks had felt by the murder. As a first step, the Lemuel Penn Memorial Committee sought to have the bridge where Penn was killed renamed in his honor.[25]

Growing international interest in restorative justice as a way for communities and nations to recognize and address the broad community harms that had been the result of political violence and oppression influenced some of those who were at the conference. Some of the groups advocated truth and reconciliation processes focused on community dialogue and healing as the best way to deal with the region's racial history. Southern Truth and Reconciliation (STAR) was created by some Atlanta residents in 2003 in response to South African Archbishop Desmond Tutu's challenge to an audience at Emory University to launch their own truth and reconciliation process to deal with America's vexed racial history. Original founders included Andrew Sheldon, the white jury consultant who had worked on so many of the civil rights cases, and Theophus Smith, a black professor of religion at Emory with a strong scholarly interest in the links between religion and violence. STAR sought to promote restorative justice in the United States by focusing on the causes and effects of racial violence in communities and by partnering with communities to tailor truth and reconciliation processes to their local needs.[26]

Community organizers in Greensboro, North Carolina also borrowed from traditions of restorative justice from outside the United States when they began to look for a means in the late 1990s to address the still-raw wounds left by the murders of five civil rights and labor activists by a combined Klan-Nazi group at a rally in 1979. In 2001, survivors of the shooting, in consultation with members of the South African Truth and Reconciliation Commission and international organizations like the International Center for Transitional Justice, launched an effort to establish an independent commission to explore the causes and consequences of the killings. Their efforts eventually resulted in the creation of the Greensboro Truth and Reconciliation Commission (GTRC), the first truth commission of its kind in the United States. In 2005, at the same time that Edgar Ray Killen went on trial for the Freedom Summer murders, the GTRC was holding public hearings and conducting open community discussions that it hoped would ultimately "lead Greensboro into becoming a more just, understanding, and compassionate community."[27]

The groups that gathered at the 2006 conference saw themselves as the foot soldiers of a new movement; civil rights veteran Lawrence Guyot even compared the gathering to the 1960 meeting at Shaw University in North Carolina where different student groups came together to form the Student Nonviolent Coordinating Committee. Those involved in this modern movement, which included not only the organizations meeting at the Winter Institute that would join together in a loose coalition known as the Alliance of Truth and Racial Reconciliation but also journalists like Donna Ladd and some veterans of the 1960s struggles, insisted that there was a relationship between how a community or society understood its history and its political priorities and perspective in the present. Shaping people's views of America's racial history was thus an important part of achieving a more equitable society. They shared the belief, as famed Birmingham civil rights leader Fred Shuttlesworth put it, that "if you don't tell it like it was, it can never be as it ought to be."[28]

Echoing arguments made by political theorists and philosophers, these on-the-ground practitioners had specific ideas about what kinds of understanding of history would serve their political project to build stronger communities, foster racial healing, and promote racial, social, and economic justice. They insisted, first, that the racism of the Jim Crow era could not be dismissed as the acts of prejudiced individuals; it had to be understood as sanctioned by governmental actors and as embedded in institutions and structures. For the Mississippi Coalition for Justice, a group of religious and community leaders that formed in response to the open letter Rita Bender had written to Haley Barbour after the Killen trial in 2005, the most pressing task for changing the state was fostering an understanding of the systemic nature of racism. Inspired to explore "what Mississippi might look like if it were a social justice state," they launched the Mississippi Truth Project, a grassroots effort to organize a statewide truth and reconciliation commission to bring to light the full history of civil rights–era racial violence. In their "Declaration of Intent," the Truth Project organizers explained that they hoped to spur a "truthful engagement" with history that would make clear the "economic, environmental, legal, political, educational, and social systems" that had shackled the state's "potential and promise." The stories of racism in the Jim Crow era too often focused "on individuals and not institutions," but it was only by acknowledging the history of "deliberate, insidious and systematic racism" that Mississippians would be able to achieve a more equitable future.[29]

Only an understanding of the systemic and institutionalized practices designed to subordinate blacks and privilege whites would foster an awareness of how historic racial practices had shaped and contributed to contemporary political and economic inequalities. "Deepening our understanding of history and its continuing effects" was one of the key goals articulated by the Alliance for Truth and Racial Reconciliation, while Southern Truth and Reconciliation insisted that any full accounting with the past must "'connect-the-dots' between past human rights abuses and current affairs." Donna Ladd too sought to help her readers understand the connections between then and now. "You can't understand why Jackson is the way it is right now if you don't understand Jim Crow laws, if you don't understand the Citizens' Council, or the terrorist arm of the Klan, or if you don't understand the sovereignty commission files, if you don't understand redlining," she insisted.[30] America's history of racial domination shaped political and economic structures that continued to disadvantage African Americans and the poor. Failing to acknowledge the legacies of the Jim Crow era enabled defenders of the status quo to explain contemporary racial inequalities as the result of a dysfunctional black culture or "black people's genetic inability," which, as one black journalist pointed out, re-created the "logic and the system that produced" civil rights murders in the first place.[31] Refusing to recognize the legacies of past racial practices in the present was for these activists another manifestation of racism.

The groups who came together at the Southern Exposure conference and their allies also argued that the unaddressed racial violence of the Jim Crow era had caused long-lasting damage to the fabric of local communities that could be repaired only through a more honest reckoning with history. As Southern Truth and Reconciliation charged, "Racial terrorism" enabled or condoned by "community-wide conspiracies" resurfaced in debilitating ways if left unaddressed. Legal scholar and STAR consultant Sherilynn Ifill argued that lynchings and racial murders generated distrust that continued to divide blacks and whites decades later. "Where communities are, white and black today, is very much a product of their history, including the history of lynching and racial terrorism," she told the audience at the 2006 meeting. Systematic racial terrorism affected the political, educational, social, and economic development of both blacks and whites, and it still resonated in divisions between them.[32]

Given their understanding of the legacies of government and community-sanctioned systemic racism, the community groups and activists pushing for a confrontation with the past insisted that even individuals who had not been born at the time, or who had not personally engaged in racial violence, had a responsibility to explore and rectify a history of racial subordination. There would be no meaningful justice or racial equality, Rita Schwerner Bender argued, until Americans today understood "the responsibility they carry with them for the actions of their community and their state." Current generations had to have the courage to own up to the past that many of their ancestors had "enabled, or even helped facilitate," Donna Ladd insisted on the pages of the *Jackson Free Press*. Activists sought to reframe the debate about the need to address historic injustices in terms of legacies and responsibilities rather than collective guilt. Americans, they charged, could not portray themselves as outsiders to their own history.[33]

This expansive vision of corporate or political responsibility challenged deeply held American political traditions that portrayed historical obligations as an obstacle to individual autonomy and an unfair burden. American political thought, from Thomas Jefferson to homages to the "self-made man," has proven highly suspect of any claims that individuals bear some kind of responsibility for wrongs they did not personally commit.[34] Calls to understand a broader responsibility for the crimes of the civil rights era generated familiar denials of responsibility. When the *Jackson Free Press* called on Mississippians to own up to and address the state's racial history, one reader angrily responded that he, a white man born in 1973, had no wrongs to claim. What should he apologize for? "That I was born in Mississippi, that I am white? Or both?" He could see no ways in which he was implicated in, or should be accountable for, the racial murders of the era. Broadening that perspective was a vital aspect of this larger political project. All Americans, North and South, needed to own the nation's history of racism. "We are all Mississippians," the William Winter Institute stated baldly. When Americans—whether from Mississippi or not—comforted themselves by believing that "Mississippi is not us, that we do not all harbor these fears of those we deem the 'other,' that we have not all inherited this tortured history," they lied to themselves in ways that made it impossible to tackle disadvantage and privilege.[35]

For these groups, building a more democratic and equitable society required that Americans fully confront and hold themselves accountable for the centrality of racial domination in the nation's past. As the Mississippi Truth Project founders explained, only a "truthful engagement" with history would lead to a "just and inclusive future." Donna Ladd put it far more colorfully. It was "sheer dumbassedness," she argued, to think you could convince people to "support policies to help the inner-cities and equalize public education" if they remained "ignorant of how things got they way they are."[36] Anyone who hoped to create a "social justice state" had to reframe the ways in which Americans understood their past.

Given this understanding of what kind of political engagement with the past was necessary for creating a more just present, it should not be surprising that many of those who embraced this political project recognized the limitations of the criminal legal process as a form of redress for historic racial violence. The title of the session about the work of the Philadelphia Coalition at the 2006 Southern Exposure conference—"Is a Verdict Enough?"—suggested from the start that the likely answer to that question was no.

A trial, they knew, offered little opportunity to hold government actors accountable for their role in racial violence or to expose the systemic and institutionalized nature of racism. The crimes of the civil rights era might be "heavily tainted with government misconduct," in the words of Rita Schwerner Bender, but she recognized that "the overarching complicity of government" was not easily highlighted by a criminal trial. Birmingham minister Fred Shuttlesworth agreed that a criminal prosecution had only a limited ability to reveal the history of state-sanctioned racial terror. The church bombing trials, he argued, would produce only "slivers" of truth, not the kind of official "confession" about the city's complicity with the racial violence that he felt Birmingham needed.[37]

Critics of trials worried too that the criminal legal process, which focused on the actions of a few Klansmen, did little to inculcate a sense of responsibility for or ownership over the past among current generations. As one astute observer noted in response to the Killen trial, it seemed to allow those in the North to blame racism on people in the South and those in the South to blame it on "people in the past." Neither strategy encouraged ownership over history that might lead people to challenge "racism here and now." Diane McWhorter, a journalist and native of Birmingham, concurred that the church bombing trials did not encourage the people of Birmingham to understand that they had "any collective sin for which to atone." In her view, the city was still "dodging the verdict of history."[38]

And the criminal courtroom offered few opportunities for linking the racial oppression and violence of the civil rights era to contemporary racial problems. Longtime activists recognized that even the most celebrated civil rights trials would not lead to the kinds of conversations about the legacies of racism that they saw as vital. Horace Huntley, the director of the Birmingham Civil Rights Institute Oral History Project, insisted that despite two men being brought to trial for the 1963 church bombing, Birmingham still needed a forum to uncover the continued economic consequences of slavery and segregation. To get at those legacies, he advocated "an American-style Truth and Reconciliation Commission."[39] As Huntley recognized, the trials told a story about the relationship between past and present very different from the one he considered necessary to address contemporary inequalities. The framing adopted by the Greensboro Truth and Reconciliation Commission—three public hearings, one focused on the historical causes of a

1979 murder of five activists, one on what actually happened on the day of the shooting, and one focused on the legacies of the shooting—could not have taken place in a courtroom.

Some of those who wanted to expose the systemic nature of racism and to hold state actors accountable for their role in civil rights–era violence believed that civil law might have more potential than criminal law to do so. In a civil case, a plaintiff seeks compensation for an injury from the parties who committed or enabled the harm. Civil litigation allows for a broader scope of accountability than criminal law, making it possible to hold city governments or police departments responsible for the actions of an employee, for example. Civil law provided an avenue to try to expose governmental complicity with civil rights–era violence, and some families of victims achieved some limited success in civil cases. The family of Ben Brown, a twenty-two-year-old shot in the back and killed when police opened fire on the campus of Jackson State College in 1967, turned to civil courts after a Hines County grand jury determined in 2001 that both shooters had died. The family filed a lawsuit seeking $20 million in damages from the estates of the assailants, the City of Jackson, and the State Department of Public Safety, which resulted in a settlement award of $50,000 in 2002.[40]

Relatives of Charles Moore and Henry Dee who wanted to hold public officials in Franklin County accountable for the role they had played in the 1964 murder of the two young black men also turned to a civil lawsuit. Although James Ford Seale had been found guilty of kidnapping and conspiracy to kidnap for his role in the crime in a 2007 criminal prosecution, that trial had only briefly explored the complicity of the Franklin County Police in the crime. With the assistance of Margaret Burnham of the Civil Rights Restorative Justice Project, relatives filed a civil lawsuit in 2008 charging that Franklin County assisted the Klan's campaign of racial terror "by conspiring with the Klan to commit the criminal acts; by refusing to investigate and to prosecute crimes committed by the Klan; and by covering up the commission of such crimes." In 2010, the Board of Supervisors of Franklin County settled the case for an undisclosed sum.[41]

Civil litigation had greater potential than criminal trials to document a more complete record of civil rights–era violence and to hold state actors accountable for it, but it proved limited in its own ways. The discovery process for a civil trial involved very extensive research, but if a case settled, most of those findings would not be made public. As Rita Bender Schwerner noted in a commentary on the Dee and Moore civil ligation, the ability of civil suits to encourage a confrontation with the historical record "may be procedurally more limited than in a criminal trial." And although Thomas Moore believed that if not for the civil suit, "Franklin County would still be in denial" about its role in the murders of his brother and Henry Dee, the resolution settling the case made clear that the county government had accepted neither the historical narrative presented by the prosecution nor responsibility for its role in the crime. They agreed to settle not because they admitted culpability, the Board of Supervisors explained, but because they worried about losing their insurance coverage if they went to trial. "These deaths," the settlement resolution maintained, "are believed to have resulted solely from the criminal actions of the Ku Klux Klan." And the historical account of the crimes put forward by the plaintiffs, the Board insisted, was based on "unsubstantiated accounts which would not be considered in a court of law." Since the county refused to admit to the facts presented by the plaintiffs, it was "a bit of a stretch to say they were 'held accountable,'" Margaret Burnham admitted.[42]

Given the limitations of the legal process as a tool for recasting history, it would be understandable if those committed to the pursuit of social and racial justice viewed trials as inconsequential, or even cynically dismissed them as a distraction from the real work that needed to be done to achieve change. Yet most of the same activists who believed in the need to reframe the nation's understanding of history also supported the legal process taking place in courtrooms around the region. Some, like Donna Ladd and Rita Schwerner Bender, had played a major role in getting cases reopened and pushing for prosecutions. The William Winter Institute not only provided key support for groups working on the community level for restorative justice through truth processes, but also encouraged the pursuit of legal justice and provided assistance to those working on the ground to move the legal process forward. Jury consultant Andrew Sheldon, an instrumental figure in most of the trial convictions, also helped found STAR.[43]

Ladd, Sheldon, Bender, and others were not politically naïve; they were aware of the limitations of the legal process. But they still saw real value in pursuing legal actions when it was possible to do so. Trials deserved support if for no other reason than they were meaningful to the families of victims. When Thee Smith, founding director of STAR and a professor of religion at Emory, told the group gathered at the 2006 Southern Exposure conference that he favored a form of restorative justice that eschewed accusations and instead sought to restore honor to both victims and perpetrators, civil rights movement veteran Lawrence Guyot was horrified. The pursuit of legal justice was not a theoretical issue, he insisted: "There are real people in this room who've lost relatives and there've been convictions in those cases. We cannot say to them, we were wrong," he insisted. "I WILL NOT join in saying that," he added for emphasis. Guyot expressed one of the most basic reasons that many activists supported efforts to reopen cases and seek prosecutions: that the legal process was important for the relatives of victims. Andrew Sheldon admitted that he saw truth commissions as a better way to foster "a new way of looking at ourselves and our country," but felt that activists first had to finish the work of prosecutions because of the huge debt owed to victims and their families. Once the work of trials had been dispatched, they could move on to a better process.[44]

Some also saw prosecutions as necessary to create a level of basic civility and trust important to any further steps towards exploring the legacies of history. Despite their functional limitations, trials mattered, Rita Schwerner Bender told the audience gathered at a 2007 conference on crimes of the civil rights era, because they offered evidence that a community did not condone the criminal act. A trial served as "an affirmation of the values that make civil society possible." Affirming those basic values was a necessary first step for communities that had been torn apart by racial violence, legal scholar Patryk Labuda insisted. Ending the "dominant culture of impunity" was vital to healing the mistrust among blacks that the failure of the justice system had generated. Although Labuda hoped to see a truth and reconciliation commission in Mississippi someday, he described criminal prosecutions as a symbolically important "first phase" of reckoning with the legacies of the violence of the Jim Crow era. Thomas Moore made a similar point when he described the prosecution of his brother's murderer as vital to "begin the process" of removing the fear in Franklin County generated by the 1964 crime, fear, he charged, that you could still "hear," "smell," and "breathe."[45]

Many activists pushing for a reorientation towards the nation's history in order to promote the cause of social justice also saw ways in which the pursuit of legal justice could serve their cause. It could play a vital role, for example, in generating attention towards the past and in directing resources towards recovering histories of violence that had long been silenced or buried.[46] Activists welcomed the potential of the legal process to draw attention to the crimes of the civil rights era in ways that could then spur the kind of historical exploration that they hoped to see. As they knew, there could not be a reckoning with history if people knew nothing about the past. The possibility of getting cases reopened was crucial for generating media interest in and attention to these murders; without the legal angle, it seems unlikely that murders like that of Ben Chester White or Charles Moore and Henry Dee would ever have received the extensive media coverage that they did. As Donna Ladd noted, Americans probably would not "go back and look at these stories if there's not some element of revenge up in the prosecution and the justice-seeking because that's the way we are."[47] The American commitment to and investment in legal processes opened avenues for exploration that might have remained closed otherwise.

Indeed, some advocated pursuing legal prosecutions as a way to get more attention paid to the history, even if it might be difficult or impossible to secure convictions. For historian Stephen Whitfield, however "elusive" legal justice might be in Emmett Till's murder, reinvestigating the case could help remind Americans "of how perilous were the conditions under which black Southerners were so recently obliged to live." Reopening the murder investigation, he believed, could offer a history lesson that might "finally be more significant than the judicial resolution to be achieved." An editorial in the *Memphis Commercial Appeal* also touted the benefits of reopening the investigation into Till's murder even if there was scant hope of a successful conviction. The investigation needed to move forward if only because of the "necessity of filling in the details of a dark period in Mississippi history," the paper suggested.[48] Criminal investigations could be a lever to encourage Americans to learn about histories of racial violence.

The legal process could also offer some limited space for people to talk honestly with each other across racial lines. Although during a trial itself it proved difficult for witnesses who were subject to cross-examination to discuss their views and experiences on their own terms, the voir dire process—when potential jurors were questioned about their personal experiences with race and racism—offered at least some opportunity for people to talk about their personal histories and perspectives. Donna Ladd described the emotional testimony of potential jurors in the Seale trial about their own encounters with racial and sexual violence as "the closest thing we've ever had to a truth commission." Outside of the courtroom, community organizing around trials could also foster cross-racial dialogue. Members of the Philadelphia Coalition felt that their meetings provided an unprecedented opportunity for community members with different backgrounds and beliefs to listen to and learn from each other. Just working together in a coalition encouraged more cross-racial discussion and understanding than most members had experienced during their lives in Neshoba County. Many involved with the group emphasized the cathartic nature of sitting down and talking about the 1964 events with people from different racial groups. Meeting at a local church every week with Susan Glisson of the William Winter Institute facilitating the conversation, Coalition members talked openly about how the murders and the stigma associated with them made them feel. These meetings were a lot like counseling sessions and some participants even described them as "soul cleansing."[49] On this small scale, the legal process could sometimes generate conversations somewhat like those associated with truth and reconciliation commissions.

Some activists also believed that working for prosecutions could serve as a focal point for grassroots organizing that might help transform communities and generate momentum for other forms of activism. As Rita Schwerner Bender put it, she hoped that trials could serve as "a tool" for some residents "in local communities to reach for political empowerment." Organizing to reopen a legal case could bring together people in a local community interested in change, give them a goal to work towards, and provide an avenue to raise concerns about ongoing community challenges. To many who gathered at the Southern Exposure conference in 2006, the Philadelphia Coalition offered an example of how the pursuit of legal justice could drive social and political change on the local level. Activists praised the work of the Philadelphia Coalition and defended the group from critics who questioned its motives. "I know the Coalition has its detractors," Lawrence Guyot told those at the conference, but "let's understand success when we see it." That success, members of the Coalition argued, included opening constructive dialogues across race lines and increasing the representation of blacks and Choctaw Indians in the county's decision-making process. "This was not so much about convicting an eighty year old man," Leroy Clemons insists. "This was about a community coming together." Now working as the director of community relations for the William Winter Institute, Clemons hopes to spread the model of the Philadelphia Coalition to other communities around the state.[50]

But activists knew that if trials were to participate in the creation of a "social justice state," as the Mississippi Coalition on Justice described its political project, they had to be viewed as a first step towards creating a more equitable political and economic system, not as the final step that proved justice had been achieved. Prosecutions, Donna Ladd insisted, needed to be understood "as a beginning, not an ending, as so many people seemed to believe." Describing trials as a way to close the door on the past or as proof that history had been fully dealt with was, to Ladd, a form of "institutionalized racism." Ladd criticized too the refrain taken up by the media with each trial that it was likely to be the last of its kind or "the end of an era." These predictions implied that the goal of revisiting the past was simply prosecuting a few old men rather than helping people better understand their own history. "The bottom line is that we need to pursue these cases, and most importantly the *details of the stories* so that Mississippians can really know our own history," she insisted. "It's not just about prosecutions."[51]

Those invested in seeking social justice made it their constant refrain that trials should be understood as only a first step towards their goal of racial justice. "What happened today is just the beginning," Rita Bender announced hopefully on the day of the verdict in the Killen trial. Jury consultant Andrew Sheldon lamented that there seemed to be no word for "opening" that was as powerful as the term "closure." Only if the trials could be framed as a beginning rather than an ending could they play any role in working towards what many of these activists saw as their ultimate goal: to "prod a national conversation on race" and to foster "a new way of looking at ourselves and our country."[52]

Yet civil rights trials did not offer a neutral site for those who sought to promote racial and economic justice. Without political intervention, activists recognized, the legal process offered a version of history that supported the status quo. Moreover, the political project of trying to use trials to do the work of social justice faced far more challenges than that of using trials to tell a simplistic story that racism had been overcome. As Philadelphia Coalition member Fent DeWeese acknowledged, it was very hard to move beyond a prosecution to broader political change. "Asking for justice is easy," he noted. "It's what follows is hard."[53] Trials represented a double-edged sword, but one side of that blade was sharper than the other.

Harnessing the legal process to the kind of historical project envisioned by these activists proved difficult in part because the legal process itself framed history in ways that actively worked against the understanding of the past that activists were hoping to develop. Trials did not just ignore official complicity with crimes; they framed the Klansmen as solely responsible for the racial violence of the era. They did not just fail to hold the larger community responsible; they portrayed whites, both in the 1960s and today, as innocents who were not culpable for the racial system that benefited them. And they did more than ignore the contemporary legacies of systemic racism: they promoted the view that racism was a problem of individual acts of hatred that had been solved by putting archaic Klansmen in jail. Political theorist W. James Booth notes that legal trials offer a sense of closure that other forms of reckoning with the past resist; a verdict offers "the pretext that all that can be done has been done." Civil rights trials suggested that historic injustices were a thing of the past, and that any lingering wrongs would be corrected by a conviction.[54]

Making the trials part of a broader social justice project proved especially complicated because the legal process could be relatively easily co-opted by a political elite that had no interest in transformative change or social justice. For those who saw the criminal legal process as a way to remake the South's reputation and redeem the region, civil rights trials offered the opportunity to fix history, both in the sense of repairing the historical record tainted by legal inaction in the 1960s and in the sense of resolving or settling the record in a way that would effectively limit the power of the past. For them, trials offered the opportunity to promote a version of history that emphasized the innocence of the "good people" of the South and that dismissed any connections between the past and the present. The fact that framing trials as closure or absolution could serve the ends of those who had little interest in social justice had long led some to fear that political elites would use trials as a way to appease blacks and distract attention from ongoing problems, a view voiced long before Ben Chaney and John Steele began demanding to know why Edgar Ray Killen was the only person indicted for the 1964 Freedom Summer murders. When Mississippi authorities indicted Byron De La Beckwith for Medgar Evers's murder, white Jackson movement veteran John Salter described it as a crass attempt by state authorities to "reach back and find a witch to burn" in order to counter negative publicity following the release of *Mississippi Burning*. Fifteen years later, black journalist Charles Tisdale, who had covered Emmett Till's murder in 1955, described the reopening of the case as a "classic Mississippi red herring," a "politically motivated distraction" designed to deflect attention from a spate of recent mysterious deaths of black men in Mississippi jail cells.[55] Holding legal trials, these critics charged, offered political elites an easy way to mollify those who were truly concerned about tackling racial disparities without fundamentally challenging a status quo that privileged whites.

But prosecutions, social justice advocates argued, did not have to serve the cause of upholding existing racial or economic hierarchies. Although Rita Schwerner Bender described trials as "a waste of time" if they were only part of a quest to jail eighty-year-old men, she insisted that they could be useful if they helped to frame history "the way it needed to be framed." But she knew that was unlikely if political elites with little interest in transformative justice—what she called "the Chamber of Commerce contingent"—had their way.[56] That contingent, of course, did not fully control the representations of the trials; indeed, it faced activists like her who were publicly and loudly contesting their framings of trials as redemption or closure.

Yet the "Chamber of Commerce" contingent had advantages that the activists did not. The narratives favored by those who described trials as acts of closure and redemption appealed to a media eager to tell stories of racial progress, and they were culturally familiar in a way that the arguments of those who hoped to use trials to open a discussion about systemic racism or the legacies of the Jim Crow era were not. In a nation forged around the idea of individual responsibility, social justice activists sought to tell stories of community complicity, political responsibility, and systemic racism. Instead of pointing out a clear villain who could be felled by decisive legal action, they offered a complex account, where redemption, if possible, could only come from slow and deep social and community transformation, and where there were no simple heroes or villains. Susan Glisson noted the challenge of trying to tell a different story through the trials. While Americans typically looked for, and the media rushed to create, "white male heroes," what happened in Neshoba County was about "complicated human beings, none of whom are perfect, but all of whom are trying hard to discern a path to a better community for all." Donna Ladd recognized too the comfort provided by the "whitewashed" version of history, "filled with easy heroes and demons, and one in which it's always white guys saving the day."[57] The media preferred the story of stalwart white heroes taking a stand against depraved white racists over that of a complex portrait of ordinary people, with a range of motivations, trying to do the hard work of social justice.

The power of the narratives of closure and redemption, and the difficulty of displacing them, was evident in all kinds of public responses to the trials. Even in the case of the Killen trial, where grassroots organizers had succeeded in broadening the agenda at the local level beyond legal prosecutions, the common response to the trial reflected the established narratives. The trope of closure dominated representations of Killen's conviction. Newspaper coverage claimed that the Killen verdict "closed one of the most shocking chapters in the movement to end segregation across the South" and that the verdict had closed an "evil chapter" in history. A black man who traveled to Philadelphia from Greenville, Mississippi, to be in the courtroom expressed his relief when the verdict was handed down: "It's closed. This chapter in history is closed." The innocence of the larger white community also proved an entrenched idea. As one white man told a reporter, he came to witness the trial because he felt the crime "caused the black people to feel bad about something the younger (white) generation had nothing to do with." He hoped the verdict would enable the community to "put all this behind us."[58]

The idea of southern exceptionalism—with Mississippi being the retrograde state that needed to atone for its racial sins—remained powerful too. A column in *Newsday* described Killen's conviction as evidence that "bloody Mississippi" had finally "made its peace with some bedrock tenets of American democracy." With the verdict, "a region that had suffered as a third-world, caste-ridden country within a country was finally liberated." These descriptions of the trial fully embraced the notions that the verdict closed the door on the past, that whites had no responsibility for the racism of the Jim Crow era, and that racist Mississippi should be understood as unlike the rest of the egalitarian United States.[59]

These culturally familiar frames influenced scholarship on the trials too. In the only book yet published on the 2005 Killen trial, *Justice in Mississippi* by University of Vermont history and law professor Howard Ball, the heroes of the story were white prosecutors and white journalists, like Stanley Dearman and Jerry Mitchell. Edgar Ray Killen was the embodiment of evil, and whites in Neshoba County were described as "bystanders" who had been "mortified" by the murders but silenced by fear of the Klan, rather than as supporters or beneficiaries of the system of white supremacy. Ball's book, one critical reviewer noted, fell into "the *Mississippi Burning* trap of emphasizing white heroes, offering a superficial story of good vs. evil, and relegating blacks to the role of passive victims or virtually invisible backdrop." Ball had effectively "fashioned a superficial redemption story."[60] It was a story that was very easy for the trials to tell.

Activists in the South embraced historical narrative as a political tool that could be used to promote and sustain social justice initiatives.[61] They had faith that if Americans changed the way they understood their past, it would lead to political change in the present. As Donna Ladd insisted on the pages of her newspaper, "We must face our past and *understand* what was wrong with it and how it still affects our present and future for *ourselves.*" She called on Mississippians of all races to "tell our own stories . . . with love and hopefully some forgiveness, and with unflinching honesty." Only then would they be able to understand their history in a way that would enable them to address present-day inequality. The power of storytelling had to be harnessed to the cause of social justice.[62]

But civil rights trials lent themselves to some stories more easily than others. Indeed, their power and influence stemmed largely from the narratives that they so easily communicated: that the American justice system had become color-blind, that racism was confined to a few evil men, and that the South had joined the rest of the nation by overcoming the burden of its racial history. This celebratory narrative of redemption and closure dominated the national media, motivated people like Jim Prince and Haley Barbour, and presented an obstacle to those who wanted the legal process to be a launching pad for a deeper understanding of the region's history and its legacies. Although activists struggled to harness the legal process to what they considered to be more progressive political ends, trials could easily reinforce the very understandings of history that they were working so hard to change.

Conclusion

"We Are All Mississippians"

I really do believe that we can all become better than we are. I know we can. But the price is enormous and people are not yet willing to pay it.

—James Baldwin, in *James Baldwin: Price of the Ticket*, 1990

In 2008, the man who had lobbied federal authorities to create a process and structure to reinvestigate civil rights–era murders celebrated the passage of the Emmett Till Unsolved Civil Rights Crime Act, which dedicated federal resources to investigating and assisting in prosecutions of unresolved racially motivated murders from the 1950s and 1960s. "The greatest criminal manhunt in this country's history" had begun, Alvin Sykes told the media. Finally, those perpetrators who thought they had "gotten away with their lynchings a long time ago" would be held accountable.[1] But within five years, it had become clear that despite the new federal law, few perpetrators of civil rights–era violence would ever face trial. After assisting with only two trials, cases that had begun before the passage of the Till Act, the FBI determined that prosecutions were not viable in the vast majority of civil rights–era murders. In 2013, the Department of Justice announced that it had closed all but twenty of the 112 unresolved cases that had been reopened under the law.

Although the Department of Justice acknowledged that "very few prosecutions" had resulted from its efforts, it insisted that the federal government had done everything it could to resolve civil rights cold cases. The FBI, Civil Rights Unit Chief Cynthia Deitle claimed, had undertaken a "tremendous amount of work" since the project began in 2007. "Our agents have worked tirelessly, reaching out to victims' families and interviewing witnesses, along with police officers, prosecutors, and judges," she explained in 2009. They had "combed through old police records, grand jury transcripts, and court transcripts" in their efforts to piece together decades-old stories. They had not been successful in bringing more charges because of the challenges of locating evidence, establishing jurisdiction, and finding live suspects so many years after the original crimes had taken place. While people might feel like they knew who committed these crimes, one FBI agent explained, "we have to prove it in a court of law."[2]

Despite the failure to bring new charges in most cases, the Department of Justice believed the Till Act had accomplished its primary goal: federal investigations had "helped bring closure to many family members of the victims," a 2012 DOJ report insisted. As part of that effort to bring "some sense of closure" to relatives of victims, the Department decided to devote "considerable resources" to locating the next of kin of each victim so the FBI could write each of them letters explaining what steps had been taken to investigate the case and why it was being closed. The DOJ signaled its sense of responsibility to the families and the seriousness they accorded the process by making the effort to deliver these letters by hand whenever possible.[3]

While some of the activists who had lobbied for the Till Act and who had long fought to reopen unresolved civil rights–era murders praised the agency for "the dignity with which they are accepting responsibility for letting families know how justice failed them," as Margaret Burnham of the Civil Rights and Restorative Justice Project put it, many of those who had fought for the law expressed disappointment with the DOJ and FBI's implementation of it. There had been no manhunt, Alvin Sykes complained, no passionate and aggressive pursuit of the perpetrators of civil rights–era murders. Janis McDonald and Paula Johnson, the founders of Syracuse University's Cold Case Justice Initiative, demanded that Congress hold hearings to determine why the FBI had not done more to act quickly before suspects died. To activists who had hoped that the federal government would take over the burden of investigating and prosecuting these cases after the passage of the Till Act, federal authorities still seemed to be sitting on the sidelines.[4]

The widespread disappointment with the results of the federal law reflected the different perspectives of those who had pushed for the law and the political authorities who had enacted it. Alvin Sykes and others had hoped that the Till Act would prompt a national reckoning with the extent and nature of civil rights–era violence. "From the beginning," Sykes maintained, "our focus was not just to prosecute cases but to find the truth." To Sykes, finding "the truth" meant uncovering murderers regardless of whether a crime could ever be brought to trial. To Janis McDonald of Syracuse University's Cold Case Justice Initiative, truth would require "a full accounting of all the people who were killed as the result of the Klan and other racial hatred and violence during the era." She had wanted the Justice Department to create a regional task force to determine how many people had been killed in civil rights–era violence, something that the DOJ proved unwilling to do. Rita Schwerner Bender had hoped the legislation would provide an opportunity to expose not only the scope of the violence, but also the structures of racism that had fostered it. The law, she had argued before Congress, would help Americans understand the truth about "the overreaching societal and governmental conduct that both enabled these crimes and which continues to cause racial inequality."[5] These activists sought a full accounting for the nation's history of racial violence, not just a list of which cases were prosecutable.

The legal process did not generate this kind of reckoning. Whatever the hopes for the Unsolved Civil Rights Crime Act, its limitations reflected those of the legal process more generally. That is not to say that civil rights trials were not significant. The search for evidence that took place over the course of a legal investigation could help uncover new information about a crime. A trial could offer comfort and closure to families who had been wounded by these crimes. Myrlie Evers could hardly put into words the sense of release she felt when her husband's murderer was finally convicted at his third trial. When the verdict was read, she "felt as though all of the demons in my soul, in my body, were coming out through every pore of my body." She savored the fact that after the trial she could call Beckwith a "convicted" assassin, not just an

Trials, whatever their limitations, have proven incredibly meaningful for many of the relatives of slain victims. Here Myrlie Evers, left, celebrates with her daughter Reena Evers-Everett after Byron De La Beckwith was finally convicted in 1994 for murdering Medgar Evers in 1963. (AP Photo/Rogelio Solis)

accused one. Ben Chester White's son, Jesse, explained his feelings after Ernest Avants's 2003 conviction this way: "It's like being hungry for long and you get a good meal under your belt. You're not so hungry anymore." And after the conviction of James Ford Seale in the 1964 murders of Charles Moore and Henry Dee, Moore's brother Thomas declared that he felt he could once again call Mississippi home.[6]

But as important as convictions could be to relatives of victims, the legal process inherently defined the goal of any reckoning with historic racial violence in terms of prosecutions: when prosecutions were no longer possible, no further action was necessary. As happened time and again, when cases did move forward, the legal format narrowed the scope of any inquiry to the actions of individual defendants outside of a broader historical context in ways that minimized societal responsibility for the racial terror of the civil rights era, obscured the systemic nature of racial violence, and did little to address the relationship between the racial structures of the past and racial inequalities in the present. In the courtroom, systemic white supremacy was reduced to the work of a few bad Klansmen. The media, attracted by the drama and spectacle of a legal trial, then helped turn the convictions of a few Klansmen into narratives of redemption that suggested that racism was a thing of the past.

Most of the existing commentary on the contemporary prosecution of civil rights murders focuses on what these trials tell us about the South, and especially about Mississippi, where the majority of the trials have taken place. Journalist Adam Nossiter, for example, begins his book on the 1994 Beckwith trial by explaining that the trial made sense only within the context of Mississippi history and culture, a place "where the past jutted into the present to a startling degree." The 2005 trial of Edgar Ray Killen was, historian Howard Ball claims, "the story of changes in Mississippi over the past four decades . . . the prism through which we can understand and appreciate the nature of change in Mississippi." To Harry MacLean, a crime journalist who wrote a book about the 2007 prosecution of James Seale, the trial was the "latest act in Mississippi's great morality play," one that served as a window into "the ineluctable paradox that is Mississippi."[7] Like most writings on the trials, these works reinforce the notion of southern exceptionalism, whether by suggesting that the trials make sense only in the context of Mississippi's peculiar history or by portraying Mississippi and the South as the locus of racism in the United States, even as they see new trials as proof of the state's progress since the Jim Crow era.

But as the William Winter Institute reminds us, "We are all Mississippians." Civil rights trials cannot be limited to a history of Mississippi, and they cannot be understood only in the context of changes in the South. Civil rights trials are the stuff of American history, a window not only into the "ineluctable paradox" of Mississippi, but also into the nature of America's contemporary racial reckoning.

That reckoning, a history of the contemporary prosecutions makes clear, has most commonly taken the form of legal actions because the idea of legal justice could appeal to people with a wide range of personal and political interests. People with very different agendas could come together around the shared goal of a trial. For families of victims, a criminal trial served as proof that their loved ones were full citizens who were worthy of legal protection. They also pushed for a more complete legal process because they understood the symbolic importance of unbiased treatment in a court of law. For activists who became involved in efforts to reopen cases, the law offered an opportunity for crafting a fuller record of the history of the racial violence, for attracting public attention to it, and potentially for starting a process that could reframe Americans' under-standing of the depth and power of racism in the civil rights era and its legacies for the present. At the same time, the legal process offered those with an interest in rehabilitating the reputation of their communities or states a potent arena for the performance of new civic and racial identities. Southern states and communities long stigmatized as backwards could use reopenings and trials as a way to renounce overt white supremacy publicly and to rehabilitate a white southern identity tarnished by iconic images of racist white sheriffs and hateful Klansmen.

Yet while the trials brought together a diverse group of supporters who had very different hopes for them, the contemporary prosecutions became part of a narrative of racial progress and redemption that best served those who hoped prosecutions would serve to close the door on the past. Contemporary civil rights trials thus shed light on the evolution that enabled new structures of racial inequality to rise from the ashes of the older racial system. In particular, they suggest how easy it has been for examples of legal justice—equal treatment before the law—to become evidence that the United States is now a "postracial" society. The ideology of colorblindness or postracialism insists that the government no longer needs to undertake racial remedies or engage in race-based decision making because the United States has made such racial prog-ress since the Jim Crow era. It suggests that racism is a thing of the past and thus race no longer needs to be a central consideration of our social thinking or our public policy. It is an ideology that has gained traction across the political spectrum in the past three decades as many have come to favor policies that are universal and race neutral over those that continue to consider and address racial inequities.[8]

A host of public intellectuals have attacked postracial thinking as a dangerous fiction, the equivalent, black cultural commentator Touré suggested in 2011, of an "intellectual Loch Ness monster," and have pointed out the reams of evidence that contradict claims that race no longer matters in American society.[9] In 2012, for example, white families had fourteen times the median household wealth of black families and African Americans were nearly three times more likely than whites to live below the poverty line. Blacks drop out of high school at a far higher rate than whites and are much less likely than whites to attend college. Perhaps most disturbing, of the 2.3 million Americans now in prison, a number that began to increase dramatically after 1980, fully one million are African Americans. African Americans are incarcerated at a rate six times the national average.[10]

The political rhetoric about and media discussion of contemporary civil rights trials provides insight into how the narrative of racial progress so central to postracial ideology has been widely accepted despite the fact that race so clearly continues to structure American society. The postracialist retreat from race is only possible, one legal scholar argues, "in a society that is perceived as having made significant strides in racial equality, at least symbolically." Denying the continued salience of race depends upon constructing a plausible narrative of racial progress, one that can point to "big events" that signify that the "racial eras of the past have been and should be transcended."[11] Civil rights trials could be—and were—framed as symbolic "big events" that proved the nation had transcended its racial past. The media coverage of trials equated the formal legal justice offered by the trials as a form of redemption for the racial sins of the past. In the trial narrative, the contemporary prosecutions of civil rights murders symbolized that the legal system was now free of bias, that racism was an aberration in American life, and that American institutions treated everyone equally.

Civil rights trials seemed to affirm the foundational claims at the heart of the postracial claims of racial progress: that the civil rights movement had purged racism from the state, that whites had embraced the changes of the 1960s, and that any remaining injustices stemmed from individual acts of prejudice rather than institutional practices. "Colorblind justice" became proof that the nation had finally overcome its racial history. By any measure, this is at best a narrow conception of racial justice, and it was one that at least some conservative advocates of civil rights trials embraced as they looked for ways to prove how much the South had changed since the dark days of the Jim Crow era.

Yet even as a study of the contemporary civil rights trials suggests some of the reasons that Americans can imagine that the United States has moved beyond race, it also highlights the energy and urgency of the political movement to challenge the dominant racial discourse and its refusal to recognize the ways in which race continues to structure opportunities and privilege in America. Those who argued that trials must be seen as a first, rather than last, step towards a more equitable American society insisted that racial justice required more than fair treatment in the courtroom. It required that people of all races have similar economic opportunity, that they are valued equally in society, that they have the same chance to be healthy and secure. Civil rights–era murder cases, which had the potential to reveal the systemic nature of the racial violence of the Jim Crow era and to highlight its legacies for today, offered an opportunity to foster what Rita Bender Schwerner described as a "long overdue" confrontation with our "common legacy of racism."[12] The struggle of activists to force that confrontation will certainly continue long after the last possible defendant in a civil rights murder case has died; the range of organizations working on the ground in the South to foster a different understanding of the nation's racial history offers hope that we will one day, as black writer and social critic James Baldwin believed, "become better than we are."[13]

In the last sermon he would ever give, just four days before his assassination, Martin Luther King Jr. used words he had said many times before. "The arc of the moral universe is long," he said, "but it bends toward justice." The contemporary prosecutions of civil rights–era murders in some ways offer evidence that King was right; although justice was long delayed in civil rights murders, it was finally delivered. The arc of the moral universe bent towards legal justice.

But civil rights trials are also evidence of what James Baldwin described as the unhappy but remarkable ability of Americans "to alchemize all bitter truths into an innocuous but piquant confection." Americans, he charged, seemed able to transform even their public discussion of their moral contradictions into a "proud decoration, such as are given for heroism on the field of battle."[14] Baldwin wrote long before the contemporary civil rights trials, but he offered an uncanny assessment of what has been the nation's most extensive and publicized reckoning with its racial history to date. In civil rights trials, even the most horrific stories of racial violence became an opportunity to tell a mythic tale of racial progress. Prosecutions of civil rights–era violence became part of a narrative of redemption that affirmed the United States as an exceptional nation committed to equality, justice, and democracy. America's bitter truths deserve a more honest reckoning.

Notes

Introduction

1. On the debates about what actually happened, see Devery S. Anderson, "A Wallet, a White Woman, and a Whistle: Fact and Fiction in Emmett Till's Encounter in Money, Mississippi," *Southern Quarterly* 45 (Summer 2008): 10–21.
2. William Bradford Huie, "A Shocking Story of Approved Killing in Mississippi," *Look*, January 24, 1956, 46–49; Clenora Hudson-Weems, *Emmett Till: The Sacrificial Lamb of the Civil Rights Movement* (Troy, MI: Bedford Publishers, 1994).
3. Martha Minow, *Between Vengeance and Forgiveness: Facing History after Genocide and Mass Violence* (Boston: Beacon Press, 1998), 1–2. For more on these developments, see Elazar Barkan, *Guilt of Nations: Restitution and Negotiating Historical Injustices* (New York: W. W. Norton, 2000), xii, xxii; Kathryn Sikkink, *The Justice Cascade: How Human Rights Prosecutions Are Changing World Politics* (New York: W. W. Norton, 2011); Priscilla Hayner, *Unspeakable Truths: Confronting State Terror and Atrocity* (New York: Routledge, 2000); Greg Grandin and Thomas Miller Klubock, eds., "Truth Commissions, State Terror, History, and Memory," special issue, *Radical History Review* 97 (Winter 2007).
4. Bishop Desmond Tutu, "Reconciliation in Post-Apartheid South Africa: Experiences of the Truth Commission" (remarks at the Nobel Peace Laureates conference, University of Virginia, November 5, 1998), http://www.virginia.edu/nobel/transcript/tutu.html.
5. For more on Mamie Till Mobley's struggle to ensure her son not be forgotten, see Mamie Till Mobley and Christopher Benson, *The Death of Innocence: The Story of the Hate Crime That Changed America* (New York: One World; New York: Ballantine Books, 2003); Ruth Feldstein, *Motherhood in Black and White: Race and Sex in American Liberalism, 1930–1965* (Ithaca, NY: Cornell University Press, 2000).
6. The FBI agent charged with collecting forensic evidence from the corpse expected the remains to be skeletonized. He was astonished by how little Till's corpse had decomposed. Anthony Raap and Jennifer Leigh Oprihory, "A Further Look into Emmett Till Case," *Austin Weekly News*, November 21, 2012, http://www.austinweeklynews.com/News/Articles/11–21–2013/A-further-look-into-Emmett-Till-case/.

7. The Greensboro Truth and Reconciliation Commission, the only truth commission in the United States to date, took place in 2004–2005 as an independent community initiative to explore the 1979 killing of five labor activists by the Ku Klux Klan. On the Tulsa Commission, see Alfred Brophy, *Reconstructing the Dreamland: The Tulsa Riot of 1921; Race, Reparations, and Reconciliation* (New York: Oxford University Press, 2003).

8. Congress apologized for lynching in 2005, although the two senators from Mississippi, the state that experienced the most lynchings, refused to sign the resolution. An apology for slavery and Jim Crow laws (which made explicit that it should not be construed as authorizing or supporting claims for restitution or reparations) followed in 2009.

9. For a discussion of the common representations of the civil rights struggle, see Renee Romano and Leigh Raiford, eds., *The Civil Rights Movement in American Memory* (Athens: University of Georgia Press, 2006), especially the introduction.

10. The three most intense race riots of the period alone—those in Watts in 1965 and in Detroit and Newark in 1967—resulted in 103 deaths, approximately 90 percent of them of African Americans.

11. Accounts from the time, and later in the trials, revealed that some York policemen had attended "White Power" rallies in the wake of Officer Schaad's shooting and had encouraged local whites to protect their neighborhoods by killing blacks if necessary. "York (Pennsylvania) Riots of 1969," *Encyclopedia of American Race Riots*, vol. 2, ed. Walter Rucker and James Nathaniel Upton (Westport, CT: Greenwood Press, 2007), 723–729; Melissa Tyrrell, "The Desire to Forget Remains Strong," *York Daily Record*, June 25, 1999.

12. Darryl Fears, "In Pa. City, Balancing Two Deaths; Officials' Tenacity Led to Break in '69 Cases," *Washington Post*, November 4, 2001, A3; William Bunch, "Handcuffed by History," *New York Times*, September 2, 2001, SM28.

13. Jeanne Theoharis offers an excellent overview of the ways in which "foregrounding the South has constricted popular understandings of race and racism in the United States during and after World War II." See the introduction to Jeanne Theoharis and Komozi Woodard, eds., *Freedom North: Black Freedom Struggles outside the South, 1940–1980* (New York: Palgrave MacMillan, 2003), 2.

14. "The Attorney General's Second Annual Report to Congress Pursuant to the Emmett Till Unsolved Civil Rights Crime Act of 2007," October 2012, http://www.justice.gov/crt/about/crm/documents/cold_case_report_2012.pdf.

15. David Garrow, "Unfinished Business: Yes, We Should Revisit Civil Rights 'Cold Cases.' But Not Just Those from the '60s and Deep South," *Los Angeles Times*, July 8, 2007, M1. For a more extended critique of the law as framing racism as a thing only of the past, see Barbara Schwabauer, "The Emmett Till Unsolved Civil Rights Crime Act: The Cold Case of Racism in the American Justice System," 71 *Ohio St. L.J.* 653 (2010).

16. Jackson quoted in Monica Davey and Gretchen Ruethling, "After 50 Years, Emmett Till's Body Is Exhumed," *New York Times*, June 2, 2005, A12; Everett quoted in Charles Sheehan, "Body of Emmett Till Exhumed in Illinois," *Chicago Tribune*, June 2, 2005.

17. Deavours Nix died before his case could come to trial. Charles Noble's trial ended in a mistrial after charges of illegal contact between the prosecutor and a witness. Noble has not been retried.

18. *United States v. Ernest Henry Avants*, the United States District Court for the Southern District of Mississippi, Western Division, Jackson, MS, 2003; Jerry Mitchell, "The Last Days of Ben Chester White," *Clarion-Ledger*, February 23, 2003.

19. *United States vs. James Seale*, U.S. District Court, Southern District of Mississippi, Jackson Division, 2007; Civil Rights and Restorative Justice Project, "The Dee-Moore Case," http://nuweb9.neu.edu/civilrights/dee-moore-documentary/; Donna Ladd, "The Klansman Bound: The Crime," *Jackson Free Press*, May 22, 2007; *Mississippi Cold Case*, directed by David Ridgen (Canadian Broadcasting Company, 2007).

20. There have been four books by scholars or journalists about contemporary civil rights trials to date. See Maryanne Vollers, *Ghosts of Mississippi: The Murder of Medgar Evers, the Trials of Byron De La Beckwith, and the Haunting of the New South* (Boston: Little, Brown and Company, 1995); Adam Nossiter, *Of Long Memory: Mississippi and the Murder of Medgar Evers* (Reading, MA: Addison-Wesley, 1994; repr., Cambridge, MA: Da Capo Press, 2002); Howard Ball, *Justice in Mississippi: The Murder Trial of Edgar Ray Killen* (Lawrence: University of Kansas Press, 2006); and Harry MacLean, *The Past Is Never Dead: The James Seale Trial and Mississippi's Struggle for Redemption* (New York: Basic Civitas Books, 2009). In addition, Bobby DeLaughter, the lead prosecutor in the Beckwith trial, has written a memoir about that experience. Doug Jones, a prosecutor in the 2001 and 2002 Birmingham church bombing trials, is currently writing a book about those trials, and Jerry Mitchell, a reporter for Jackson's *Clarion-Ledger* whose investigations have spurred the reopenings of many of these cases, is writing a book about the trials.

1. Crimes and Complicity during the Civil Rights Era

1. Martin Luther King Jr., "A Witness to Truth," March 15, 1965, reprinted in *InSpire*, a publication of the Princeton Theological Seminary, Winter 2002, 28, http://www.ptsem.edu/Publications/inspire2/6.2/pdf/feature4.pdf; Martin Luther King Jr., eulogy for Addie Mae Collins, Denise McNair, and Cynthia Wesley, delivered at Birmingham's Sixth Avenue Baptist Church, September 18, 1963, reprinted in James M. Washington, ed., *A Testament of Hope: The Essential Writings and Speeches of Martin Luther King, Jr.* (San Francisco: Harper and Row, 1986), 221.

2. Boutwell quoted in *Birmingham News*, September 16, 1963, 21. Boutwell's sense that he was an innocent victim stemmed in part from his lack of power as mayor; in the fall of 1963, extreme segregationist Bull Connor still held most of the political power in the city despite voters' recent approval of a new form of municipal government there.

3. On the colonial era, see Kirsten Fischer, *Suspect Relations: Sex, Race, and Resistance in Colonial North America* (Ithaca, NY: Cornell University Press, 2002), 160; quote from Carol Emberton, *Beyond Redemption: Race, Violence, and the American South after the Civil War* (Chicago: University of Chicago Press, 2013), 187.

4. On lynching, see W. Fitzhugh Brundage, *Lynching in the New South: Georgia and Virginia, 1880–1930* (Urbana: University of Illinois Press, 1993); Philip Dray, *At the Hands of Persons Unknown: The Lynching of Black America* (New York: Modern Library, reprint ed., 2003); Sherilynn Ifill, *On the Courthouse Lawn: Confronting the Legacy of Lynching in the Twenty-First Century* (Boston: Beacon Press, 2007).

5. Robert Patterson quoted in Michael Newton, *The Ku Klux Klan in Mississippi: A History* (Jefferson, NC: McFarland and Co. Publishers, 2010), 108.

6. National Association for the Advancement of Colored People, "M is for Mississippi and Murder," November 1955, pamphlet from the Campbell (Will D.) Papers, University of Southern Mississippi Digital Collections, http://digilib.usm.edu/cdm4/document.php?CISOROOT=/manu&CISOPTR=2834&REC=6.

7. The FBI released a list of 125 cold cases in 2012, but it believes that 20 percent of those cases should not be considered hate crimes. In 2012, the Cold Case Justice Initiative, a project launched by two law professors at Syracuse University, came up with a list of 196 "suspicious deaths" in ten states from the civil rights era that they believed demanded further investigation. "Justice Department Provided New List of Suspected Civil Rights Era Murders," *Concordia Sentinel*, October 7, 2012.

8. Ashraf Rushdy, *The End of American Lynching* (New Brunswick, NJ: Rutgers University Press, 2012), 94–98.

9. Quote of Clarence Rowe from Eric Deggans, "Lest We Forget," *St. Petersburg Times*, January 15, 2001, 1D. For more on Harry Moore see Ben Green, *Before His Time: The Untold Story of Harry T. Moore, America's First Civil Rights Martyr* (New York: Free Press, 1999).

10. Kaylie Simon, "Lost Life, A Miscarriage of Justice: The Death of John Earl Reese," http://nuweb9.neu.edu/civilrights/wp-content/uploads/Lost_Life_a_Miscarriage_of_Justice_The_Death_of_John_Earl_Reese.pdf; Tim Padgett and Frank Sikora, "The Legacy of Virgil Ware," *Time*, September 22, 2003, 53–59.

11. Bill Shipp, *Murder at Broad River Bridge: The Slaying of Lemuel Penn by Members of the Ku Klux Klan* (Atlanta: Peachtree Publishers Limited, 1981), 7, 59, 14.

12. Quoted in William Bradford Huie, "A Shocking Story of Approved Killing in Mississippi," *Look*, January 24, 1956, 46–49, http://www.pbs.org/wgbh/amex/till/sfeature/sf_look_confession.html.

13. Frank Morris's death has been the subject of extraordinary reporting by Stanley Nelson of the *Concordia Sentinel*. Many of the over 120 stories Nelson has written about Morris's murder are available at the Civil Rights Cold Case Project, http://coldcases.org/cases/frank-morris-case.

14. Two of the bodies were those of Henry Dee and Charles Moore. The third body belonged to fourteen-year-old Herbert Oarsby, found wearing a Congress of Racial Equality t-shirt. Marshall Jones, "In the Mississippi River," *Voices of the Civil Rights Movement: Black American Freedom Songs* (Smithsonian Folkways, 1997).

15. Evers quoted in Jerry Mitchell, "Klan Fear Hampered Justice in Slayings," *Clarion-Ledger*, February 13, 2000, http://www.clarionledger.com/crimes/moore2–13.html; Hodding Carter, "We Are Paying and Will Continue to Pay a Price for It, Both in the Sight of God and Our Fellow Man," *Delta Democrat-Times*, September 21, 1955, quoted in M. Susan Orr-Klopfer with Fred and Barry Klopfer, *Where Rebels Roost: Mississippi Civil Rights Revisited*, 2nd ed. (Lulu.com, 2005), 2666.

16. Newton, *The Ku Klux Klan in Mississippi*, 115, 118; David Chalmers, *Backfire: How the Ku Klux Klan Helped the Civil Rights Movement* (Lanham, MD: Rowman and Littlefield, 2003), 5, 20; interview with David Cunningham, "'Klansville, U.S.A.' Chronicles the Rise and Fall of the KKK," *Fresh Air*, National Public Radio, February 14, 2013.

17. David Cunningham, "The Civil Rights–Era Ku Klux Klan in Mississippi," http://nuweb9.neu.edu/civilrights/?page_id=978; Chalmers, *Backfire*, 15–16, 52.

18. "Central casting" quote from Adam Cohen, "The Widow and the Wizard," *Time*, May 18, 1998; "elimination" from Roy K. Moore to Edwin B. Zeigler, Chief US Probation Officer, Gulfport, MS, December 11, 1967, Fact Sheet on Sam Holloway Bowers, Box 42, Folder 2, Helfrich (Robert B.) Papers, M410, McCain Library and Archives, University of Southern Mississippi, Hattiesburg, MS. For more on Sam Bowers, see Charles Marsh, *God's Long Summer: Stories of Faith and Civil Rights* (Princeton, NJ: Princeton University Press, 1997), chapter 2.

19. On the Cahaba boys, see Elizabeth Cobbs/Petric Smith, *Long Time Coming: An Insider's Story of the Birmingham Church Bombing That Rocked the World* (Birmingham, AL: Crane Hill Publishers, 1994), 56–58; Diane McWhorter, *Carry Me Home: Birmingham, Alabama, the Climatic Battle of the Civil Rights Revolution* (New York: Touchstone, 2002), 483–485. On other Klan splinter groups, see *Intimidation, Reprisal, and Violence in the South's Racial Crisis*, published jointly by Southeastern Office, American Friends Service Committee, Dept. of Racial and Cultural Relations, National Council of the Churches of Christ

in the United States of America [and] Southern Regional Council (Atlanta: Southern Regional Council, 1959); Stanley Nelson, "Klansman's Son Recalls Shamrock, Silver Dollar Group, Meeting Joe Edward," *Concordia Sentinel,* January 15, 2009; Newton, *The Ku Klux Klan in Mississippi,* 159.

20. Newton, *The Ku Klux Klan in Mississippi,* 133–134; Chalmers, *Backfire,* 56.
21. Paul Good, "Klan Hand Seen in Most Acts of Rights Violence," *Washington Post,* March 27, 1965, A15. See for example the letter sent by James Ford Seale to the *Franklin Advocate,* July 23, 1964, http://www.clarionledger.com/assets/pdf/D065560312.pdf.
22. Jeff Woods, *Black Struggle, Red Scare: Segregation and Anti-Communism in the South, 1948–1968* (Baton Rouge: Louisiana State University Press, 2004), 3, 2.
23. See Gail Williams O'Brien, *The Color of Law: Race, Violence, and Justice in the Post-WWII South* (Chapel Hill: University of North Carolina Press, 1999).
24. Seth Cagin and Philip Dray, *We Are Not Afraid: The Story of Goodman, Schwerner, and Chaney and the Civil Rights Campaign for Mississippi* (New York: Macmillan, 1988), 303–305, campaign quote from 8; Florence Mars with the assistance of Lynn Eden, *Witness in Philadelphia* (Baton Rouge: University of Louisiana Press, 1977), 77–78; "maggot" quote from Stanley Nelson, "DeLaughter, Poissot Linked to Criminal Acts in 1964–65," *Concordia Sentinel,* March 23, 2011, http://www.concordiasentinel.com/news.php?id=6024.
25. "2 Now-Dead Officers Blamed in '67 Death at Jackson State Riot," *Commercial Appeal,* May 31, 2001; Civil Rights and Restorative Justice, "Benjamin Brown," http://nuweb9.neu.edu/civilrights/benjamin-brown/. On Fowler, see John Fleming, "The Death of Jimmie Lee Jackson," *Anniston Star,* March 6, 2005, http://www.annistonstar.com/pages/full_story/push?article-The+Death+of+Jimmie+Lee+Jackson%20&id=2746471&instance=special.
26. Cunningham, "The Civil Rights–Era Ku Klux Klan in Mississippi."
27. Local blacks had, in fact, recently begun organizing in their own self-defense, forming what was likely an unofficial chapter of the Deacons of Defense. The Klansmen were likely responding to rumors about these organized self-defense efforts, although efforts never involved any importation of guns.
28. Killen quote from Jerry Mitchell, "Atmosphere in '60s Made Violence Possible," *Clarion-Ledger,* June 28, 2010, http://blogs.clarionledger.com/jmitchell/2010/06/28/atmosphere-of-violence-in-1960s/. Cecil Price statement to Tony Shelburn and Jim Gilliand of the State of Mississippi Office of the Attorney General, 1999, http://www.clarionledger.com/assets/pdf/D093035121.pdf.
29. Karl Fleming, *Son of the Rough South: An Uncivil Memoir* (New York: Public-Affairs, 2005), 253; "Sheriff Says Shots Fired by Agitators," *Clarion-Ledger,* September 11, 1962; Cunningham, "The Civil Rights–Era Ku Klux Klan in Mississippi."

30. A. L. Hopkins, "Investigation of Whippings and Armed Robberies of Negro Men in Adams County by Hooded or Masked White Men," February 20, 1964, SCR ID# 2-63-1-114-1-1-1, Series 2515: Mississippi State Sovereignty Commission Records, Mississippi Deparmtent of Archives and History, http://mdah.state.ms.us/arrec/digital_archives/sovcom/result.php?image=images/png/cd04/025910.png&otherstuff=2|63|1|114|1|1|1|25417|; Journal of Reverend Clyde Briggs, 1964, http://www.jacksonfreepress.com/foi_pdfs/briggs_journal.pdf.

31. Jason Sokol, *There Goes My Everything: White Southerners in the Age of Civil Rights* (New York: Knopf, 2006), 307; Fleming, *Son of the Rough South*, 244.

32. Newton, *The Ku Klux Klan in Mississippi*, 108, 115; Neil McMillen, *The Citizens' Council: Organized Resistance to the Second Reconstruction* (Urbana: University of Illinois Press, 1994), 152.

33. CC leader quoted in Joseph Crespino, *In Search of Another Country: Mississippi and the Conservative Counterrevolution* (Princeton, NJ: Princeton University Press, 2007), 26; McWhorter, *Carry Me Home*, 15, 17; McMillen, *The Citizens' Council*, 343.

34. For more on the backlash, see Michael Klarman, "How *Brown* Changed Race Relations: The Backlash Thesis," *Journal of American History* 81 (June 1994): 81–118.

35. Dan T. Carter, *The Politics of Rage: George Wallace, the Origins of the New Conservatism and the Transformation of American Politics* (New York: Simon and Schuster, 1995), 96, 320.

36. Crespino, *In Search of Another Country*, 43–44. For more on the Mississippi Sovereignty Commission, see Yasuhiro Katagiri, *The Mississippi State Sovereignty Commission: Civil Rights and States' Rights* (Jackson: University Press of Mississippi, 2001). On the Alabama Commission, see Wayne Greenhaw, *Fighting the Devil in Dixie: How Civil Rights Activists Took on the Ku Klux Klan* (Chicago: Lawrence Hill Books, 2011), 101–102. Similar commissions also existed in Georgia, Louisiana, and Florida.

37. Maryanne Vollers, *Ghosts of Mississippi: The Murder of Medgar Evers, the Trials of Byron De La Beckwith, and the Haunting of the New South* (Boston: Little, Brown and Company, 1995), 53.

38. Lee Cole to Erle Johnston Jr., November 15, 1967, SCR ID #2-49-0-64-1-1-1, Mississippi State Sovereignty Commission, http://mdah.state.ms.us/arrec/digital_archives/sovcom/result.php?image=images/png/cd04/025910.png&otherstuff=2|63|1|114|1|1|1|25417|; Howard Ball, *Justice in Mississippi: The Murder Trial of Edgar Ray Killen* (Lawrence: University Press of Kansas, 2006), 33.

39. Erle Johnston Jr. to Hon. Herman Glazier, Executive Assistant, Office of the Governor, January 25, 1965, Box 37, Folder 1, Paul B. Johnson Family Papers, M191, McCain Library and Archives, University of Southern

Mississippi, Hattiesburg, MS; Erle Johnston Jr. to Laurance S. Carlson, April 23, 1965, Box 137, Folder 4, Johnson Papers.

40. McComb mayor quoted in Erle Johnston, *Mississippi's Defiant Years, 1953–1973: An Interpretive Documentary with Personal Experiences* (Forest, MS: Lake Harbor Publication, 1990), 313; Johnson quote from "No Signs of Violence Found in the Disappearance of 3 Men," *Meridian Star*, June 24, 1964, reprinted in Associated Press State and Local Wire, December 29, 1999; Cagin and Dray, *We Are Not Afraid*, 341–342.

41. Rita Schwerner Bender comments on *Morning Edition*, National Public Radio, November 2, 2000; Quote from Paul Good, "Klan Hand Seen in Most Acts of Rights Violence," *Washington Post*, March 27, 1965, A15.

42. Charles Morgan Jr., *A Time to Speak* (New York: Harper and Row, 1964), 164.

43. Andrew M. Manis, "'Dying from the Neck Up': Southern Baptist Resistance to the Civil Rights Movement," *Baptist History and Heritage* 34 (Winter 1999): 33–48; Bill J. Leonard, "A Theology for Racism: Southern Fundamentalists and the Civil Rights Movement," *Baptist History and Heritage* 34 (Winter 1999): 49–68; Andrew W. Manis, "Silence or Shockwaves: Southern Baptist Reponses to the Assassination of Martin Luther King, Jr.," *Baptist History and Heritage* 15 (October 1980): 19–27, 35.

44. Alabama pastor quoted in Leonard, "A Theology for Racism," 63; Charles Marsh, *The Last Days: A Son's Story of Sin and Segregation at the Dawn of a New South* (New York: Basic Books, 2001), 44, 104.

45. Davis Houck, "Killing Emmett," *Rhetoric and Public Affairs* 8, no. 2 (2005): 231; "Accused in 1964 Mississippi Race Slayings Wrote Hate Letter," *CBC News*, http://www.cbc.ca/world/story/2007/03/08/cold-case.html. For more on the southern media in the 1950s and 1960s, see David R. Davies, *The Press and Race: Mississippi Journalists Confront the Movement* (Jackson: University Press of Mississippi, 2001); Bill Minor, "Minor Redeems the *Clarion-Ledger*," *Neshoba Democrat*, November 16, 2005; Janis L. McDonald, "Heroes or Spoilers? The Role of the Media in the Prosecutions of Unsolved Civil Rights Era Murders," 34 *Ohio N.U.L. Rev.* 797 (2008).

46. "Meddling in Local Case Creates Problems," *Greenwood Morning Star*, September 6, 1955, reprinted in Christopher Metress, ed., *The Lynching of Emmett Till: A Documentary Narrative* (Charlottesville: University of Virginia Press, 2002), 28; *Meridian Star* quoted in Claude Sitton, "Tragedy in Mississippi," *New York Times*, August 9, 1964, E6.

47. Carter quote from Jerry Mitchell, "44 Days Changed Mississippi: Newspaper Stories 'Maintained Status Quo,'" *Clarion-Ledger*, June 18, 2000, A18.

48. Marsh, *The Last Days*, 18–19; Morgan Jr., *A Time to Speak*, 93.

49. Chalmers, *Backfire*, 27; Claude Sitton, "Inquiry into the Mississippi Mind," *New York Times Magazine*, April 28, 1963, 13.

50. "Designed to Inflame," *Jackson Daily News*, September 2, 1955, reprinted in Metress, ed. *The Lynching of Emmett Till*, 21.

51. Excerpts of Whitaker's thesis were published in 2005. Hugh Stephen Whitaker, "A Case Study in Southern Justice: The Murder and Trial of Emmett Till," *Rhetoric and Public Affairs* 8 (2005): 189–224, quote from 198. For an excellent analysis of the changing press coverage, see Davis W. Houck, "Killing Emmett," *Rhetoric and Public Affairs* 8 (2005): 225–262.

52. Vollers, *Ghosts of Mississippi*, 155–156; Adam Nossiter, *Of Long Memory: Mississippi and the Murder of Medgar Evers* (Reading, MA: Addison-Wesley, 1994: repr., Cambridge, MA: Da Capo Press, 2002), 107–109.

53. Ira B. Harkey Jr., *The Smell of Burning Crosses* (Jacksonville, IL: Harris-Wolfe & Co., 1967), 13–19, quotes from 15, 17.

54. Virgina Durr to Clark and Mairi Foreman, February 27, 1957, in Patricia Sullivan, ed., *Freedom Writer: Virginia Foster Durr, Letters from the Civil Rights Years* (New York: Routledge, 2003), 140; Durr to Clark Foreman, July 22, 1957, *Freedom Writer*, 150. See also Mary Stanton, *Journey towards Justice: Juliette Hampton Morgan and the Montgomery Bus Boycott* (Athens: University of Georgia Press, 2006).

55. The Heffners' story is recounted in Johnston, *Mississippi's Defiant Years*, 312–316, quote from 316. Hodding Carter recounted their story in *So the Heffners Left McComb: What Happens to an Innocent Family When Violence Goes Unchecked* (New York: Doubleday, 1965).

56. Cagin and Dray, *We Are Not Afraid*, 345–348, quote from 246; Mars describes her treatment in *Witness in Philadelphia*, xvi, 134–140.

57. Mr. Rosen to F. L. Price, FBI Memo, August 29, 1955, 2, in "Emmett Till Murder FBI–White House–State of Mississippi Files," CD-ROM, BACM Research (Paperless Archive, 2008); F. L. Price to Rosen, September 2, 1955, "Emmett Till Murder," BACM Research.

58. Quote from Marsh, *The Last Days*, 19. On the FBI's relationship to and view of the civil rights struggle, see Kenneth O'Reilly, *"Racial Matters": The FBI's Secret File on Black America, 1960–1972* (New York: Free Press, 1989); David Cunningham, *There's Something Happening Here: The New Left, the Klan, and FBI Counterintelligence* (Berkeley: University of California Press, 2004); Michael Belknap, *Federal Law and Southern Order: Racial Violence and Constitutional Conflict in the Post-Brown South* (Athens: University of Georgia Press, 1987).

59. Belknap, *Federal Law and Southern Order*, ix, 73.

60. "Eulogies for James Chaney, August 7, 1964," Document # 7INT30, Project on Lived Theology, University of Virginia, Charlottesville, VA.

61. See Belknap, *Federal Law and Southern Order*, for a detailed history of this shift. In his account of the FBI's COINTELPRO operations against the Klan, David Cunningham finds, though, that unlike the COINTELPRO operations directed at black power groups and the New Left, those directed at the Klan sought only to contain the organization, not to destroy it. Cunningham, *There's Something Happening Here*.

62. Howard Zinn, "The Federal Bureau of Intimidation," in Howard Zinn with Donaldo Macedo, *Howard Zinn on Democratic Education* (Boulder, CO: Paradigm Publishers, 2008), 179.

63. "Lawyer in Birmingham Blames Whites, Saying 'We All Did It,'" *New York Times*, September 17, 1963, 24; Morgan, *A Time to Speak*, 11–13, 167.

2. *"Jim Crow" Justice*

1. "City Pledges All-Out Hunt for Bomber," *Birmingham News*, September 16, 1963, 1; "Bomber Challenge Must Be Met," *Birmingham News*, September 16, 1963, 25; "The Shock and the Shame," *Birmingham News*, September 16, 1963, 4.

2. Southern Regional Council, "Southern Justice: An Indictment," October 18, 1965, 24, Civil Rights in Mississippi Digital Archive, University of Southern Mississippi Digital Collections, http://digilib.usm.edu/cdm/compoundobject/collection/manu/id/3201/rec/5.

3. W. E. B. Du Bois, "Race Relations in the United States, 1917–1947," *Phylon* 9 (1948): 237, quoted in Neil R. McMillen, *Dark Journey: Black Mississippians in the Age of Jim Crow* (Chicago: University of Illinois Press, 1990), 197.

4. "Southern Justice: An Indictment," 5; Neil Maxwell, "The Liuzzo Case," *Wall Street Journal*, May 4, 1965, 16.

5. Mississippi Civil Rights Project. "Rev. George Lee and Gus Courts," William Winter Institute, http://www.winterinstitute.org/county/?q=node/102; J. Todd Moye, *Let the People Decide: Black Freedom and White Resistance Movements in Sunflower County, Mississippi, 1945–1985* (Chapel Hill: University of North Carolina Press, 2004), 80; John Dittmer, *Local People: The Struggle for Civil Rights in Mississippi* (Chicago: University of Illinois Press, 1995), 54.

6. Hugh Stephen Whitaker, "A Case Study in Southern Justice: The Murder and Trial of Emmett Till," *Rhetoric and Public Affairs* 8, no. 2 (2005): 212; "Alabama Sets Murder Charge in Killing of Postman in March," *New York Times*, April 28, 1963, 84; "Alabama Jury Refuses to Indict in Murder of Hiking Postman," *New York Times*, September 14, 1963, 11. McDowell quote from Christopher Sullivan, "Part II: No Action by Prosecutors in Many Unsolved Cases," *Associated Press*, October 21, 1991.

7. Grand jury report quoted in Howard Ball, *Justice in Mississippi: The Murder Trial of Edgar Ray Killen* (Lawrence: University Press of Kansas, 2006), 45.

8. *State of Mississippi v. James "Doc" Caston, Charles E. Caston, Harold Spivey Crimm, and Dennis Howell Newton*, Circuit Court of Humphreys County, Belzoni, MS, March 18, 1999, vol. 1-A, 84A; "1970 Murder Case Gains Impetus," *Associated Press State and Local Wire*, September 23, 1998, PM Cycle.

9. Kenneth O'Reilly, *"Racial Matters": The FBI's Secret File on Black America, 1960–1972* (New York: Free Press, 1989), 24.

10. J. Edgar Hoover, "Racial Tension and Civil Rights," confidential report to the Cabinet, March 1, 1956, in "Emmett Till Murder FBI–White House–State of Mississippi Files," CD-ROM, BACM Research (Paperless Archives, 2008), 24.

11. Ben Green, *Before His Time: The Untold Story of Harry T. Moore, America's First Civil Rights Martyr* (New York: Free Press, 1999), 229. For a detailed description of the FBI investigation, see ibid., 229–238.

12. "Cold Case: The Murder of Louis Allen," *Sixty Minutes*, April 7, 2011, transcript, http://www.cbsnews.com/2100–18560_162–20051850–2.html?pageNum =2&tag=contentMain;contentBody.

13. A. B. Caldwell quoted in Michael Belknap, *Federal Law and Southern Order: Racial Violence and Constitutional Conflict in the Post-*Brown *South* (Athens: University of Georgia Press, 1987), 17. On the lack of action by the Eisenhower and Kennedy administrations, see ibid., chapters 2–4.

14. Warren Brown Washington, "Ex-Klan Informer Hits Birmingham Police," *Washington Post*, July 30, 1978, A2; Howell Raines, "Inquiries Link Informer for the F.B.I. to Major Klan Terrorism in '60s," *New York Times*, July 17, 1978, A1, A12. For a detailed history of the FBI's relationship with Gary Thomas Rowe, see Gary May, *The Informant: The FBI, the Ku Klux Klan, and the Murder of Viola Liuzzo* (New Haven, CT: Yale University Press, 2005). See also Diane McWhorter, "Bureau's Blunders," *Birmingham News*, May 20, 2001.

15. In her memoir, *Long Time Coming: An Insider's Story of the Birmingham Church Bombing That Rocked the World* (Birmingham: Crane Hill Publishers, 1994), Elizabeth Cobbs/Petric Smith, niece of one of the eventually convicted bombers, accuses state officials of working with the Klan to impede the FBI investigation (102). Diane McWhorter agrees with this take on the arrests. See McWhorter, *Carry Me Home: Birmingham, Alabama, the Climatic Battle of the Civil Rights Revolution* (New York: Touchstone, Simon and Schuster, 2001), 548–549.

16. See Renee Romano, "Narratives of Redemption: The Birmingham Church Bombing Trials and the Construction of Civil Rights Memory," in *The Civil Rights Movement in American Memory*, ed. Renee Romano and Leigh Raiford (Athens: University of Georgia Press, 2006), 109–111. Diane McWhorter notes that Rowe's FBI handlers instructed him to steer clear of the scene of the bombing for at least a week after it happened so that he would not show up as a suspect in any state or local investigations. McWhorter, *Carry Me Home*, 547, 553.

17. Cobbs/Smith, *Long Time Coming*, 138.

18. McNair quoted in Susan Willoughby Anderson, "The Past on Trial: The Sixteenth Street Baptist Church Bombing, Civil Rights Memory and the Remaking of Birmingham" (PhD diss., University of North Carolina, Chapel Hill, 2008), 98.

19. Although this is by no means an exhaustive list, I have found that state trials were held in the case of the following murders: Emmett Till (killed in MS

in 1955); Clifford Melton (MS, 1955); Howard Bromley (VA, 1955); James Earl Reese (TX, 1955); C. H. Baldwin (AL, 1956); Bessie McDowell (AL, 1956); Woodrow Wilson Daniels (1958, MS); Hattie Carroll (MD, 1963); Virgil Ware (AL, 1963); Medgar Evers (MS, 1963); Johnnie Mae Chappell (FL, 1964); Lemuel Penn (GA, 1964); Willie Brewster (AL, 1965); Viola Liuzzo (AL, 1965); James Reeb (AL, 1965); Jonathan Daniels (AL, 1965); Clarence Triggs (LA, 1966); Ben Chester White (MS, 1966); Vernon Dahmer (MS, 1966); Sammy Younge (AL, 1966). Most of the defendants faced charges of murder or manslaughter, although two of the trials were on arson charges rather than murder in the firebombing of Vernon Dahmer's house in 1966. Eight of these murder cases resulted in some kind of conviction (with a total of eleven men being convicted in court), twelve cases resulted in acquittals (for a total of seventeen men being acquitted), and eight trials ended with hung juries.

20. *State of Mississippi v. Sam Holloway Bowers*, Court Reporter's Transcript of Trial, vol. 3, Circuit Court of Forrest County, MS, August 19, 1998, 472–473; Virginia Durr to Jessica Mitford, May 31, 1965, reprinted in Patricia Sullivan, ed., *Freedom Writer: Virginia Foster Durr, Letters from the Civil Rights Years* (New York: Routledge, 2003), 334.

21. "Charleston Sheriff Says Body in River Wasn't Young Till," *Memphis Commercial Appeal*, September 4, 1955, reprinted in Christopher Metress, ed., *The Lynching of Emmett Till: A Documentary Narrative* (Charlottesville: University of Virginia Press, 2002), 36; "Grand Jury Gets Case: Troops Posted in Delta as Mob Violence Feared in Aftermath to Slaying," *Jackson Daily News*, September 5, 1955, reprinted in Metress, *The Lynching of Emmett Till*, 38.

22. The blacks who testified had to be protected by armed guards during the trial, and all subsequently fled the state. See testimony of Willie Reed, September 22, 1955, trial transcript, *State of Mississippi v. J. W. Milam and Roy Bryant*, September Term 1955, Circuit Court, 2nd District of Tallahatchie County, available on "Emmett Till Murder," CD-ROM; Whitaker, "A Case Study in Southern Justice," 214.

23. M. Susan Orr-Klopfer, *The Emmett Till Book* (self-published, 2005), 23–31; James L. Hicks, "Sheriff Kept Key Witness Hid in Jail during Trial," *Cleveland Call and Post*, October 8, 1955, reprinted in Metress, ed., *The Lynching of Emmett Till*, 155–160.

24. Maryanne Vollers, *Ghosts of Mississippi: The Murder of Medgar Evers, the Trials of Byron De La Beckwith, and the Haunting of the New South* (Boston: Little, Brown and Company, 1995), 188–189.

25. Jerry Mitchell, "The Last Days of Ben Chester White," *Clarion-Ledger*, February 23, 2003; *United States of America v. Ernest Henry Avants*, trial transcript, United States District Court for the Southern District of Mississippi, Western Division, 2003, 215; *U.S. v. Ernest Henry Avants*, "Motion to Preclude

Introduction of Preliminary Hearing Transcript and Motion to Dismiss," United States District Court, Southern Division of Mississippi, Jackson, MS, September 1, 2000, 7–8.

26. Testimony of Daniel Bickford, special counsel for the Unitarian Universalist Association, U.S. Senate Judiciary Committee Subcommittee on Constitutional Rights. "Civil Rights, Part 1," Session 89–2 (1966), 497–506.

27. Rev. Walter Jones testimony, "Civil Rights, Part 1," 497.

28. Mary Stanton, *From Selma to Sorrow: The Life and Death of Viola Liuzzo* (Athens: University of Georgia Press, 2000), 114, 116.

29. Charles Eagles, *Outside Agitator: Jon Daniels and the Civil Rights Movement in Alabama* (Chapel Hill: University of North Carolina Press, 1993), 195, 236; Jack Nelson, "Coleman Trial Skipped 8 Witnesses for State," *Los Angeles Times*, October 20, 1965, 22.

30. Eagles, *Outside Agitator*, 245.

31. See McMillen, *Dark Journey*, 221–222. All-white, all-male juries heard most of these cases. Mississippi and Alabama did not even allow women to serve as jurors until 1966, and while a handful of black men were sometimes called as jurors, they were very rarely selected. In the first trial of Collie Wilkins for the murder of Viola Liuzzo, for example, the potential juror pool consisted of one hundred white men and one black man.

32. A. L. Hopkins, "Assisting Honorable Stanney Sanders, Defense Attorney for Byron De La Beckwith, Charged with Murdering Medgar Evers, c/m, in Checking the Background of Prospective Jurors," April 9, 1964, Series 2515: Mississippi State Sovereignty Commission Records, Mississippi Department of Archives and History, http://mdah.state.ms.us/arrec/digital_archives/sovcom/result.php?image=images/png/cd04/025910.png&otherstuff=2|63|1|114|1|1|1|25417|#; Paul Johnston, *Mississippi's Defiant Years, 1953–1973* (Forest, MS: Lake Harbor Publishers, 1990), 186–187.

33. Bill Shipp, *Murder at Broad River Bridge: The Slaying of Lemuel Penn by Members of the Ku Klux Klan* (Atlanta: Peachtree Publishers Limited, 1981), 53.

34. Jared Taylor, "The Many Deaths of Viola Liuzzo," *The National Review*, July 10, 1995, p. 38; Roy Reed, "Klansmen Freed in Liuzzo Killing," *New York Times*, October 23, 1965, p. 1; Belknap, *Federal Law and Southern Order*, 140.

35. "Calahan notes," notes taken from the files of the FBI for use in 1998 Bowers Murder Trial, undated, Box 26, Folder 9, Helfrich (Robert B.) Papers, M410, McCain Library and Archives, The University of Southern Mississippi, Hattiesburg, MS; FBI Memo, June 18, 1968, Box 42, Folder 1, Helfrich Papers; Jerry Mitchell, "Bowers Admitted Jury Tampering, Documents Show," *Clarion-Ledger*, March 12, 1998.

36. *State of Mississippi v. Byron De La Beckwith*, trial transcript, Circuit Court of the First Judicial District of Hinds County, MS, January 31, 1964, 9–12.

37. Shipp, *Murder at Broad River Bridge*, 55.

38. For background on this system of sexual racism, see Renee Romano, *Race Mixing: Black-White Marriage in Postwar America* (Cambridge, MA: Harvard University Press, 2003).

39. *MS v. Milam and Bryant*, trial transcript, 49, 176; Eagles, *Outside Agitator*, 231; Jack Nelson, "Jury Acquits Deputy in Rights Death," *Los Angeles Times*, October 1, 1965, 10.

40. For more on the gendered nature of the slandering of Viola Liuzzo, see Jonathan Entin, "Viola Liuzzo and the Gendered Politics of Martyrdom," review essay of *From Selma to Sorrow: The Life and Death of Viola Liuzzo* by Mary Stanton, 23 *Harvard Women's L.J.* 249 (2000).

41. Stanton, *From Selma to Sorrow*, 53–54, 119, 117, 121.

42. Vollers, *Ghosts of Mississippi*, 162; Adam Nossiter, *Of Long Memory: Mississippi and the Murder of Medgar Evers* (Reading, MA: Addison-Wesley, 1994: repr., Cambridge, MA: Da Capo Press, 2002), 153–154. Nossiter provides an excellent discussion of Waller's strategy on 146–155.

43. Stanton, *From Selma to Sorrow*, 113.

44. Patricia Michelle Buzard, "Worth Dying For: The Trials of Vernon F. Dahmer" (MA thesis, University of Southern Mississippi, 2002), 150. Pitts, a Klansman who had participated in the murder, testified before at least four grand juries and served as the star witness in ten state trials and in the federal conspiracy trial. In return, he received FBI protection and payment, which eventually totaled over $10,000. "Calahan Notes"; SAC Jackson to FBI Director, "DABURN State Trial Proceedings, Circuit Court, Forrest County Summary," January 23, 1970, Box 42, Folder 1, Helfrich Papers; Memo, US Dept. of Justice, FBI, Jackson, May 27, 1968. FBI Summary Report on the trial of James Franklin Lyons, JN44–1512, undated, Box 25, Folder 7, Helfrich Papers.

45. Douglas Linder, "Bending toward Justice: John Doar and the 'Mississippi Burning' Trial," 72 *Mississippi L. J.* 731 (Winter 2002), quote from 752.

46. Carpetbagger was a derogatory term coined during the Reconstruction era to refer to Northerners who came South with their suitcases—or "carpet bags"—to impose the will of the Republican federal government on the defeated white Confederacy.

47. Shipp, *Murder at Broad River Bridge*, 68.

48. Vollers, *Ghosts of Mississippi*, 201.

49. The trial transcript does not include the closing arguments. These quotes are drawn from media coverage. See Murray Kempton, "2 Face Trial as 'Whistle' Kidnappers—Due to Post Bond and Go Home," *New York Post*, September 25, 1955, reprinted in Metress, ed., *The Lynching of Emmett Till*, 110, 108.

50. Matt Murphy quoted in William Chapman and Thomas Kendrick, "Alabama Official Says State Will File Murder Charges," *Washington Post*, March 27, 1965, A15; Shipp, *Murder at Broad River Bridge*, 68.

51. Eagles, *Outside Agitator*, 240–241.

52. Shipp, *Murder at Broad River Bridge*, 81–92.

53. Rev. Walter Jones testimony, "Civil Rights, Part 1," 497.

54. In the Dahmer case, Mississippi tried seven men for arson and murder in a series of trials beginning in 1968. When juries returned guilty verdicts against four of the men, it became the first time that the state of Mississippi convicted white men for the murder of a black man.

55. Adam Bernstein, "William Zantzinger, Convicted of Killing Hattie Carroll and Denounced in Bob Dylan Song, Dies at 69," *Los Angeles Times*, January 10, 2009, http://www.latimes.com/news/obituaries/la-me-zantzinger10–2009jan10,0,4825718.story.

56. "Texas: Bad Day in Longview," *Time*, May 6, 1957, http://www.time.com/time/magazine/article/0,9171,809409,00.html.

57. Quoted in "The Legacy of Virgil Ware," *Time*, September 22, 2003, http://www.time.com/time/magazine/article/0,9171,1005718,00.html.

58. "Hometown of Victim Shocked by Acquittal," *Los Angeles Times*, October 1, 1965, 11; *New York Post* quoted in Eagles, *Outside Agitator*, 246; Jack Nelson, "Alabama Court Charade Cries Out for Intervention," *Los Angeles Times*, October 3, 1965, K2.

59. David Nevin, "A Strange, Tight Little Town, Loath to Admit Complicity," *Life*, December 18, 1964, 28.

60. See *United States v. Price et al.*, 383 U.S. 787, 86 S. Ct. 1152 (1966); *United States v. Guest*, 383 U.S. 745 (1966). For more on these two cases and the complexities of the Supreme Court ruling, see Belknap, *Southern Law and Federal Order*, 172–182.

61. *United States v. Cecil Ray Price et al.*, trial transcript, United States District Court, Southern District of Mississippi, 1967, 2386; Howard Ball, *Murder in Mississippi: United States v. Price and the Struggle for Civil Rights* (Lawrence: University Press of Kansas, 2004), 128; Linder, "Bending toward Justice," 760–761.

62. James L. Dickerson and Alex A. Alston Jr., *Devil's Sanctuary: An Eyewitness History of Mississippi Hate Crimes* (Chicago: Chicago Review Press, 2009), 127.

63. Buzard, "Worth Dying For," 131, 133, 191; Roy Reed, "Release of Klansman, Jailed for Killing Black Leader, Is Decried in Mississippi," *New York Times*, December 24, 1972, 17.

64. Linder, "Bending toward Justice," 773.

3. Reopening Civil Rights–Era Murder Cases

1. Jerry Mitchell, "The Case of the Supposedly Sealed Files—And What They Revealed," *Nieman Reports*, Fall 2011, http://www.nieman.harvard.edu/reports/article/102664/The-Case-of-the-Supposedly-Sealed-FilesAnd-What-They-Revealed.aspx; Jerry Mitchell, interview by Terry Gross, *Fresh Air*, National Public Radio, November 22, 2005; Myrlie Evers-Williams with Melinda Blau, *Watch Me Fly: What I Learned on the Way to Becoming the Woman I Was Meant to Be* (Boston: Little, Brown, and Co., 1999), 200.

2. Maryanne Vollers provides a detailed account of Beckwith's two 1964 trials in *Ghosts of Mississippi: The Murder of Medgar Evers, the Trials of Byron De La Beckwith, and the Haunting of the New South* (Boston: Little, Brown and Company, 1995), 161–208.

3. "Evers's Widow Says Files Justify Reopening Assassination Case," *Clarion-Ledger*, October 3, 1989; Evers-Williams, *Watch Me Fly*, 200–201.

4. Bobby DeLaughter, *Never Too Late: A Prosecutor's Story of Justice in the Medgar Evers Case* (New York: Scribner, 2001), 71.

5. Mamie Till Mobley and Christopher Benson, *The Death of Innocence: The Story of the Hate Crime That Changed America* (New York: One World; New York: Ballantine Books, 2003), 130–132; Bo Emerson, "'Town Where They Killed Those Guys' Seeks Justice; Residents Confront Civil Rights Shame," *Atlanta Journal-Constitution*, June 20, 2004, 1A; "Chaney Brother Calls for Additional Inquiry," *Los Angeles Sentinel*, May 31, 1995, A3; Steven Brody, "A Chance for Meridian," *Meridian Star*, undated, http://www.meridianstar.com/archivesearch/local_story_182235121.html/resources_printstory.

6. Yasuhiro Katagari, *The Mississippi State Sovereignty Commission: Civil Rights and States' Rights* (Jackson: University Press of Mississippi, 2001), 228–229. Paul Connerton labels these efforts by governing authorities to coercively expunge an event from historical memory "repressive erasure." See Connerton, "Seven Types of Forgetting," *Memory Studies* 1, no. 1 (2008): 60, http://mss.sagepub.com/content/1/1/59.

7. Lynda Edwards, "Money Residents Say Till Killing Not Often Discussed," *Associated Press State and Local Wire*, May 10, 2004; Carolyn Maull McKinstry with Denise George, *While the World Watched: A Birmingham Bombing Survivor Comes of Age during the Civil Rights Movement* (Carol Stream, IL: Tyndale House Publishers, 2011), 79.

8. Bo Emerson, "'Town Where They Killed Those Guys' Seeks Justice: Residents Confront Civil Rights Shame," *Atlanta Journal-Constitution*, June 20, 2004, 1A; Donna Ladd, "Dredging Up the Past," *Jackson Free Press*, May 29, 2007, http://www.jacksonfreepress.com/news/2007/may/30/dredging-up-the-past-why-mississippians-must-tell; Dearman quoted in Paul Hendrickson, "20 Years Ago, in the Heat of the Night: On the Anniversary of the Murders, Mississippi Guards Its Memories," *Washington Post*, July 10, 1984, C1. See also Dudley Clendinen, "'3 Rights Deaths' Legacy: Peace but No Consensus," *New York Times*, June 24, 1984, 16.

9. Mamie Till Mobley and Christopher Benson, *Death of Innocence: The Story of the Hate Crime That Changed America* (New York: One World; New York: Ballantine Books, 2003), xxii, 243–244, 254.

10. Myrlie Evers with William Peters, *For Us, the Living* (Jackson, MS: Banner Books, University Press of Mississippi, 1967; repr. 1996), 338, 344.

11. Chaney quoted in "Chaney Brother Calls for Additional Inquiry," *Los Angeles Sentinel*, May 31, 1995, A3; telephone interview with John Steele,

November 16, 2007; telephone interview with John Gibson, October 30, 2007.

12. "60 Honor Memory of Rights Workers," *New York Times*, June 25, 1984, D13; Chaney, interview by Kisselhoff, 2000; James Earl Chaney Foundation, http://www.jecf.org. Ben Chaney founded the Chaney Foundation in 1989.

13. Evers, *Watch Me Fly*, 12, 195–196; Till Mobley quoted in Bob Longino, "The Unfinished Story of Emmett Till," *Atlanta Journal-Constitution*, January 5, 2003, 1A; Dahmer quoted in "Activists Family Renews Call for Trials," *Atlanta Journal and Constitution*, April 1, 1995, 5B.

14. *ABC Nightline*, May 29, 1998; Ben Chaney on *The Tavis Smiley Show*, National Public Radio, June 21, 2004, transcript, http://www.lexisnexis. com/lnacui2api/api/version1/getDocCui?lni=4CNT-RGS0-00KC-W13D&c-si=8398&hl=t&hv=t&hnsd=f&hns=t&hgn=t&oc=00240&perma=true; Evers, *Watch Me Fly*, 196.

15. Mark Weiner, *Black Trials: Citizenship from the Beginning of Slavery to the End of Caste* (New York: Alfred A. Knopf, 2004), 9–12.

16. Evers, *Watch Me Fly*, 202, 195; Tamara Lush, "Mother, Then Justice, Stolen Away," *Tampa Bay Times*, October 12, 2005, http://www.sptimes.com/2005/ 10/12/State/Mother__then_justice_.shtml.

17. Evers with Peters, *For Us, the Living*, 5–6; Evers, *Watch Me Fly*, 6; Bender quoted in "Jury Finds Killen Guilty of Manslaughter in Civil Rights Killings," *New York Daily News*, June 22, 2005, and Jerry Mitchell, "Bowers: Klansman Got Away with Murder," *Clarion-Ledger*, December 27, 1998.

18. While other female victims of violence, such as Viola Liuzzo, could be blamed for acting outside traditional gender norms in a way that led to their deaths, these four girls—dressed in their Sunday best and often described as heading to the church bathroom to apply a little makeup before the service when the bomb exploded—were neither engaged in political activism nor violating any gender boundaries.

19. Baxley quoted in Frank Sikora, *Until Justice Rolls Down: The Birmingham Church Bombing Case* (Tuscaloosa: University of Alabama Press, 1991), 39–40; telephone interview with Bill Baxley, September 11, 2006.

20. Joseph Blank, "The Day They Bombed the Church," *Reader's Digest*, November 1978, 117. Initially the FBI insisted that the state investigator ask specifically for the files he wanted to see, an impossible request since he did not really know what information the FBI had. Baxley interview; Bill Cornwell, "The Birmingham Bombing of 1963," *The Nation*, November 5, 1977, 463–465.

21. Bill Cornwell, "Baxley Tells of Push for New Indictments," *Birmingham Post-Herald*, November 19, 1977, A2; "Baxley Expects More Indictments in '60s Birmingham Bombings," *Birmingham News*, September 30, 1977, 1.

22. Gary May, *The Informant: The FBI, the Ku Klux Klan, and the Murder of Viola Liuzzo* (New Haven, CT: Yale University Press, 2005), 289–315; Mary Stanton, *From Selma to Sorrow: The Life and Death of Viola Liuzzo* (Athens: University

of Georgia Press, 1998), 206–210. For a harsh critique of the FBI's actions in response to the 1970s investigations, see Diane McWhorter, "Bureau's Blunders—The FBI Got Caught with Dirty Hands in Birmingham," *Birmingham News*, May 20, 2001.

23. DeWayne Wickham, "Hoover Role in Bombing Case Deserves Our Condemnation," *USA Today*, May 8, 2001, 13A; Bill Baxley, "Why Did the FBI Hold Back Evidence?" *New York Times*, May 3, 2001, A25. For more on the FBI's foot-dragging in this case, see Howell Raines, "Rounding Up the 16th Street Suspects," *New York Times*, July 13, 1997, E16; Raines, "Federal Report Says Hoover Barred Trial for Klansmen in '63 Bombing," *New York Times*, February 18, 1980, A1; *San Diego Union-Tribune*, May 5, 2001, B8.

24. Bill Baxley, interview by Susan Willoughby Anderson, quoted in Anderson, "The Past on Trial: The Sixteenth Street Baptist Church Bombing, Civil Rights Memory and the Remaking of Birmingham" (PhD diss., University of North Carolina, Chapel Hill, 2008), 135; Bill Montgomery, "Trial Opens Monday," *Atlanta Constitution*, November 13, 1977; B. Drummond Ayres Jr., "Case Goes to Jury in Birmingham in '63 Bombing Fatal to 4," *New York Times*, November 18, 1977, A18.

25. "The Chambliss Verdict," *Birmingham News*, November 19, 1977, 9.

26. Quote from Howell Raines, "The Birmingham Bombing," *New York Times Magazine*, July 24, 1983, 25; Baxley interview. Many media articles at the time mentioned the criticism that Baxley was "simply stoking his political ambitions." See for example Richard Boeth with Vern E. Smith, "The South: Arrest in Birmingham," *Newsweek*, October 10, 1977, 32; "More Indictments to Be Sought in '63 Birmingham Bombing," *Washington Post*, October 2, 1977, 5; Bill Cornwell, "The Birmingham Bombing of 1963," *The Nation*, November 5, 1977, 464; Ron Casey, "Baxley Expects More Indictments in '60s Birmingham Bombings," *Birmingham* News, September 30, 1977, 8.

27. Quoted in Raines, "The Birmingham Bombing," 29.

28. Roy L. Brooks, *Rethinking the American Race Problem* (Berkeley: University of California Press, 1992), 25, 26; Weiner, *Black Trials*, 18.

29. Lawrence Bobo, James R. Kluegel, and Ryan A. Smith, "Laissez-Faire Racism: The Crystallization of a Kinder, Gentler, Antiblack Ideology," in *Racial Attitudes in the 1990s: Continuity and Change*, ed. Steven A. Tuch and Jack K. Martin (Westport, CT: Praeger, 1997), 15–41. Tuch and Martin's essay in the same volume documents the slower pace of change in attitudes in the South. See "Regional Differences in Whites' Racial Policy Attitudes," 165–174. On the emergence of color blindness, see Joseph Crespino, *In Search of Another Country: Mississippi and the Conservative Counterrevolution* (Princeton, NJ: Princeton University Press, 2007); Tim Wise, *Colorblind: The Emergence of Post-Racial Politics and the Retreat from Racial Equity* (San Francisco: City Light Publishers, 2010).

30. Till Mobley and Benson, *Death of Innocence*, 254.

31. The SPLC also published a book about the victims listed on the monument, *Free at Last*, which it updated in 2004. This research enabled the memorial to become "an instrument of justice," according to reporter Jerry Mitchell, who consulted *Free at Last* as his guide when he embarked on his project of researching civil rights–era murders. Southern Poverty Law Center, "Civil Rights Memorial History," http://www.splcenter.org/civil-rights-memorial/ history#.UaH0Kb9RHww; Glenn Eskew, "Commemorating the Civil Rights Movement with Monuments in the Urban South," in *Commemoration in America: Essays on Monuments, Memorials, and Memory*, ed. David Gobel and Daves Russell (Charlottesville: University of Virginia Press, 2013), Kindle edition; "SPLC Provides List of Unresolved Civil Rights Era Deaths to FBI," Southern Poverty Law Center Press Release, February 21, 2007.

32. Christopher Metress found over 140 literary works that made notable reference to Till written between 1955 and 2008. Of those, sixty-two were produced in the 1950s and 1960s. Only fifteen appeared in the two subsequent decades, but since 1990, another sixty-two works that mention Till have been produced, including six novels and five plays. See Christopher Metress, "Literary Representations of the Lynching of Emmett Till: An Annotated Bibliography," in *Emmett Till in Literary Memory and Imagination*, ed. Harriet Pollack and Christopher Metress (Baton Rouge: Louisiana State University Press, 2008), 223–250.

33. Baxley quoted in David Holmberg, "The Legacy of Emmett Till," *Palm Beach Post*, September 4, 1994, 1A; Dees quoted in Anne Rochell Konigsmark, "Civil Wrongs: Pressure Builds to Reopen the Unsolved Murders of Civil Rights Activists in 1960s," *Atlanta Journal and Constitution*, February 21, 1999, 1M.

34. The United States and other allies imposed the Nuremburg trials on Germany in order to teach Germans a lesson about the democratic norms and the proper rule of law. In fact, they resembled more the federal trials held in the 1960s when southern states failed to prosecute anyone for racial murders than these contemporary trials in which southern authorities took the lead. On the nature of the Nuremberg trials, see Donald Bloxham, *Genocide on Trial: War Crimes Trials and the Formation of Holocaust History and Memory* (Oxford: Oxford University Press, 2001); Elizabeth Borgwardt, "A New Deal for the Nuremberg Trials: The Limits of Law in Generating Human Rights Reform," *Law and History Review* 26 (Fall 2008): 679–705.

35. John Gibeaut, "Confronting a Dark Past: Recently Released Miss. Files May Aid Retrial of Klansman," *American Bar Association Journal*, June 1998, 26–28, quote from 26; Mitchell quoted in Lauri Lebo, "York Riots Trial Part of a National Pattern," *York Sunday News*, October 6, 2002.

36. Steve Ritea, "Opening Old Wounds," *Times-Picayune*, June 15, 2004, 1; Debra Pickett, "Mississippians Say Till's Killers Won't Go to Jail," *Chicago Sun-Times*, May 16, 2004, 2.

37. DeLaughter, *Never Too Late*, 25; Philip Martin, "Pursuing Byron De La Beck-with," *Arkansas Democrat-Gazette*, February 1, 1994, 7B; "Justice Delayed, Not Denied," *Denver Post*, April 17, 2001, B10.

38. Adams County Sheriff Thomas Ferrell quoted on *20/20*, November 29, 1999 episode.

39. *Mississippi Burning*, directed by Alan Parker (Orion Films, 1988); Stanley Dearman, "Meridian-Laurel Plot Nets Two Neshobans," *Neshoba Democrat*, October 26, 1967, quoted in Mars, *Witness in Philadelphia*, 266; Adam Nossiter, *Of Long Memory: Mississippi and the Murder of Medgar Evers* (Reading, MA: Addison-Wesley, 1994; repr., Cambridge, MA: Da Capo Press, 2002), 227.

40. Molpus quoted in Bill Minor, "Image in Film Worries Mississippians," *New York Times*, January 15, 1989, 16; Peter J. Boyer, "The Yuppies of Mississippi: How They Took Over the Statehouse," *New York Times Magazine*, February 28, 1988, 24; Nossiter, *Of Long Memory*, 222–229, quote from 225; For more on Molpus, see John Sugg, "Racial Healing in Mississippi," *Creative Loafing Atlanta*, June 29, 2005, http://atlanta.creativeloafing.com/gyrobase/racial_healing_in_mississippi/Content?oid=19637.

41. Jack Elliott, "State OKs Marker Near Site of 'Mississippi Burning' Murders," *Associated Press*, May 5, 1989. In his moving apology, Molpus told the audience gathered at the Mount Zion Church, "We wish we could undo it. We are profoundly sorry that they were gone." Remarks by Secretary of State Dick Molpus at the Ecumenical Memorial Service, Mount Zion Church, June 21, 1989, http://www.neshobajustice.com/molpus/1989.htm.

42. On the politics behind the building of the Birmingham Civil Rights Institute, see Glenn Eskew, "The Birmingham Civil Rights Institute and the New Ideology of Tolerance," in *The Civil Rights Movement in American Memory*, ed. Renee Romano and Leigh Raiford (Athens: University of Georgia Press, 2006), 28–66. Vann quote from *Birmingham Post-Herald*, November 19, 1992, cited in Eskew, 29.

43. Trent Watts, "Mississippi's Giant House Party: Being White at the Neshoba County Fair," *Southern Cultures* 8 (June 2002): 38–55, quote from 50.

44. DeLaughter, *Never Too Late*, 59; J. L. Martin quoted in Laurie Evants, "Dahmer Case Changed Racial Strife, Ex-FBI Agent Says," *Hattiesburg American*, February 11, 1990, Box 1, Folder 5, Vernon Dahmer Papers, M250, McCain Library and Archives, University of Southern Mississippi, Hattiesburg, MS.

45. DeLaughter, *Never Too Late*, 62–63.

46. Vollers, *Ghosts of Mississippi*, 259–260; Clay Harden, "The Changing Face of Jackson," *Clarion-Ledger*, October 5, 2003.

47. Myrlie Evers, comments at Crimes of the Civil Rights Era conference, Boston, MA, April 28, 2007.

48. Andrew Jacobs, "In Mississippi Delta Town, an Unwelcome Past Calls," *New York Times*, May 12, 2004, A17; Holmberg, "The Legacy of Emmett Till," *Palm Beach Post*, September 4, 1994, 1A.

49. Interview with Doug Jones, Birmingham, AL, February 11, 2013.

50. Mary Schmich, "New Medgar Evers Trial May Help Mississippi Cleanse Its Past," *Chicago Tribune*, December 23, 1990; "Reno Help Sought for Dahmer Files," *Commercial Appeal* (Memphis), February 17, 1995, 2B; "Survivors of Activist Take Sen. Lott to Task," *Commercial Appeal*, March 28, 1995, 1B.

51. Jerry Mitchell told this story at a university forum at the University of Southern Mississippi in 2000. "Pursuing a Late Justice," video recording (university forum held at University of Southern Mississippi, August 29, 2000), Cook Library, University of Southern Mississippi.

52. Media can be defined as "one of the means or channels of general communication, information, or entertainment in society, as newspapers, radio, or television." The term encompasses the news media, the entertainment media, and those that lie somewhere between the two, or the "infotainment" media. This definition is taken from Matthew Robinson, *Media Coverage of Crime and Criminal Justice* (Durham, NC, Carolina Academic Press, 2011), introduction, http://www.pscj.appstate.edu/media/introduction.html.

53. Interview with Jerry Mitchell, April 1, 2005, Jackson, MS; Sherry Ricchiardi, "Out of the Past," *American Journalism Review*, April–May 2005, http://www.ajr.org/article_printable.asp?id=3852; "Still Seeking the Truth in the South; Jerry Mitchell Has Kept the Fires of Justice Burning," *Charleston Daily Mail*, January 19, 2005; Sheila Hardwell, "Crusading Journalist Tackles One of Mississippi's Darkest Secrets," *Associated Press State and Local Wire*, June 20, 1999; Jerry Mitchell, "Finding Joy in Justice," Journey to Justice blog, March 29, 2010, http://blogs.clarionledger.com/jmitchell/tag/billy-roy-pitts/.

54. Marcel Dufresne, "Exposing the Secrets of Mississippi Racism," *American Journalism Review*, October 1991, http://www.ajr.org/article.asp?id=1311.

55. For more on the popularity and economics of newsmagazines, see David Zurawik and Christina Stoehr, "Eclipsing the Nightly News," *American Journalism Review*, November 1994, http://www.ajr.org/article.asp?id=1706; "Newsmagazine," "*20/20*," "*60 Minutes*," and "*Dateline NBC*" pages on Wikipedia.

56. Ray Surette, "Prologue: Some Unpopular Thoughts about Popular Culture," in *Popular Culture, Crime, and Justice*, ed. Frankie Y. Bailey and Donna C. Hale (Belmont, CT: West/Wadsworth Publishing Company), xxii.

57. Ladd, "Dredging Up the Past."

58. Lee Shearer, "A New Call for Justice," *Athens Banner Herald*, March 27, 2005.

59. *Unsolved Mysteries*, November 14, 1990; "Program Features Firebombing Death of Mississippi Civil Rights Figure," *Associated Press State and Local Wire*, January 6, 2003. The *Cold Case* episode "Strange Fruit" aired in April 2005. It focused on the murder of a black teen in 1963; it included the Martin Luther King Jr. quote, "Our lives begin to end when we become silent about the things that matter." "Wednesday's Woman," an episode from October 2008, told the story of the murder of a young white woman who secretly traveled

to Mississippi in 1964 to volunteer during Freedom Summer. Coldcasepedia, http://www.coldcasepedia.com/episode/2x19-strange-fruit.

60. W. James Booth, *Communities of Memory: On Witness, Identity, and Justice* (Ithaca, NY: Cornell University Press, 2006), 67; Molpus quoted in Ricchiardi, "Out of the Past."

61. On the trend towards coverage of secondary victims, see Carrie Rentschler, *Second Wounds: Victims' Rights and the Media in the U.S.* (Durham, NC: Duke University Press, 2011), 2, 21.

62. "Seeking Justice for a Racial Killing, 40 Years Later," *Dateline NBC*, September 7, 2005, transcript, http://www.msnbc.msn.com/id/8670054/ns/dateline_nbc/t/seeking-justice-racial-killing-years-later/#.UEoDqULbxUQ.

63. *Four Little Girls*, directed by Spike Lee (40 Acres and a Mule Filmworks, 1997).

64. This was the language former Mississippi Secretary of State Dick Molpus used to praise Jerry Mitchell. See Ricchiardi, "Out of the Past."

65. The exception would be the three cases (that of Medgar Evers, Willie Edwards, and Emmett Till) where bodies were exhumed and new autopsies performed in order to prove cause of death or to find bullet fragments. The absence of new scientific evidence in these cases is striking especially given the popularity of DNA evidence and forensic investigations in today's media culture.

66. Holbrook Mohr, "Reward Offered for Info in Unsolved Miss. Civil Rights Murders," *Associated Press State and Local Wire*, December 8, 2005.

67. Donna Ladd, "I Want Justice, Too," *Jackson Free Press*, February 1, 2007, http://www.jacksonfreepress.com/news/2007/feb/01/i-want-justice-too/.

68. Interview with Donna Ladd, February 13, 2013, Jackson, MS; Sheila Weller, "Two Women, Joined by Murder," *Glamour*, July 2004, 150–163. Quote from Donna Ladd, "[Editor's Note] Damned If We Don't," *Jackson Free Press*, October 26, 2005.

69. Ladd interview; David Ridgen, "It Takes a Hard-Driving Team to Uncover the Truth of a Cold Case," *Nieman Reports: Nieman Foundation for Journalism at Harvard*, Fall 2011, http://www.nieman.harvard.edu/reports/article/102662/It-Takes-a-Hard-Driving-Team-to-Uncover-the-Truth-of-a-Cold-Case.aspx.

70. Sheila Dewan, "Push to Resolve Fading Killings of Rights Era," *New York Times*, February 3, 2007, 11. In the course of the investigation, Ridgen and the journalists from the *Jackson Free Press* came into conflict about journalistic methods and ethics, and Moore and Ridgen do not acknowledge the role the *Free Press* played in investigating the case in their public statements.

71. Robin Finn, "Bringing History to Life and a Crime to Light," *New York Times*, May 21, 2004, B2; Amy Goodman, interview by Keith Beauchamp, "The Untold Story of Emmett Till: New Documentary Uncovers Evidence in 1955 Murder," *Democracy Now*, June 15, 2005, transcript, http://www.

democracynow.org/2005/6/15/the_untold_story_of_emmett_louis; "Cong. Rangel and Sen. Schumer Demand: Reopen Emmett Till Case," Congressman Charles B. Rangel Press Releases, U.S. House of Representatives, April 13, 2004, www.house.gov/list/press/ny15_rangel/CBRSchumerEmmettTill-Case041304.html; quote from "Revisiting a Martyrdom," *Time*, May 24, 2004, 57.

72. For the 2008 TV One series *Murder in Black and White* Beauchamp directed four hour-long episodes, each on a different civil rights cold case. *Wanted Justice: Johnnie Mae Chappell* was run by the History Channel in 2009. Then, in 2011, Beauchamp launched the *Injustice Files*, a cable television program aired on the Investigation Discovery Channel that featured a different cold case from the FBI cold case list in each episode. "The Injustice Files Digs Deep into Civil Rights Era Cold Cases," *The Early Show*, February 17, 2011, transcript, http://www.cbsnews.com/stories/2011/02/17/earlyshow/main20032887.shtml?tag=mncol;lst;1; Felicia Lee, "TV Series Tries to Revive Civil Rights Cold Cases," *New York Times*, February 15, 2011; "The Injustice Files: Investigation Discovery," http://investigation.discovery.com/tv/injustice-files/.

73. Michael Hill, "Not Denied, but Delayed 30 Years," *Washington Post*, July 10, 1994, Y6; Nisa Islam Muhammad, "FBI Cold Case Initiative Offers Little Comfort for Families," *Final Call*, December 4, 2009, http://www.finalcall.com/artman/publish/article_6638.com.

74. "Beckwith, Byron De La," Mississippi State University Poll, *Polling the Nations*, April 1994, http://poll.orspub.com/document.php?id=quest94.out_881&type=hitlist&num=0; Jerry Mitchell, "Almost Half in Neshoba Survey Favored Trial in '64 Killings," *Clarion-Ledger*, July 5, 2005; "Americans Seek Justice in Mississippi Burning Murders," Zogby Interactive Poll, May 31, 2005, www.angus-reid.com/polls/18031.americans_seek_justice_in_mississippi_burning_murders.

75. Clyde Smith, "Bring Up Past to Ensure Justice Now," letter to the editor, *Clarion-Ledger*, June 22, 2005; Mike Boteler on News 42, WJTV.com website on response to Edgar Ray Killen's arrest, January 12, 2005; Barbara Marbury, "Letters to the Editor," *Virginian-Pilot*, May 24, 2004, B8; Steve Ritea, "Opening Old Wounds," *Times-Picayune*, June 15, 2004, 1.

76. Reed Branson, "Trial to Revisit '66 Racial Slaying—Miss. Doggedly Persists in Atoning," *Commercial Appeal* (Memphis), February 24, 2003, A1; Baxley interview; DeLaughter, *Never Too Late*, 26, 297.

77. Donna Ladd, "I Felt the Earth Move," *Jackson Free Press*, June 23, 2004, http://www.jacksonfreepress.com/news/2004/jun/23/i-felt-the-earth-move/; Ladd interview; Ladd, "Damned If We Don't," *Jackson Free Press*, October 26, 2005, http://w.jacksonfreepress.com/comments.php?id+7629_0_7_0_C.

78. Emily Wagster Pettus, "Haley Barbour Appears to Have a Confederate Problem," *Huffington Post*, February 17, 2011, http://www.huffington

post.com/2011/02/18/haley-barbour-appears-to-_n_824969.html; Benjamin Greenberg, "Adopt a Racist Boor for Martin Luther King Day," *Hungry Blues*, December 15, 2005, http://www.crmvet.org/comm/core0512.htm; Andrew Ferguson, "The Boy from Yazoo City," *Weekly Standard*, December 27, 2010.

79. "Excerpts from Barbour Speech," *Neshoba Democrat*, June 26, 2004; Tom Gordon, "Barbour: Trial Will Help State," *Birmingham News*, June 18, 2005, 15A ; Julie Goodman, "Miss. Closer to Civil Rights Museum," *USA Today*, June 20, 2007; Executive Order No. 969: Governor's Commission to Establish a National Civil Rights Museum in Mississippi, September 21, 2006, http://www.governorbarbour.com/proclamations/Executive%20Order%20Home%20age/EO-CivilRightsMuseum969.htm; Haley Barbour, "Remarks at the Inaugural Meeting of the Governor's Commission to Establish a National Civil Rights Museum in Mississippi," September 21, 2006, http://www.governorbarbour.com/speeches/CivilRightsMuseuemCommissionRemarks.htm.

80. The language of "infrastructure" is borrowed from Dan Berger, "Rescuing Civil Rights from Black Power: Collective Memory and Saving the State in Twenty-First Century Prosecutions of 1960s-Era Crimes," in *We Have Not Been Moved: Resisting Racism and Militarism in 21st Century America*, ed. Elizabeth "Betita" Martinez, Matt Meyer, and Mandy Carter (Oakland, CA: PM Press, 2012), 152.

81. Robert J. Rosenthal, "The Enduring Ambition of the Civil Rights Cold Case Project," *Nieman Reports*, Fall 2011; Civil Rights Cold Case Project, "About," accessed May 20, 2013, http://coldcases.org/about/about; David Ridgen, "The Bonds of Our Reporting: The Civil Rights Cold Case," *Nieman Reports*, Fall 2011; W. Winston Skinner, "Journalists' Work Solving Cold Cases from Civil Rights Era," *Newnan Times-Herald*, March 5, 2011.

82. Ericka Blount Davies, "Cold-Case Murders from the Civil Rights Movement May Be Solved," *BV Black Spin*, April 28, 2010, http://www.bvblackspin.com/2010/04/28/cold-case-justice-initiative/; "Cold Case Justice Initiative and Civil Rights Era Murders Promo," video created by NSBL Network, 2009, YouTube, http://www.youtube.com/watch?v=oghZ-6JoXCM; Cold Case Justice Initiative, http://www.syr.edu/coldcaselaw/fast_facts.html.

83. Elaine McCardle, "Resurrection: A Brutal Execution, a Landmark Case, Justice at Last," *Northeastern School of Law Magazine*, Summer 2010, 10–15; Civil Rights and Restorative Justice Project, http://www.northeastern.edu/civilrights/; program, Crimes of the Civil Rights Era conference, Boston, MA, April 27–28, 2007, copy in author's possession.

84. Alvin Sykes, comments at Crimes of the Civil Rights Era conference, Boston, MA, April 27–28, 2007, http://nuweb9.neu.edu/civilrights/wp-content/uploads/Sykes_The_Emmett_Till_Bill2.pdf; Drew Jubera, "Civil Rights-Era Murder Cases: 'Another Day for Justice,'" *Atlanta Journal-Constitution*, June 3, 2007. Bob Longino, "Rights Group Joins Calls for New Till Slaying Probe," *Atlanta Journal-Constitution*, January 9, 2003, 3B; Scott Lauck, "A Mission to

Perform: Unsolved Civil Rights Crime Act Was Quest of K.C. Activist," *Kansas City Daily Record*, October 9, 2008.

85. Jerry Mitchell, "Senator Eyes Cold-Case Unit for Civil Rights Killings," *Clarion-Ledger*, June 12, 2005. The legislation in the Senate was cosponsored by Jim Talent and Connecticut Senator Chris Dodd. It would be introduced in the House in 2005 by Bob Filner, a Democrat from California, and reintroduced in 2006 by John Lewis, a Democrat from Georgia. Talent would cite his conversations with Sykes as impetus for the legislation. "Talent and Dodd Announce Unsolved Civil Rights Crime Act," June 29, 2005, Project Vote Smart, https://votesmart.org/public-statement/109163/talent-dodd-announce-unsolved-civil-rights-crime-act#.UZoNDL9RHww.

86. Federal Bureau of Investigation Press Release, "Partnerships Established with NAACP, the National Urban League, and the Southern Poverty Law Center," February 27, 2007, http://www.fbi.gov/pressrel/presssrel07/coldcase022707.htm.

87. The legislation also provided for $2 million per year for grants to state and local law enforcement agencies to help them pay for cold case investigations and $1.5 million per year for the DOJ's Community Relations Service to bring together law enforcement agencies and communities in investigating cases. Only a fraction of the money authorized for the act would ever be appropriated. For a critical account of the Till Bill, see Barbara Schwabauer, "The Emmett Till Unsolved Civil Rights Crimes Act: The Cold Case of Racism in the American Justice System," 71 *Ohio St. L.J.* 653 (2010); "The Attorney General's Fourth Annual Report to Congress Pursuant to the Emmett Till Unsolved Civil Rights Crime Act of 2007," October 2012.

88. FBI Director Robert Mueller, "Major Executive Speeches: News Conference on the Civil Rights Cold Case Initiative," Department of Justice, Washington, DC, February 2007; "Conference Addresses Unfinished Business," *Syracuse University Magazine*, Summer 2012, http://sumagazine.syr.edu/2010summer/orangematters/coldcase.html.

89. Attorney General Alberto Gonzales quoted in "A Final Chapter for Cold Cases," *News and Record* (Greensboro), March 9, 2007, A12; Senator Christopher Dodd, press conference, "Justice Department Office to Investigate and Prosecute Civil Rights-Era Murders," *Federal News Service*, June 29, 2005; Sykes quoted in David Goldstein, "House OKs 'Cold Case' Squad for Civil Rights-Era Murders," *McClatchy-Tribune News Service*, June 20, 2007.

90. Hank Klibanoff, "Here's What People Want to Know: Why Do Journalists Tell These Stories," *Nieman Reports*, Fall 2011; Cold Case Justice Initiative, http://www.syr.edu/coldcaselaw/fast_facts.htm; "Confronting Anti-Civil Rights Violence," pamphlet from the Northeastern University Project on Civil Rights and Restorative Justice, n.d., in author's possession; Sykes quoted in Jerry Mitchell, "National Push Likely to Pursue Cold Cases of Civil Rights Era," *Clarion-Ledger*, June 15, 2007.

91. Robert S. Mueller, comment at the news conference on the Civil Rights Cold Case Initiative, Department of Justice, Washington, DC, February 27, 2007, http://www.fbi/gov/pressrel/speeches/mueller022707.htm.

92. Jerrold Nadler statement, U.S. House of Representatives Subcommittee on the Constitution, Civil Rights, and Civil Liberties and the Subcommittee on Crime, Terrorism, and Homeland Security of the Committee on the Judiciary, "Joint Hearing on the Emmett Till Unsolved Civil Rights Crime Act," June 12, 2007, 12; Statement of Senator Christopher Dodd, "Introduction of the Emmett Till Unsolved Civil Rights Crime Act," 153 Cong. Rec. S1788 (daily ed. February 8, 2007).

93. DeLaughter, *Never Too Late*, 74.

94. Evers, *Watch Me Fly*, 203, quote from 89.

95. Ibid., 205.

4. Civil Rights Crimes in the Courtroom

1. Bobby DeLaughter, *Never Too Late: A Prosecutor's Story of Justice in the Medgar Evers Case* (New York: Scribner, 2001), 234.

2. Ibid., 281.

3. For more on trials as civic rituals, see Mark S. Weiner, *Black Trials: Citizenship from the Beginning of Slavery to the End of Caste* (New York: Alfred A. Knopf, 2004), introduction.

4. Andrew Sheldon and Beth Bonora, interview by Beth Foley, "Working for Justice in Neshoba County, Mississippi," *Jury Expert*, September 1, 2010, http://www.thejuryexpert.com/2010/09/working-for-justice-in-neshoba-county-mississippi/. On the legal complications of trying civil rights–era cases, see Margaret Russell, "Cleansing Moments and Retrospective Justice," 101 *Michigan L. Rev.* 1225 (March 2003), and Michael Rowe, "Contemporary Prosecutions of Civil Rights Era Crimes: An Argument against Retroactive Application of Statute of Limitations Amendments," Northwestern University School of Law, *Journal of Criminal Law and Criminology* 101, no. 2 (2011): 699–726.

5. Author interview with Doug Jones, February 11, 2013, Birmingham, AL; News Release, "Pryor Appoints Veteran Prosecutors for Birmingham Church Bombing Case," January 4, 2002.

6. Vershal Hogan, "District Attorney Looks into Possibility of Seale Murder Trial in Natchez," *Natchez Democrat*, October 1, 2008.

7. Peters quoted in *Clarion-Ledger*, August 17, 1987, from Adam Nossiter, *Of Long Memory: Mississippi and the Murder of Medgar Evers* (Cambridge, MA: Da Capo Press, 2002), 237.

8. *Byron De La Beckwith v. State of Mississippi*, 707 So 2d 547 (Supreme Court of Mississippi, 1997); Paul Hoffman, "Double Jeopardy Wars: The Case for a Civil Rights Exception," *Special Issue: The Rodney King Trials: Civil Rights Prosecutions and Double Jeopardy*, 41 *UCLA L. Rev.* 649 (February 1994).

9. "Beckwith Ruling Could Affect Other Civil Rights Cases," *Commercial Appeal*, October 16, 1992, B1.

10. *Beckwith v. Mississippi*, 45; Also see Sarah Campbell, "Beckwith's Appeal Claims Rights Violated," *Commercial Appeal*, April 19, 1995, C2. For more background on the legal issues related to speedy and fair trials, see Warren Freedman, *The Constitutional Right to a Speedy and Fair Criminal Trial* (New York: Quorum Books, 1989).

11. Jerry Mitchell, "Seale Charges Stand: May 29 Trial Date Set," *Clarion-Ledger*, May 3, 2007; Maryanne Vollers, *Ghosts of Mississippi: The Murder of Medgar Evers, the Trials of Byron De La Beckwith, and the Haunting of the New South* (Boston: Little, Brown and Company, 1995), 343; trial transcript, *United States v. Ernest Avants*, U.S. District Court, Southern Division of MS, Jackson, MS, February 27, 2003, 123–124.

12. See for example "Supplemental Memorandum Brief in Support of the Motion to Dismiss for Violation of the Accused's Constitutional and Statutory Rights to a Speedy Trial," *State of Mississippi v. Charles Noble*, 31–32, Box 35, Folder 2, Helfrich (Robert B.) Papers, M410, McCain Library and Archives, University of Southern Mississippi, Hattiesburg, MS; "Motion to Preclude Introduction of Preliminary Hearing Transcript and Motion to Dismiss," *U.S. v. Ernest Henry Avants*, U.S. District Court, Southern Division of MS, Jackson, MS, September 1, 2000, 71, 72; *Thomas E. Blanton v. State of Alabama*, Appeal to Alabama Court of Criminal Appeals, Motion to Dismiss, vol. 1, 106–118; "Defense: Prosecution Intentionally Delayed '63 Church Bombing Case," *Associated Press State and Local Wire*, November 15, 2000, BC Cycle.

13. Pretrial hearing in *State of MS v Joe Oliver Watson, James "Doc" Caston, Charles E. Caston, Harold Spivey Crimm, and Dennis Howell*, Circuit Court of Humphreys County, Belzoni, MS, March 18, 1999, 79A.

14. Rothstein quoted in Henry J. Reske, "The Pitfalls of Prosecuting Old Cases: Memories Fade and Evidence Disappears, as in a Recent Civil Rights Prosecution," 80 *A.B.A.J.* 30 (1994); Rick Bragg, "Ex-F.B.I. Agent Testifies of Bloody Time in Mississippi," *New York Times*, February 28, 2003, A18; AGamma627, June 12, 2007, comments in response to Matt Saldana, "Day 10: A Final Dagger," *Jackson Free Press*, June 12, 2007, http://www.jacksonfreepress.com/comments.php?id=13928_0_59_0_C.

15. The circuitous legal debate over the case is explained in great detail in Rowe, "Contemporary Prosecutions of Civil Rights Era Crimes." See also Harry MacLean, *The Past Is Never Dead: The Trial of James Ford Seale and Mississippi's Struggle for Redemption* (New York: Basic Books, 2009), 77–78, 240, 267.

16. For more on political trials, see Steven E. Barkan, "Political Trials and the 'Pro Se' Defendant in the Adversary System," *Social Problems* 24 (February 1977): 324–336.

17. Brief of Appellant, *Byron De La Beckwith v. State of Mississippi in the Supreme Court of MS*, 70, Box 31, Folder 11, Helfrich Papers.

18. Richard Barrett, "Seventh Amendment Fomenting Outrage," February 27, 2003, published by The Nationalist Movement, 2003, http://www.national-ist.org/alt/2003/feb/avants.html; Barrett quoted in Bob Johnson, "Second Ex-Klansman Convicted in Deadly 1963 Church Bombing," *Associated Press State and Local Wire*, May 2, 2001.

19. Howard Ball, *Justice in Mississippi: The Murder Trial of Edgar Ray Killen* (Lawrence: University Press of Kansas, 2006), 134. For more on the challenges of prosecuting symbolic political cases, see Mark Osiel, *Mass Atrocity, Collective Memory, and the Law* (New Brunswick, NJ: Transaction Publishers, 1997), 65, 61.

20. DeLaughter, *Never Too Late*, 222.

21. Statement of Doug Jones, U.S. House of Representatives Joint Hearing before the Committee on the Constitution, Civil Rights, and Civil Liberties and the Committee on Crime, Terrorism, and Homeland Security of the Committee on the Judiciary, "Emmett Till Unsolved Civil Rights Crime Act," 110th Congress, June 12, 2007, 49.

22. See for example Brief of Appellant, *Beckwith v. Mississippi.*

23. DeLaughter, *Never Too Late*, 221; "About Us," SheldonSinrich Jury and Trial Consultants, www.sheldonsinrich.com.

24. Andrew Sheldon, "Remarks Prepared for Service at Mt. Zion United Methodist Church," 2004, http://www.crmvet.org/comm/csg40as1.htm; Andrew Sheldon and Beth Bonora, interview by Beth Foley, "Working for Justice in Neshoba County, Mississippi," *Jury Expert*, September 1, 2010, http://www.thejuryexpert.com/2010/09/working-for-justice-in-neshoba-county-mis-sissippi/. Additional information from telephone interview with Andrew Sheldon, July 2, 2006; SheldonSinrich, "Our Work—Civil Rights," www.sheldonsinrich.com.

25. Maclean, *The Past Is Never Dead*, 25, 36.

26. DeLaughter, *Never Too Late*, 229.

27. Maclean, *The Past Is Never Dead*, 212.

28. Ernest Avants's lawyer, for example, asked jurors if they could be fair even if there was evidence that Avants was a racist, belonged to the Klan, and used the "n" word. But, at least during the Beckwith trial, the judge took such questions to be a rather transparent way to keep blacks off the jury and told lawyers that he would not excuse any juror just because they said they would be offended by racist language. Jack Elliott Jr., "Prospective Jurors in Civil Rights Murder Trial Quizzed on Racial Views," *Associated Press State and Local Wire*, June 6, 2003, BC cycle; Emily Wagster Pettus, "Avants Trial Jurors Questioned Extensively on Race," *Associated Press State and Local Wire*, June 10, 2003, BC Cycle; *United States v. Ernest Avants*, Status Conference, December 12, 2002, 26; Sarah Campbell, "11 Join List of Eligibles for Beckwith Trial Jury," *Commercial Appeal*, January 22, 1994, 2B.

29. DeLaughter, *Never Too Late*, 227.

30. Joe Sam Owens, "Motion in Limine III," 3, *State of Mississippi vs. Charles Noble*, May 25, 1999, Circuit Court of Forrest County, MS, Box 34, Folder 11, Helfrich Papers.

31. "Hearing before Henry T. Wingate," *United States of America v. James Ford Seale*, April 14, 2007, U.S. District Court, Southern District of Mississippi, Jackson Division, 7, 19.

32. Sarah Campbell, "11 Join List of Eligibles for Beckwith Trial Jury," *Commercial Appeal*, January 22, 1994, 2B; William Booth, "Bias and Race Still Pertinent as 3rd Beckwith Trial Opens," *Washington Post*, January 21, 1994, A2.

33. Dr. Andrew Sheldon and Matthew McCusker, "Racially Charged Cases: Advice from a Trial Consultant's Perspective," SheldonSinrich, http://www.sheldonsinrich.com/articles.php?articleID=58. See also Beverly Pettigrew Kraft, "Lawyers Seek Expert Advice during Jury-Screening Phase of Bowers Trial," *Clarion-Ledger*, August 17, 1998, 8A.

34. See for example the jury questionnaire used during the Bowers trial. "Juror Questionnaire," Box 33, Folder 2, Helfrich Papers.

35. Sheldon and McCusker, "Racially Charged Cases." The questionnaires used in each trial differed slightly. The one used in the Bowers case had sixty-six questions and was designed by the prosecution. In the Blanton case, the defense and prosecution worked together to develop a one hundred–item questionnaire. But all the questionnaires covered basically the same terrain.

36. That point was made very clearly when defense lawyers for Byron De La Beckwith objected after the judge ruled that Beckwith could be tried only in counties that had a racial composition similar to the country where the crime took place rather than in one of the majority-white counties that the defense preferred. It was reverse discrimination to mandate demographic similarity, defense lawyers insisted. The judge was arbitrarily making a decision "based on constitutionally impermissible racial considerations." M. Shanara Gilbert, "An Ounce of Prevention: A Constitutional Prescription for Choice of Venue in Racially Sensitive Criminal Cases," 67 *Tulane L. Rev.* 1886 (June 1993).

37. Sarah Campbell, "Queries Trim Beckwith Jury Pool," *Commercial Appeal*, January 19, 1994, 1B.

38. Interview with Andrew Sheldon; Sarah Campbell, "Queries Trim Beckwith Jury Pool," *Commercial Appeal*, January 19, 1994, 1B; interview with Doug Jones; Trisha Renaud, "Juries and Beyond," *National Law Journal*, July 30, 2001. A friend of Sheldon's who had lost a child used that phrase in a letter to him.

39. "Jury Finds Beckwith Guilty of Murder in Mississippi," *CNN News Report*, February 5, 1994.

40. Shoshana Felman, "Forms of Judicial Blindness: Traumatic Narrative and Legal Repetitions," in *History, Memory, and the Law*, ed. Austin Sarat and Thomas R. Kearns (Ann Arbor: University of Michigan Press, 1999), 43.

41. Laura Parker, "Reliving the Evers Death: Mississippi Haunted by '63 Murder of Black," *Washington Post*, February 9, 1991, A1.

42. *U.S. v. Avants*, 283.

43. See testimony by Devours Nix in *State of Mississippi v. Sam Bowers* and by Harlan Majure in *State of Mississippi v. Edgar Ray Killen*. Sheldon quote from author interview with Andrew Sheldon.

44. Doug Jones in *State of Alabama v. Thomas Blanton*, 887; Bob Helfrich in *State of Mississippi v. Sam Bowers*, August 17, 1998, 142; Paige Fitzgerald, opening argument, *United States of America v. Ernest Henry Avants*, U.S. District Court, Southern District of Mississippi, Western Division, February 26, 2003, 45.

45. DeLaughter, *Never Too Late*, 227, 284.

46. Opening statement by Helfrich, *State of Mississippi v. Bowers*, August 17, 1998, 226; Jim Hood and Mark Duncan, closing arguments, *State of Mississippi v. Edgar Ray Killen*, June 20, 2005. Quotes from the Killen trial are from author's notes from Court TV live coverage of the trial rather than the trial transcript.

47. Vollers, *Ghosts of Mississippi*, 347; notes of Andrew Sheldon on *State of Mississippi v. Sam Bowers*, August 20–21, 1998, Box 37, Folder 4, Helfrich Papers.

48. Eduardo De Silva, *Racism without Racists: Color-Blind Racism and Racial Inequality in Contemporary America*, 3rd ed. (Lanham, MD: Rowman and Littlefield, 2010), 5.

49. Doug Jones, closing argument, *State of Alabama v. Bobby Frank Cherry*, May 21, 2002. Of course, an image of a black girl from 1963 lovingly holding a white doll might not, in fact, have been considered a picture of hope at the time, when black nationalists were beginning to articulate a critique of internalized racism or blacks' acceptance of white standards of beauty.

50. Brief of Appellant, *Byron De La Beckwith v. State of Mississippi* Supreme Court of Mississippi, 60, Box 31, Folder 11, Helfrich Papers, M410; pretrial hearing in *State of Mississippi v. Joe Oliver Watson, James "Doc" Caston, Charles E. Caston, Harold Spivey Crimm, and Dennis Howell*, Circuit Court of Humphreys County, Belzoni, MS, March 18, 1999, 56a; Jerry Mitchell, "Opening Statements in Seale Trial Expected This Afternoon," *Clarion-Ledger*, June 4, 2007.

51. *State of Mississippi v. Thomas Blanton*, 868–870; *Beckwith v. Mississippi* (1997).

52. Doug Jones, "Justice for Four Little Girls: The Bombing of the Sixteenth Street Baptist Church Cases," *Young Lawyer*, American Bar Association, February–March 2010, http://www.americanbar.org/content/dam/aba/publishing/young_lawyer/yld_tyl_febmar10_justice.authcheckdam.pdf.; DeLaughter, *Never Too Late*, 226; Paige Fitzgerald, opening argument, *United States of America v. Ernest Henry Avants*, U.S. District Court, Southern District of Mississippi, Western Division, February 26, 2003, 45; motion hearing, February 21, 2003, *U.S. v. Avants*, Feb. 21, 2003, 10; Paige Fitzgerald, *U.S. v. Seale*, 1617.

53. *State of Mississippi v. Thomas Blanton*, 1776.

54. DeLaughter, *Never Too Late*, 235; Bob Johnson, "Defense to Try to Unravel Government's Case in Church Bombing Trial," *Associated Press State and*

Local Wire, April 30, 2001; Matt Saldana, "Day Four: Fueled by a Racism So Extreme," *Jackson Free Press*, June 5, 2007.

55. David Snyder, "Do Right Thing, Beckwith Jury Told," *Times-Picayune*, February 5, 1994, A4; *State of Mississippi v. Thomas Blanton*, 913.

56. Mitch Moran, closing argument, *MS v. Killen*, June 20, 2005. Byron De La Beckwith's lawyers, for example, hoped to introduce the claim that Beckwith had made in 1964 that his rifle, which had killed Evers, had been stolen before the murder. But when the judge told them they would need to put Beckwith on the stand rather than just read in his testimony from the 1964 trial, they decided not to do so.

57. The black district attorney pursuing the investigation noted that while she would give "some weight" to the fact that blacks had to be subservient to whites in 1950s Mississippi, she also felt that individuals had a "moral obligation for right and wrong." Allen G. Breed, "The Murder of Emmett Till, 50 Years Later," *Associated Press*, updated August 28, 2005, http://www.msnbc. msn.com/id/9056380/ns/us_news-life/t/murder-emmett-till-years-later/#. UIr-CULbxUQ.

58. Robbie Brown, "45 Years Later, an Apology and Six Months," *New York Times*, November 15, 2010.

59. "Then and Now: Justice and Byron De La Beckwith," *Arkansas Democrat-Gazette*, January 30, 1994, 6B; DeLaughter, *Never Too Late*, 157; "Ex-Klansman's Fate in Jury's Hands," *CNN.com/Law Center*, May 22, 2002, http://www.cnn. com/2002/LAW/05/21/church.bombing.trial/.

60. Robbins quoted in Chanda Temple and Val Walton, "39 Years Later, Last Suspect Trial Begins," *Birmingham News*, May 5, 2002; Maclean, *The Past Is Never Dead*, 26; Nossiter, *Of Long Memory*, 252.

61. Mitchell Landsberg, "De La Beckwith Called 'Back-Shooting Coward,'" *New York Beacon*, February 11, 1994, 23; Manuel Roig-Franzia, "Reopened Civil Rights Cases Evoke Painful Past," *Washington Post*, January 10, 2005, A01; Richard Cohen, "Not Too Late for Justice," *Washington Post*, January 11, 2005, A15; David Molpus, "Suspect in Murder of Medgar Evers to Be Retried," *Morning Edition*, National Public Radio, January 18, 1994, transcript #1262–14.

62. This is language used about the Beckwith trial in "Then and Now: Justice and Byron De La Beckwith," *Arkansas Democrat-Gazette*, January 30, 1994, 6B.

63. Ben Chaney, quoted in *National Public Radio News*, with Tanya Cox, January 11, 2005, and in Donna Ladd, "After Killen: What's Next for Mississippi?" *Jackson Free Press*, June 22, 2005; Ellis Cose, "A Reckoning in Birmingham," *Newsweek*, June 3, 2002, 31.

64. This is language borrowed from Dan Berger, who describes trials as the "juridical equivalent of the Rosa Parks myth." See Dan Berger, "Rescuing Civil Rights from Black Power: Collective Memory and Saving the State in

Twenty-First-Century Prosecutions of 1960s-Era Crimes," in *We Have Not Been Moved: Resisting Racism and Militarism in 21st Century America*, ed. Elizabeth "Betita" Martinez, Matt Meyer, and Mandy Carter (Oakland, CA: PM Press, 2012), 148–164, quote from 153.

65. Leora Bilsky, "The Judge and the Historian: Transnational Holocaust Litigation as a New Model," *History & Memory* 24 (Fall–Winter 2012), 136, 123.

66. David Goodman, comments at Crimes of the Civil Rights Era conference, Boston, MA, April 27–28, 2007; author interview with Doug Jones; Diane McWhorter, interview by Jacki Lyden, "Interview: Diane McWhorter Discusses the Trial in Birmingham, Alabama, of Bobby Frank Cherry," National Public Radio, May 18, 2002.

67. Powell closing in *MS v. Caston, Caston, Crimm*, 503; Hood closing, *MS v. Killen*, June 20, 2005.

68. *U.S. v. Seale*, 2488, 2485, 2486.

69. Majority opinion, *Beckwith v. Mississippi.*

70. Martha Minow, *Between Vengeance and Forgiveness: Facing History after Genocide and Mass Violence* (Boston: Beacon Press, 1998), 78, 87.

71. *State of AL v. Thomas Blanton*, 907.

72. DeLaughter, *Never Too Late*, 235, 234–235.

73. Doug Jones, statement at the Emmett Till Unsolved Civil Rights Crime Act Hearing, 50; Doug Jones, opening argument, *State of AL v. Blanton*, 887, 890.

74. Doug Jones, presentation at Haskell Slaughter Young & Rediker law firm, Birmingham, AL, February 11, 2013; Jones, presentation at Crimes of the Civil Rights Era conference, Boston, MA, April 27–28, 2007; author interview with Doug Jones.

75. *State of Alabama v. Thomas Blanton*, 1811.

76. Vollers, *Ghosts of Mississippi*, 375; Sarah Campbell, "Jurors Weigh Beckwith Fate in Third Trial," *Commercial Appeal*, February 5, 1994, 1B.

77. Donna Ladd, "The 'Other Side' in 1964," *Jackson Free Press*, June 13, 2007.

78. Helfrich quoted in Jerry Mitchell, "Prosecutors Want Justice Served," *Clarion-Ledger*, August 17, 1998, 7A; Bob Helfrich, comments at Pursuing a Late Justice: The Prosecution of Mississippi's Civil Rights Murders, Then and Now (University Forum, Cook Library, University of Southern Mississippi, August 29, 2000), video recording.

79. DeLaughter, closing argument, reprinted in *Never Too Late*, 282; Mark Duncan, closing argument, *State of MS v. Edgar Ray Killen*, June 20, 2005; Powell, closing arguments, *State of Mississippi v. Caston, Caston, and Crimm*, 504.

80. Robert W. Gordon, "Undoing Historical Injustice," in *Justice and Injustice in Law and Legal Theory*, ed. Austin Sarat and Thomas R. Kearns (Ann Arbor: University of Michigan Press, 1996), 71.

81. Duncan quoted in Lora Hines, "High-Profile Case Puts Spotlight on Humble DA," *Clarion-Ledger*, June 15, 2005; Jones quoted in Bill Plott, "Church Bombing Also Act of Terrorism, Fairfield Chamber Told," *Birmingham News*,

January 18, 2002; Helfrich in Jerry Mitchell, "Prosecutors Want Justice Served," *Clarion-Ledger*, August 17, 1998, 7A.

82. Reed Branson, "Evers Murder May Get Retrial: Widow to Testify before Jury," *Commercial Appeal*, December 14, 1990, B1; DeLaughter, *Never Too Late*, 165–166; Adam Goldman, "Civil Rights Cases Breathing Their Last," *Birmingham News*, April 29, 2001; DeLaughter, 232.

83. Osiel, *Mass Atrocity, Collective Memory, and the Law*, 61.

84. Ball, *Justice in Mississippi*, 133; Duncan, closing arguments, *State of MS v. Edgar Ray Killen*, June 20, 2005.

85. Tom Robbins, opening and closing arguments, *State of Alabama v. Thomas Blanton*, 915–916, 1793; Nester, closing arguments, *U.S. v. Seale*, 2523; Maclean, *The Past Is Never Dead*, 206; Moran, closing arguments, *State of MS v. Edgar Ray Killen*, June 20, 2005.

86. Nossiter, *Of Long Memory*, 253; Maclean, *The Past Is Never Dead*, 49.

87. Rita Schwerner Bender, "Searching for Restorative Justice—The Trial of Edgar Ray Killen," comments at the Crimes of the Civil Rights Era Conference, Boston, MA, April 28, 2007, http://nuweb9.neu.edu/civilrights/dee-moore-documentary/essay/.

88. Doug Jones, opening argument, *State of Alabama v. Thomas Blanton*, 900.

5. Civil Rights Trials and Narratives of Redemption

1. *Sins of the Father*, VHS, directed by Robert Dornhelm (Artisan, 2002). The movie was loosely based on Pamela Colloff, "The Sins of the Father," *Texas Monthly* 28 (April 2000): 130–137, 150–154.

2. In *Sins of the Father*, that role would be played by Garrick, the black man Tom befriends in Texas as they build a house together. Garrick teaches Tom what life was like in Birmingham for black people in the 1960s and prods him to renounce his racist upbringing.

3. Doug Jones, the lead prosecutor in Cherry's trial, claims that Tom Cherry "didn't give us crap." Cherry, Jones says, only offered further evidence that his dad was a racist Klansman, which prosecutors already knew. Cherry testified that he'd never heard his father admit to the bombing and that he didn't know whether he was guilty. Yet Tom's own daughter, Teresa, who was featured in *Glamour* for her own renunciation of her racist upbringing, testified that, when she was only ten years old, she had heard her grandfather boast of "blowing up a bunch of niggers." She too believed that her father knew more than he told the grand jury. Interview with Doug Jones, February 11, 2013, Birmingham, AL; Barry Yeoman, "A Hideous Hate Crime: It's My Family's Secret No More," *Glamour*, August 2000, 226.

4. Kristen E. Hoerl, "Representing Byron De La Beckwith in Film and Journalism: Popular Memories of Mississippi and the Murder of Medgar Evers," in *Rhetorical Agendas: Political, Ethical, Spiritual*, ed. Patricia Bizzell (Mahwah,

NJ: Lawrence Erlbaum Associates, 2006), 243–249; Jerry Mitchell, "'Human Story' behind Killings Draws World Media to Miss.," *Clarion-Ledger*, June 12, 2005; Patsy Brumfield, "Being in Philadelphia Mattered—The World Was Watching," *Northeast Mississippi Daily Journal*, June 23, 2005.

5. Lieve Gies, *Law and the Media: The Future of an Uneasy Relationship* (New York: Routledge, 2008), 13.

6. Willie Morris, *The Ghosts of Medgar Evers: A Tale of Race, Murder, Mississippi, and Hollywood* (New York: Random House, 1998), 264, 57.

7. See "Fewer Americans Say Black-White Relations Have Gotten Worse," May 27, 2003, Gallup poll, http://www.gallup.com/poll/8479/Fewer-Americans-Say-BlackWhite-Relations-Gotten-Worse.aspx.

8. "Finally Convicted," *Washington Post*, February 8, 1994, A18; "Finally, Justice Is Done," *Commercial Appeal*, February 8, 1994, Viewpoint, 1A; "The De La Beckwith Verdict," *Times-Picayune*, February 8, 1994, B6; "Evers Verdict: Mississippi Learning," *Atlanta Journal and Constitution*, February 8, 1994, A22.

9. On the power of framing, see Irwin Iwona-Zarecka, *Frames of Remembrance: Social and Cultural Dynamics of Collective Memory* (New Brunswick, NJ: Transaction Publishers, 1994).

10. Cynthia Tucker, "Our Opinion: Klansman Not Too Old to Pay," *Atlanta Journal-Constitution*, June 26, 2005, 6B.

11. For more on the force of redemption as an idea in American culture, see George Shulman, *American Prophecy: Race and Redemption in American Political Culture* (Minneapolis: University of Minnesota Press, 2008); Dan P. McAdams, *The Redemptive Self: Stories Americans Live By*, rev. ed. (New York: Oxford University Press, 2013).

12. Michiko Kakutani, "Faith Base: As American as Second Acts and Apple Pie," *New York Times*, February 4, 2001, WK1.

13. Quoted in Barbara Kantrowitz and Pat Wingert, "A New Era of Segregation," *Newsweek*, December 27, 1993, 44.

14. "Justice at Last: A Killer of Children Convicted 39 Years On," *Pittsburgh Post-Gazette*, May 29, 2002, A8.

15. Kenneth Lavon Johnson, "Mississippi Takes Steps to Rectify Sins of Past," *Baltimore Sun*, June 26, 2005, 5C.

16. There is an extensive literature detailing—and criticizing—the claim that the election of Barack Obama heralded the arrival of a new, postracial America. See for example Kevern Verney, Mark Ledwidge, and Inderjeet Parmar, eds., *Barack Obama and the Myth of the Post-Racial America* (New York: Routledge, 2013); Michael Tesler and David O. Sears, *Obama's Race: The 2008 Election and the Dream of a Post-Racial America* (Chicago: University of Chicago Press, 2010); and Thomas J. Sugrue, *Not Even Past: Barack Obama and the Burden of Race* (Princeton, NJ: Princeton University Press, 2010).

17. "Closing the Books: A New Generation Fights for Racial Justice," *Nightline*, ABC News, May 28, 2002.

18. Mark Golub, "History Died for Our Sins: Guilt and Responsibility in Hollywood Redemption Histories," *Journal of American Culture* 21 (Fall 1998): 23–45.

19. Sherry Ricchiardi, "Out of the Past," *American Journalism Review*, April–May 2005, http://www.ajr.org/article_printable.asp?id=3852.

20. Mary Orndorff, "FBI Agents in Church Bomb Investigation Get Top Awards," *Birmingham News*, November 14, 2002; Bill Fleming and Bob Herren, interview by Bob Edwards, *Morning Edition*, National Public Radio, November 13, 2002.

21. Lisa Ison-Rodriguez, "Prosecuting a 31-Year-Old Mississippi Murder Case," *American Lawyer*, April 1994, 33; "Evil Man, Evil Deed," *Augusta Chronicle*, January 24, 2001, A4; "SCLC Honors Nunn, Lawyer," *Birmingham News*, April 5, 2003; "The Digest," *Birmingham News*, December 17, 2002; "FBI Agents in Church Bomb Investigation Get Top Awards." One of the FBI agents, Bill Fleming, also received a 2002 Department of Justice Award for Excellence in Law Enforcement. "The Digest," *Birmingham News*, July 12, 2002. For an example of Moore being featured in articles on the Killen case, see Jerry Mitchell, "New Witnesses Surface in Probe of '64 Killings," *Clarion-Ledger*, June 11, 2000; Lora Hines, "High-Profile Case Puts Spotlight on Humble DA," *Clarion-Ledger*, June 15, 2005.

22. Colin Chapell, "'You Might Be a Redneck If . . . ': Advertising Southern Male Deviancy, 1960–1992," in *Black and White Masculinity in the American South, 1800–2000*, ed. Lydia Plath and Sergio Lussana (Newcastle upon Tyne: Cambridge Scholars Publishing, 2009), 181; Allison Graham, *Framing the South: Hollywood, Television, and Race during the Civil Rights Struggle* (Baltimore: Johns Hopkins University Press, 2001), 148, 154.

23. "Let Freedom Summer Ring," *St. Louis Post-Dispatch*, June 24, 2005, B8; "Healing Old Wounds," editorial, *St. Petersburg Times*, November 15, 1999, 14A; "Dahmer: Justice for a Crime Not Forgotten," *Clarion-Ledger*, August 22, 1998.

24. "Birmingham Tries to Right '60s Wrongs," *Atlanta Journal and Constitution*, April 26, 2001, 14A. For just a few examples of the coverage of prosecutors, see "Alabama's Long Search for Justice," *New York Times*, May 18, 2000, A30; Stevie Lacy-Pendleton, "Old Southern Murders and the 'Arc of Justice,'" *Staten Island Advance*, January 26, 2007, 22; "At Last, Justice in Alabama," *Economist*, May 5, 2001; "No Justice, No Peace," *Los Angeles Times*, June 24, 2005, B10.

25. "Simonton Key in Reopening of White Case," *Natchez Democrat*, June 25, 2000; *Morning Edition*, National Public Radio, November 13, 2002; Judge W. O. "Chet" Dillard, *Caveats from the Bench: Warnings about the Erosion of our Constitutional Rights from a Mississippi Trial Court* (Jackson, MS: Lawyer's Publishing Press, 1994), 112.

26. Graham, *Framing the South*, 12, 153; Eduardo De Silva, *Racism without Racists: Color-Blind Racism and Racial Inequality in Contemporary America*, 3rd ed. (Lanham, MD: Rowman and Littlefield, 2010), 15.

27. *San Diego Union-Tribune*, May 5, 2001, B8; "Courting Justice in Alabama," *Omaha World Herald*, April 19, 2001, 26; "Birmingham Sunday Revisited," *St. Louis Post-Dispatch*, May 18, 2000, B6; "Justice Delayed, but Not Denied," *Daily News* (New York), May 19, 2000, 42.

28. *Killed by the Klan*, directed by Charles C. Stuart, Discovery Channel [S.I.: Stuart Television Productions, Bethesda, MD; Discovery Channel Video, 1999]; Patrick Rogers, "Making Wrong Right," *People*, September 7, 1998; Billy Roy Pitts, interview by John Donvan, "Conscience of a Klansman," *ABC Nightline*, September 29, 1998.

29. Peggy Morgan with Carolyn Haines, *My Mother's Witness: The Peggy Morgan Story* (Montgomery, AL: River City Publishing, 2003); Tammy Smith, "Beckwith Witness Broke Free from Abuser—Woman Tells Life Story in Book," *Commercial Appeal*, October 13, 2003, DS4.

30. Yeoman, "A Hideous Hate Crime," 225, 251.

31. Jerry Mitchell, comments at Pursuing a Late Justice: The Prosecution of Mississippi's Civil Rights Murders, Then and Now (University Forum, Cook Library, University of Southern Mississippi, August 29, 2000), video recording.

32. "Justice Delayed in Birmingham Case," *Tampa Tribune*, May 20, 2000, 14; Yeoman, "A Hideous Hate Crime," 226.

33. James C. Cobb, *Away down South: A History of Southern Identity* (Oxford: Oxford University Press, 2005), 1–3; David R. Jansson, "The Haunting of the South: American Geopolitical Identity and the Burden of Southern History," *Geopolitics* 12, no. 3 (2007): 400–425. Cobb argues that white Southerners have long been willing to "embrace and defend even the most controversial aspects of their region's distinctiveness" (1). See also Rebecca Bridges Watts, *Contemporary Southern Identity: Community through Controversy* (Jackson: University Press of Mississippi, 2008).

34. "Stain," in Rick Bragg, "In One Last Trial, Alabama Faces Old Wound," *New York Times*, May 12, 2002, 16; "Still Sore Wounds," in "Healing Old Wounds: Reopening Till Case More than Symbolic Gesture," *Birmingham News*, May 13, 2004; Maryanne Vollers, *Ghosts of Mississippi: The Murder of Medgar Evers, the Trials of Byron De La Beckwith, and the Haunting of the New South* (Boston: Little, Brown and Company, 1995), 4. Eddie Lard, "Two States Confront Their Ghosts," editorial, *Birmingham News*, April 13, 2001. The line "The past is never dead. It isn't even past," written by William Faulkner in his 1951 novel *Requiem for a Nun*, was adapted as the title of Harry MacLean's book on the trial of James Ford Seale.

35. Jansson, "The Haunting of the South," 413; "A Long Time Coming," *San Francisco Chronicle*, May 19, 2000, A28; "Justice Delayed, but Not Entirely Denied," *Chicago Defender*, January 29, 2003, 9; Andrew Cohen, "The U.S. Confronts Its Shameful Past," *Ottawa Citizen*, March 15, 2005, A12.

36. "The FBI's Blunder Tapes Should Not Have Stayed Secret So Long," *Birmingham News*, May 8, 2001; "What Else Do They Know," *Times-Picayune*, May 5, 2001, 6.

37. Colbert I. King, "No Thanks to Hoover," editorial, *Washington Post*, May 5, 2001, A19; DeWayne Wickham, "Hoover Role in Bombing Cases Deserves Our Condemnation," *USA Today*, May 8, 2001, 13A.

38. "Time Catches Up with a Killer," *Omaha World Herald*, May 5, 2001, 16.

39. Allen G. Breed and Holbrook Mohr, "FBI Says the End Is Near for Investigations into Civil Rights-Era Cold Cases," *Huffington Post*, November 5, 2011, http://www.huffingtonpost.com/2011/11/05/fbi-says-theend-near-in-_n_1077703.html?view=print&comm_ref=false.

40. Joanna Weiss, "Justice Served as Man Finally Talks; Case Produced Unique Alliance," *Times-Picayune*, August 22, 1998, A8; Rick Bragg, "In One Last Trial, Alabama Faces Old Wound," *New York Times*, May 12, 2002, 16; Joanna Weiss, "Klan Chief Gets Life in '66 Rights Murder: Fifth Time around, Miss. Jury Convicts," *Times-Picayune*, August 22, 1998, A1; "Justice in Birmingham: An Avowed Racist Is Finally Convicted for the September 1963 Killing of Four Girls, Helping Heal That Wound," *San Antonio News-Express*, May 25, 2002, 10B. See also "Healing Old Wounds: Reopening Till Case More than Symbolic Gesture."

41. "Mississippi Justice," *Baltimore Sun*, June 22, 2005, http://articles.baltimore-sun.com/2005–06–22/news/0506220017_1_economic-justice-poetic-jus-tice-killen; Sid Salter, "Neshoba: Klan Exorcism Starts inside the Heart," *Clarion-Ledger*, June 15, 2005.

42. Davis quote in Rick Bragg, "In One Last Trial, Alabama Faces Old Wound," *New York Times*, May 12, 2002, 1, 16; Reed Branson, "Trial To Revisit '66 Racial Slaying—Miss. Doggedly Persists in Atoning," *Memphis Commercial Appeal*, February 24, 2003, A1; Emily Wagster Pettus, "Former Klansman Guilty in '64 Deaths," *Ventura County Star*, June 22, 2005, 1; Gary Younge, "'Mississippi Burning' Killer Gets 60 Years," *Guardian* (London), June 24, 2005, 15; "Catharsis—Justice in Aging Hate-Crimes Cases Remains Crucial," *Commercial Appeal*, August 12, 2000, Viewpoint, A8; Peter Sheridan, "Justice for Evil Klan Killer," *Express* (UK First Edition), June 9, 2007; Ann Woolner, "Still Burning," *American Lawyer*, January 2000.

43. Joanna Weiss, "Klan Chief Gets Life in '66 Rights Murder: Fifth Time around, Miss. Jury Convicts," *Times-Picayune*, August 22, 1998, A1; "Healing Old Wounds," *St. Petersburg Times*, November 15, 1999, 14A; "Alabama Makes Amends: The Wheels of Justice Turn Slowly—but They Turn," *Pittsburgh Post-Gazette*, April 29, 2001, E2.

44. *Ghosts of Mississippi*, VHS, directed by Rob Reiner (Castle Rock Entertainment, 1996).

45. Morris recounts his first approach to Zollo and the letter in his book *The Ghosts of Medgar Evers*, 87.

46. "Beckwith Trial Attracts Offers from Hollywood," *Commercial Appeal*, September 22, 1992, B4; Reiner quoted in Morris, *Ghosts of Medgar Evers*, 108, 112; "Righting a Wrong: Ghosts of Mississippi Offers a Spirit of ATONEMENT," *About . . . Time* (Rochester), January 31, 1997, 12.

47. Myrlie Evers discusses her feelings about the film in Myrlie Evers-Williams with Melinda Blau, *Watch Me Fly: What I Learned on Becoming the Woman I Was Meant to Be* (Boston: Little, Brown and Co., 1999), 216–222; Reiner quote from 220.

48. Steve Persall, "Missing in Mississippi," *St. Petersburg Times*, January 3, 1997, 5.

49. Evers, *Watch Me Fly*, 218; Richard Corliss, "Ghosts of Mississippi," *Time*, January 6, 1997, 140; Mal Vincent, "'Ghosts of Mississippi' Aims at Truth, Misses," *Virginian-Pilot* (Norfolk), January 5, 1997, E1. For other critiques of the film's treatment of Myrlie Evers, see Michael Paul Williams, "Hollywood Fails to Do Justice to Black Struggle," *Richmond Times Dispatch*, January 6, 1997, B1; "Movie Review: *Ghosts of Mississippi:* New Film Raises Same Old Questions," *Michigan Citizen*, January 25, 1997, B1.

50. Morris, *The Ghosts of Medgar Evers*, 131, 232–234; Michael Paul Williams, "Hollywood Fails to Do Justice to Black Struggle," B1.

51. Tom Gliatto, "Ghosts of Mississippi," *People Weekly*, January 13, 1997, 20; quoted in Morris, 239; Evers, *Watch Me Fly*, 219.

52. Steve Persall, "Missing in Mississippi," 5; Richard Corliss, "Ghosts of Mississippi," 140.

53. Max Millard, "'*Ghosts* Brings Closure to Evers' Trials," *Philadelphia Tribune*, January 31, 1997, 83; "Righting a Wrong," 12. See also Hoerl, "Representing Byron De La Beckwith in Film and Journalism," 245.

54. "'Ghost of Mississippi,' Rest in Peace Medgar Evers," *Call and Post* (Cincinnati), January 9, 1997, 1B; Reed Branson, "Latest Miss. Film a Haunting Reminder of Racial Turmoil," *Commercial Appeal*, December 16, 1996, 1A; Betsy Pickle, "'Ghosts of Mississippi' Torpedoed by Bad Script, Bad Acting, Bad Accents," *Knoxville News-Sentinel*, January 4, 1997, B6.

55. This analysis is borrowed and adapted from Golub, "History Died for Our Sins," 23–45.

56. "Alabama Makes Amends," E2; "Verdict Proves Justice Never Gives Up," *Natchez Democrat*, June 17, 2007.

57. "Justice Delayed in Birmingham Case," *Tampa Tribune*, May 20, 2000, 14; "Justice, at Last, in Mississippi," *Chattanooga Times Free Press*, January 29, 2007, B8; Roger E. Hernandez, "De La Beckwith Conviction Is a Reminder of Change," *National Minority Politics*, April 30, 1994, 11.

58. For just a few examples of this rhetoric of closure, see Ronald Smothers, "White Supremacist Is Convicted of Slaying Rights Leader in '63," *New York Times*, February 6, 1994; "It Took 38 Years," *New York* Times, May 26, 2002, sec. 4, 2; "Ex-Klansman Gets Life Sentence for '63 Birmingham Church Bombing," *Jet*, June 10, 2002; Susan Ives, "In Mississippi, an Evil Chapter Finally Ends," *San Antonio Express-News*, June 26, 2005, 3H.

59. "Closure, yet a Beginning," *Neshoba Democrat*, June 29, 2005; "Our True Character," *Neshoba Democrat*, June 22, 2005.

6. From Legal Justice to Social Justice

1. Rita Bender, open letter to Governor Haley Barbour, June 27, 2005, http://www.mississippitruth.org/documents/bender-letter.pdf.
2. Telephone interview with Rita Schwerner Bender, January 28, 2008.
3. Donna Ladd, "Dredging Up the Past: Why Mississippians Must Tell Our Own Stories," *Jackson Free Press*, May 30, 2007.
4. Rita Schwerner Bender, "Searching for Restorative Justice: The Trial of Edgar Ray Killen," comments at Crimes of the Civil Rights Era conference, Boston, MA, April 28, 2007, http://nuweb9.neu.edu/civilrights/wp-content/uploads/Bender_Trial_of_Edgar_Ray_Killen2.pdf.
5. "Mississippi 'Misses' Out on Opportunity to Prosecute 37 Year Old Civil Rights Case," *Jacksonville Free Press*, May 16, 2001, 10; "Mississippi Murders May Not Be Next Old Case Reopened," *Chattanooga Times Free Press*, May 3, 2001, A3; "Prosecute Them," *Deep South Jewish Voice*, July 1, 2002, 1, 12.
6. Interview with Leroy Clemons, February 13, 2013, Philadelphia, MS. Clemons describes being denied a promotion at his workplace to a supervisory position in the late 1980s because his manager worried that the husbands of the white female workers would object to their wives having a black supervisor.
7. Clemons interview; interview with Fenton DeWeese, February 12, 2013, Choctaw, MS; Telephone interview with Susan Glisson, March 15, 2005. See also Bill Nichols, "Residents Hope Trial Will Heal Miss. Town," *USA Today*, June 10, 2005, 3A; John Sugg, "Racial Healing in Mississippi," *Creative Loafing*, June 29, 2005, http://clatl.com/atlanta/racial-healing-in-mississippi/Content?oid=1254818
8. "We Are the People We Have Been Waiting For: Equipping Communities to Heal Themselves," resource guide from the William Winter Institute for Racial Reconciliation, 12; Clemons quoted in "'Town Where They Killed Those Guys Seeks Justice," *Atlanta Journal Constitution*, June 20, 2004, 1A; Cagin and Dray, *We Are Not Afraid*, xviii.
9. "Economic Impact of Commemoration Noted," *Neshoba Democrat*, misdated June 24, 2004, probable date June 9, 2004, http://www.neshobademocrat.com/main.asp?SectionID=20&SubSectionID=330&ArticleID=8259&TM=43214.24; Jim Prince, "Why Stir Up the Past?" *Neshoba Democrat*, misdated June 24, 2004, probable date April 21, 2004, http://www.neshobademocrat.com/main.asp?SectionID=20&SubSectionID=330&ArticleID=8251&TM=43214.24.
10. Telephone interview with John Steele, November 16, 2007. On the controversy caused by the invitation of Haley Barbour, see Bender interview, January 26, 2008; Telephone interview with Susan Glisson, June 6, 2006; Wallace Roberts, "Highway to Nowhere," Veterans of the Civil Rights Movement, http://www.crmvet.org/comm/csg40wr.htm.

11. Gibson had done some work with the Southern Student Organizing Conference, yet did not consider himself a movement veteran. But his interest in civil rights–era murders led him to incorporate himself and his wife as the nonprofit Arkansas Delta Truth and Justice Center in order to secure a copyright for the *Why Only Killen?* documentary. Chaney quoted in W. C. Shirley, "Ben Chaney Boycotts 40th Commemoration," *Neshoba Democrat*, June 23, 2004. Ben Chaney has leveled charges of whitewashing in a variety of public forums. See for example Chaney's comments in an interview with *Worker's World Newspaper*, February 10, 2005, http://www.workers.org/us/2005/chaney0210.php; interview on *NPR News with Tony Cox*, National Public Radio, January 11, 2005; interview by Amy Goodman on *Democracy Now!* June 14, 2005. On the "Why Only Killen?" refrain, see John Gibson, "Neshoba Murders: Present All Evidence to the Grand Jury," *Mississippi Headlines and Political Notes*, accessed August 22, 2007, http://www.mississippipolitical.com/letter13.htm; Arkansas Delta Truth and Justice Center, *Why Only Killen?* (documentary, 2007); Donna Ladd, "After Killen: What's Next for Mississippi?" *Jackson Free Press*, June 22, 2005.
12. Prince, "Why Stir Up the Past?"; "Economic Impact of Commemoration Noted."
13. Jim Prince, "A Different Neshoba County," *Neshoba Democrat*, June 30, 2004; Prince, "White Trash and Dusty Streets," *Neshoba Democrat*, June 8, 2005; "Our True Character," *Neshoba Democrat*, June 22, 2005. See also "Justice for All," *Neshoba Democrat*, June 8, 2005.
14. "Historic Tour on Civil Rights Said Big Draw," *Neshoba Democrat*, January 30, 2002; "Economic Impact of Commemoration Noted"; "Cracks in the Coalition," *Neshoba Democrat*, April 20, 2005.
15. "Civil Rights Battlegrounds Enter World of Tourism," *New York Times*, August 10, 2004, A1; Glisson interview, March 15, 2005; *We Are the People We've Been Waiting For*, 12–13; Deborah Burt Myers, "MDA, Tourism Council Unveil Civil Rights Brochure," *Neshoba Democrat*, June 7, 2004; Jared Story, "The 40th Neshoba Memorial: Misrepresentation and Mischaracterization," posted on Veterans of the Civil Rights Movement website, accessed November 2, 2007, http://www.crmvet.org/comm/csg40js.htm.
16. Ben Chaney quoted in Emily Sherwood, "Murdered but Still Alive: Chaney, Goodman, Scwherner: Forty-Two Years Later Family Members Speak Out," *Education Update Online*, February 2006, http://www.educatoinupdate.com/archives/2006/Feb/html/cov-murderedbutstill.htm.
17. Philadelphia Coalition, "Statement Asking for Justice in the June 21, 1964 Murders of James Chaney, Andrew Goodman, and Michael Schwerner," May 26, 2004, www.neshobajustice.com/resolution.htm; "City Resolution for Justice," posted on *Neshoba Democrat* http://neshobademocrat.com/main.asp?Search=1&ArticleID=8107&SectionID=2&SubSectionID=297&S=1, June 7, 2004; Patti Miller quoted in Richard Cotton, "Miss. Memorial Turns Divisive," *Atlanta Journal-Constitution*, June 21, 2004, 4A.

18. Jim Prince, "Cracks in the Coalition," *Neshoba Democrat*, April 20, 2005; comments by Fenton DeWeese at the Philadelphia Coalition after-party, 2004, posted by the William Winter Institute, Vimeo, http://vimeo.com/27775316; DeWeese interview; Clemons interview.

19. Donna Ladd, "Civil Rights Education Summit in Neshoba County," *Jackson Free Press*, June 22, 2005.

20. "Cracks in the Coalition," *Neshoba Democrat*, April 20, 2005; Fenton DeWeese relates that the Coalition decided to move from having black and white cochairs to having a single chair as a way to get rid of Prince, who began to distance himself from the Coalition once it became clear he would not be able to control the group. DeWeese interview.

21. Statement of the Philadelphia Coalition, March 29, 2008, accessed October 16, 2010, http://www.neshohbajustice.com/pages/2008stmt.htm; Fenton DeWeese, comments at "Plenary: Is a Verdict Enough? Reflections on Justice and Reconciliation in the Killen Trial," Southern Exposure conference, Oxford, MS, March 18, 2006, DVD; telephone interview with Susan Glisson, June 6, 2006.

22. Glisson interview, June 6, 2006. The conference was entitled Southern Exposure: Regional Summit on Racial Violence and Reconciliation (William Winter Institute for Racial Reconciliation, Oxford, MS, March 17–18, 2006). Most sessions of the conference were videotaped. DVDs are available from the Winter Institute.

23. There has been little scholarly writing about this historical moment marked by new energy to revisit histories of racial violence. One of the few works that address this emerging movement is Tracy Thompson's *The New Mind of the South* (New York: Simon and Schuster, 2013), especially 92–105. Thompson attributes this interest in history to the aging of former civil rights activists now seeking to assess their place in history, and to a religious impulse to address racial tensions through the framing of reconciliation and restorative justice. Students at Northeastern University have put together a guide to some of the groups working for truth and reconciliation in relation to racial issues. Available online at http://www.atrr.org/documents/narratives.pdf, accessed April 25, 2013.

24. William Winter Institute for Racial Reconciliation, "About Us," http://www.winterinstitute.org/pages/aboutus.htm; Glisson interview, March 15, 2005, and June 6, 2006.

25. Rich Rusk, comments at "Building Community One Project at a Time," Southern Exposure conference, March 18, 2006, DVD; Adina Chandler, comments at "Break Out Session #2: Reports from Grassroots-Community Bases Memorial Effort," Southern Exposure conference, March 18, 2006, DVD.

26. Southern Truth and Reconciliation, "About Us: History," http://www.fcd360.com/SouthernTruth/about_us_history.htm3.

27. Statement from "The Declaration" of the Greensboro Truth and Reconciliation Commission Project, http://www.gtcrp.org/declaration.asp. For more on the history of the Greensboro Truth and Reconciliation Commission, see *Greensboro Truth and Reconciliation Commission Final Report*, presented to the residents of Greensboro, the City, the Greensboro Truth and Community Reconciliation Project, and other public bodies on May 25, 2006, http://www.greensborotrc.org/; Spoma Jovanovic, *Democracy, Dialogue and Community Action: Truth and Reconciliation in Greensboro* (Fayetteville: University of Arkansas Press, 2012); James Edward Beitler III, *Remaking Transitional Justice in the United States: The Rhetorical Authorization of the Greensboro Truth and Reconciliation Commission* (New York: Spring Science and Business Media, 2013).

28. Lawrence Guyot, comments at "Contours of a Regional Collaboration," Southern Exposure conference, March 18, 2006. DVD; Shuttlesworth quoted in David Blight, "It Can Never Be as It Ought to Be," in *Slavery and Public History: The Tough Stuff of American Memory*, ed. James Oliver Horton and Lois E. Horton (Chapel Hill: University of North Carolina Press, 2006), 33. The Alliance for Truth and Racial Reconciliation currently has twenty-five member groups. They held a second conference in 2012 in Newnan, Georgia. For more information, see their website at http://www.atrr.org.

29. The MTP, with funding from grants and the William Winter Institute, hired organizers to build grassroots support for a truth commission throughout the state. Although the group has now directed its efforts towards an academic project under the auspices of the William Winter Institute rather than seeking to create a one-time commission, it remains committed to the project of "establishing a culture of truth-telling." Mississippi Truth Project, "Declaration of Intent," http://www.mississippitruth.org/; Mississippi Coalition of Justice, http://www.welcometable.net/; e-mail communication with Susan Glisson, October 31, 2013. See also Beitler, *Remaking Transitional Justice*, 131–132.

30. Alliance for Truth and Racial Reconciliation, "Mission Statement," http://www.atrr.org/pages/mission.htm; Southern Truth and Reconciliation, "About Us: Statement of Intent," http://www.fcd360.com/SouthernTruth/about_us_statement_of_intent.htm; Ladd interview.

31. Gary Younge, "Racism Rebooted," *The Nation*, July 11, 2005, 11–15.

32. Southern Truth and Reconciliation, "What Is STAR?" http://www.fcd360.com/SouthernTruth/resources_what_is_STAR.htm; Sherilynn Ifill, "Truth, Justice, and the American Way: Prospects for Reconciliation in the United States," keynote address, Southern Exposure conference, March 18, 2006, DVD; Ifill, *On the Courthouse Lawn: Confronting the Legacy of Lynching in the Twenty-First Century* (Boston: Beacon Press, 2007), xix.

33. Bender, open letter to Haley Barbour; Donna Ladd, "[Editor's Note] The Next Generation," *Jackson Free Press*, June 10, 2004; Hannah Arendt, *Eichmann in Jerusalem: A Report on the Banality of Evil* (New York: Penguin Books, 1977),

298. On political responsibility, see W. James Booth, *Communities of Memory: On Witness, Identity, and Justice* (Ithaca, NY: Cornell University Press, 2006), 17–19, 41–42, 61; Brian A. Weiner, *Sins of the Parents: The Politics of National Apologies in the United States* (Philadelphia: Temple University Press, 2005), 117–120.

34. This unwillingness to countenance political responsibility to the past has stifled debates about the legacies of American racism. Political arguments for reparations for slavery, for example, raise fierce opposition from those who insist that neither they nor their ancestors—especially those who are more recent immigrants—had anything to do with the practice. Weiner, *Sins of the Parents*, 16–19.

35. Comment of "JacksunGuy," June 23, 2005, posted on the comment board for "After Killen," *Jackson Free Press*, webpage no longer available, copy in author's possession; William Winter Institute on Racial Reconciliation, "We Are All Mississippians," http://www.winterinstitute.org/pages/we_are_all_Mississippians.html.

36. Mississippi Truth Project, "Declaration of Intent"; Southern Truth and Reconciliation, "What Is STAR"; Donna Ladd, comment posted on *Jackson Free Press* website about her article "Damned If We Don't," posted October 27, 2005, accessed February 12, 2006, http:www.jacksonfreepress.com/comments.php?id=7629_0_7_0_C.

37. Rita Schwerner Bender, "The Search for Restorative Justice"; Shuttlesworth quoted in Stephen Merelman, "An Opportunity to Erode Myths, Write New History," *Birmingham News*, April 15, 2001.

38. Comment posted by "Outsider," June 28, 2005, in response to "After Killen," *Jackson Free Press*, webpage no longer available, copy in author's possession; Diane McWhorter, "No Trial Closes Injustice's Wounds," *USA Today*, May 22, 2002; Diane McWhorter, "The Way We Live Now: 7–29–10; Aftershock," *New York Times Magazine*, July 29, 2001, 11

39. Horace Huntley on *Talk of the Nation*, National Public Radio, May 21, 2002.

40. Nikki Burns, "Wrongful Death Suit of Civil Rights Activist Settled for $50,000," *Mississippi Link*, June 12–18, 2002, 3B. On efforts to use civil litigation to address civil rights–era violence, see N. Tasmin Din, "Litigation to Vindicate Civil Rights Era Cold Cases: Ethical and Lawyering Challenges," undated, http://nuweb9.neu.edu/civilrights/wp-content/uploads/Tasmin-Essay.pdf. Jackson State College was renamed Jackson State University in 1974.

41. First Amended Complaint, *Moore v. Franklin County*, U.S. District Court for the Southern District of Mississippi, Jackson Division, civil action no: 3:09CV236TSL-FKB, filed April 23, 2010; Jonathan Saltzman, "Justice Follows Decades of Silence," *Boston Globe*, June 23, 2010.

42. Rita Bender, "More Thoughts on the Search for Restorative Justice," 2010, http://n.web9.new.edu/civilrights/?page_id=1161; Thomas Moore quoted in Jonathan Saltzman, "Justice Follows Decades of Silence," *Boston Globe*,

June 23, 2010; "Resolution Providing Consent to Settle Litigation in Civil Action No. 3:09cv236TSL-FKB," U.S. District Court for the Southern District of Mississippi, June 21, 2010, http://www.clarionledger.com/assets/pdf/D0159945622.pdf; Burnham quoted in Ben Greenberg, "A Little More Justice in Mississippi," *Hungry Blues*, June 23, 2010, http://hungryblues.net/2010/06/23/a-little-more-justice-in-mississippi/.

43. Telephone interview with Susan Glisson, March 15, 2005; telephone interview with Andrew Sheldon, June 2, 2006.

44. Reverend Theophus Smith, "Restoring Honor," opening address at Southern Exposure conference, March 17, 2006, DVD; "World Café Conversation: Fostering a New Ethos on Race and Reconciliation," Southern Exposure conference, March 17, 2006; Lawrence Guyot, response during "World Café Conversation: Fostering a New Ethos on Race and Reconciliation," Southern Exposure conference, March 17, 2006, DVD; Andrew Sheldon, comments at "Truth Commission Initiatives from around the World (and in Our Own Backyard)," Southern Exposure conference, March 19, 2006, DVD. On trials as a "debt to the dead," see Booth, *Communities of Memory*, 124.

45. Bender, "Searching for Restorative Justice: The Trial of Edgar Ray Killen"; Patryk Labuda, "Racial Reconciliation in Mississippi: An Evaluation of the Proposal to Establish a Mississippi Truth and Reconciliation Commission," *Harvard Journal of Racial and Ethnic Justice* 27, no. 1 (2011): 14, 7; Moore quoted in Donna Ladd, "I Want Justice Too," *Jackson Free Press*, July 20, 2005. Thomas Moore's comments about the lingering trauma in the community were in response to a critical editorial in the *Franklin Advocate* that argued that reopening the case would just stir up painful memories. *Franklin Advocate* editorial from July 28, 2005, and Thomas Moore's response (not printed in the *Franklin Advocate*), reprinted in the *Jackson Free Press*, accessed June 9, 2007, http://www.jacksonfreepress.com/comments.php?id+7661_0_7_0_C.

46. As Martha Minow notes, a criminal trial could be a powerful tool for uncovering historical information. The evidence collected in pursuit of a trial creates an official record of events that cannot easily be denied. Minow, *Between Vengeance and Forgiveness*, 47.

47. Ladd interview. Martha Minow argues that the legal structure can provide a focus for public attention to historic wrongs and that this focus might ultimately be more important than the remedies secured. See Martha Minow, "Why Retry: Reviving Dormant Racial Justice Claims," 101 *Michigan L. Rev.* 1133 (March 2003).

48. Stephen Whitfield, "The Resurrection of Emmett Till," *Boston Globe*, May 18, 2004, A11; "Mississippi's Unfinished Business," *Commercial Appeal* (Memphis), May 12, 2004, B4.

49. Ladd interview; "We Are the People We Have Been Waiting For," 16; telephone interview with Susan Glisson, March 15, 2005; Dawn Lea Mars

Chalmers quoted in "Community Leaders to Issue a Call for Justice in 1964 Civil Rights Slayings," *Neshoba Democrat*, May 26, 2004.

50. Bender, "Searching for Restorative Justice: The Trial of Edgar Ray Killen"; Lawrence Guyot, comments at "Is a Verdict Enough? Reflections on Justice and Reconciliation in the Killen Trial," Southern Exposure conference, March 18, 2006, DVD; Leroy Clemons, comments at "Is a Verdict Enough? Reflections on Justice and Reconciliation in the Killen Trial," Southern Exposure conference, March 18, 2006, DVD; interview with Leroy Clemons; "Institute Staff," William Winter Institute for Racial Reconciliation website, accessed April 24, 2013, http://www.winterinstitute.org/pages/aboutus. htm. See also Glisson, "Telling the Truth: How Breaking Silence Brought Redemption to One Mississippi Town."

51. Donna Ladd, "Dredging Up the Past"; Donna Ladd, comment posted on *Jackson Free Press* website in response to "I Want Justice," February 5, 2007, webpage no longer available, copy in author's possession. For claims that each case would be the last of its kind, see Christina Cheakalos, "Around the South No Big Breaks in Old Racial Slayings, Beckwith Case Seen as a Rarity," *Atlanta Journal and Constitution*, February 10, 1994, A3; Adam Goldman, "Civil Rights Cases Breathing Their Last," *Birmingham News*, April 29, 2001; Matt Volz, "Victim's Son Says He Prays for Avants—Chances Dim on Resolving Other Civil Rights Deaths," *Commercial Appeal*, March 3, 2003, B2; Jerry Mitchell, "Seale Case Could Be the Last of Its Kind," *Clarion-Ledger*, May 27, 2007.

52. Bender quoted in Gary Younge, "'Mississippi Burning' Killer Gets 60 Years," *Guardian*, June 24, 2005, 15; author interview with Andrew Sheldon; Glisson interview, March 15, 2005; Andrew Sheldon, comment at "Truth Commission Initiatives from around the World (and in Our Own Backyard)," Southern Exposure conference, March 19, 2006, DVD.

53. DeWeese interview.

54. Booth, *Communities of Memory*, 135, 136.

55. Betsy Nash, interview by John R. Salter Jr., December 26, 1990, John C. Stennis Oral History Project, Mississippi State University, 93–99; Debra Pickett, "Mississippians Say Till's Killers Won't Go to Jail: Value of Reopening Till Case Might Be Symbolic, but Locals Expect Little Else from It," *Chicago Sun-Times*, May 16, 2004, 12.

56. Rita Bender, comments at Researcher's Roundtable, Crimes of Civil Rights Era conference, Boston, MA, April 27, 2007; Rita Bender, "Searching for Restorative Justice: The Trial of Edgar Ray Killen."

57. Susan Glisson, "Telling the Truth: How Breaking Silence Brought Redemption to One Mississippi Town," in *Telling Stories to Change the World: Global Voices on the Power of Narrative to Build Community and Make Social Justice Claims*, ed. Rickie Solinger, Madeline Fox, and Kayhan Irani (New York: Routledge, 2008), 38, 37; Donna Ladd, comments in response to "The

Klansmen Bound: 43 Years Later, James Ford Seale Faces Justice," *Jackson Free Press*, May 27, 2007, http://www.jacksonfreepress.com/comments. php?id=13701_0_9_0_C.

58. Emily Wagster Pettus, "Ex-Klansman Sentenced to 60 Years in 1964 Slayings," *Ventura County Star*, June 24, 2005, 7; Susan Ives, "In Mississippi, an Evil Chapter Finally Ends," *San Antonio Express-News*, June 26, 2005, 3H; Arnold Lindsay, "Conviction Relieves Visitors from across Nation," *Clarion-Ledger*, June 22, 2005.

59. "Epitaph for South's Racist History," *Newsday*, June 25, 2005. Susan Glisson singles out this article in her critique of the coverage of the Killen trial in her essay on the Philadelphia Coalition.

60. Howard Ball, *Justice in Mississippi: The Murder Trial of Edgar Ray Killen* (Lawrence: University Press of Kansas, 2006), 46, 51. Emilye Crosby, "Truth and Reconciliation: Confronting Historic and Contemporary Racism," review of *Justice in Mississippi*, by Howard Ball, H-Net Book Review, published by H-Law@H-net.msu.edu (August 2007). Patryk Labuda agreed with this assessment. In his essay on efforts to launch a truth commission in Mississippi, he pointed to Ball's book as an example of Americans' failure to take responsibility and assume accountability for the nation's history of race. In Ball's book, there were perpetrators, victims, and the "good people" of Mississippi, who were the innocent bystanders. Labuda, "Racial Reconciliation in Mississippi," 29–30.

61. "Introduction," *Telling Stories to Change the World*, 1.

62. Donna Ladd, "Damned If We Don't."

Conclusion

1. Margarena A. Christian, "President Bush Signs Emmett Till Bill into Law," *Jet*, November 10, 2008, 16. The two cases that the Till Bill assisted with were the 2007 federal trial of James Seale for the 1964 murder of Charles Moore and Henry Dee and the 2010 case against Alabama state trooper James Bonard Fowler, who pled guilty to second-degree manslaughter and served a six-month sentence for the 1965 shooting of Jimmie Lee Jackson.

2. "The Attorney General's Fourth Annual Report to Congress Pursuant to the Emmett Till Unsolved Civil Rights Crime Act of 2007," October 2012, 2, http://www.justice.gov/crt/about/crm/documents/cold_case_report_2012. pdf; FBI Press Release, "We Need Your Help To Find Civil Rights Victims' Next of Kin," November 18, 2009, http://www.fbi.gov/news/stories/2009/ november/coldcases_111809; Krissah Thompson, "Civil Rights-Era Injustices Are Reexamined," *Washington Post*, February 20, 2011, A7.

3. "Attorney General's Report to Congress," 9.

4. Burnham quoted in Dan Barry, Cambell Robertson, and Robbie Brown, "When Cold Cases Stay Cold," *New York Times*, March 17, 2013, A1; Allen

G. Breed and Holbrook Mohr, "FBI Says the End Is Near for Investigations into Civil Rights-Era Cold Cases," *Huff Post Black Voices*, November 5, 2011, http://www.huffingtonpost.com/2011/11/05/fbi-says-the-end-near-in-_n_1077703.html; Joseph Shapiro, "Turning Up the Heat on Civil Rights-Era Cold Cases," May 18, 2013, *Weekend Edition*, National Public Radio, accessed May 24, 2013, http://www.wbur.org/npr/184936625/turning-up-the-heat-on-civil-rights-era-cold-cases; Hank Klibanoff, "Cold Cases Growing Colder by the Day," *Atlanta Journal-Constitution*, August 15, 2010, 19A.

5. Sykes quoted in Carrie Johnson, "Civil Rights Killings Yield Their Secrets: Review of Decades-Old Cases Producing Many Answers If Few Indictments, FBI Says," *Washington Post*, February 28, 2010, A1; McDonald quoted in "Justice Department Provided New List of Suspected Civil Rights Era Murders," *Concordia Sentinel*, October 7, 2012, and "When Cold Cases Stay Cold," *New York Times*, March 16, 2013; Testimony of Rita Schwerner Bender, "Emmett Till Unsolved Civil Rights Crime Act," Joint Hearing before the Committee on the Constitution, Civil Rights, and Civil Liberties and the Committee on Crime, Terrorism, and Homeland Security of the Committee on the Judiciary, House of Representatives, 110th Congress, June 12, 2007, 59.

6. Myrlie Evers-Williams quotes from *The Tavis Smiley Show*, National Public Radio, June 12, 2003, and Ronald Smothers, "White Supremacist Is Convicted of Slaying Rights Leader in '63," *New York Times*, February 6, 1994, 1; Jesse White quoted in "Ex-Klansman Guilty of 1960s Southern Mississippi Murder," *Jet*, March 17, 2003, 8; Thomas Moore quoted in LaRaye Brown, "For Families of Victims, Closure after Conviction," *Clarion-Ledger*, June 15, 2007.

7. See Adam Nossiter, *Of Long Memory: Mississippi and the Murder of Medgar Evers*, 2nd ed. (Cambridge, MA: De Capo Press, 2002), preface; Howard Ball, *Justice in Mississippi: The Murder Trial of Edgar Ray Killen* (Lawrence: University of Kansas Press, 2006), 195; Harry Maclean, *The Past Is Never Dead: The Trial of James Ford Seale and Mississippi's Struggle for Redemption* (New York: Basic Civitas, 2009), 3, 14. See also the other book on these trials, Maryanne Vollers's *Ghosts of Mississippi: The Murder of Medgar Evers, the Trials of Byron De La Beckwith, and the Haunting of the New South* (Boston: Little, Brown and Company, 1995); Vollers also frames her study as a history of Mississippi. She concludes her book by noting that while the state had achieved "a brief and shining moment of grace" after the conviction of Beckwith, what remained "was still Mississippi . . . a place at war with its own history and destined to repeat is past" until it gets it right (386).

8. Nikhil Pal Singh, *Black Is a Country: Race and the Unfinished Struggle for American Democracy* (Cambridge, MA: Harvard University Press, 2005), 10.

9. Touré, "No Such Place as Post-Racial America," Campaign Stops Blog, *New York Times*, November 8, 2011, http://campaignstops.blogs.nytimes.com/2011/11/08/no-such-place-as-post-racial-america/.

10. On the rise and domination of color blindness, see Tim Wise, *Colorblind: The Rise of Post-Racial Politics and the Retreat from Racial Equity* (San Francisco: Open Media Series, 2010). Pew Research Center, "The State of Race in America" (PowerPoint presentation at the Aspen Institute Symposium, April 22, 2013), http://www.pewresearch.org/2013/05/03/the-state-of-race-in-america/; "Black-White Student Achievement Gap Persists," *NBC News*, July 14, 2009, http://www.nbcnews.com/id/31911075/ns/us_news-education/t/black-white-student-achievement-gap-persists/#.UaU_R79RHww; "Criminal Justice Fact Sheet," NAACP, http://www.naacp.org/pages/criminal-justice-fact-sheet.

11. Sumi Cho, "Post-Racialism," 94 *Iowa L. Rev.* 1589 (2009). Quotes from 1645, 1593.

12. Margaret Burnham, comment at Researcher's Roundtable, Crimes of the Civil Rights Era conference, Boston, MA, April 27, 2007; Testimony of Rita Schwerner Bender, Hearing on Emmett Till Unsolved Civil Rights Crime Act, 57. Bender had expressed reservations about the idea for the Till Bill when Sykes first proposed it based on her mistrust of the Department of Justice and the FBI, but she decided to support it.

13. James Baldwin quoted in the film *James Baldwin: Price of the Ticket*, directed by Karen Thorson (California Newsreel, 1990).

14. Martin Luther King Jr., "Remaining Awake through a Great Revolution" (sermon, Washington National Cathedral, March 31, 1968), http://mlk-kpp01.stanford.edu/index.php/encyclopedia/documentsentry/doc_remaining_awake_through_a_great_revolution/; James Baldwin, "Many Thousands Gone" (1951), in *Notes of a Native Son* (Boston: Beacon Press, 1959), 31.

Acknowledgments

T HE WHITE CROSSES, each labeled with the name of a victim of racial violence in the civil rights era, stretched in a long line as they were placed solemnly in a row during a ceremony to honor three civil rights workers who were murdered in Neshoba County, Mississippi, in 1964. It was a blazing hot Mississippi day in 2010, and I was gathered with people who had traveled from near and far for the annual ceremony to honor those who had been killed during the civil rights movement. I have tried to keep that afternoon in mind as I have written this book, as a reminder that the history I have tried to document in these pages is still present and painful for people who lived through it.

Writing a book is at once a solitary and a communal process. The time that I have spent by myself in the past eight years doing research and typing away at my keyboard would never have resulted in this book if I had not had the assistance, support, and encouragement of so many people along the way. First and foremost, I owe an enormous debt of gratitude to the people involved in efforts to revisit civil rights–era racial violence who shared their experiences and perspectives with me. Bill Baxley, Rita Schwerner Bender, Leroy Clemons, Stanley Dearman, Fenton DeWeese, John Gibson, Susan Glisson, Doug Jones, Donna Ladd, Jerry Mitchell, Andrew Sheldon, John Steele, Joya Wesley, and Jill Williams all graciously agreed to speak with me about their experiences as I pursued my research. I learned a tremendous amount from my conversations with them, and I am grateful to them for the time they gave me as I sought to understand the movement to revisit Jim Crow–era racial violence and the phenomenon of the contemporary prosecution of civil rights–era murders. I am grateful also to all the archivists and court clerks who helped me locate trial transcripts and other records related to the court proceedings that are the main subject of this book. The many helpful people I met on research trips to Jackson, Hattiesburg,

Philadelphia, Belzoni, Birmingham, and Montgomery convinced me that the South's reputation for hospitality was richly deserved.

Institutional support from Wesleyan University, where I began working on this project, and Oberlin College, where I finished it, made my work possible. At Wesleyan, several project grants enabled me to take my first research trips to locate sources, while a semester spent at Wesleyan's Center for the Humanities in 2005 gave me time to immerse myself in the extensive literature about the pursuit of justice in response to historic violence. I moved to Oberlin in 2008 in the midst of working on this book and found wonderful colleagues and a supportive intellectual environment there. At Oberlin, I was able to take advantage of a Research Status grant to take leave for a year so I could write the bulk of this manuscript. Giving campus presentations to colleagues from many disciplines helped me sharpen my argument, and the structure provided by an informal research group helped keep me on track as I moved to a new institution. I am thankful also for the help of Ana Weibgen, Jen Graham, and Claire Molholm, student research assistants who helped me with crucial tasks at different stages in the project.

I am grateful too to all of the scholars whose work I drew on and learned from during every stage of this project and to the many colleagues who provided me with valuable feedback as I developed my ideas and arguments. The thoughtful comments and critiques I received when I presented my work at meetings of the Organization of American Historians, the American Society for Legal History, the Association for the Study of African American History and Culture, the Southern Intellectual History Circle, and the Law and Society Workshop at the University of Southern California pushed me to ask hard questions about my evidence, my argument, and my own unconscious assumptions as I researched and wrote this book. I benefitted especially from the very thoughtful and conscientious reviews of the manuscript provided by the readers for the press and from the careful reading of my editor, Joyce Seltzer. Their suggestions have made this a better book.

A challenging project always seems more manageable when discussed over a glass of wine, and I am so fortunate to belong to a wonderful group of women who meet regularly to share wine, good meals, and great discussions of our work. Ariela Gross, Wendy Wall, Leslie Harris, Karen Dunn-Haley, Alice Yang, and Wendy Lynch have functioned for the past fifteen years as part writing group, part professional advisors, and part therapists. They have witnessed the evolution of this project from the very beginning and have provided useful feedback on everything from grant applications to book proposals to early chapters. I am so grateful for their friendship and their support.

I owe a special debt to two colleagues in particular. Claire Potter, formerly at Wesleyan and now at the New School for Social Research, has been my partner in crime for many of my scholarly pursuits of the past five years as we have worked together on an edited collection and the book series we coedit. Her advice and encouragement have proved invaluable over the last five years, as has her good cheer in picking up the bulk of the work on our shared projects at times when I needed to devote myself fully to this manuscript. I only hope that I can cover for Claire as effectively as she has covered for me when she needs to focus on her own book.

I owe an even greater debt to Wendy Kozol of the Comparative American Studies program at Oberlin. Getting to know Wendy has been one of the unexpected joys of coming to Oberlin, and she has shaped this work more than she knows. Wendy read drafts of every chapter of the manuscript, and her exceptionally thoughtful and substantive feedback helped me to sharpen my thinking and analysis. She never complained as I spent countless hours talking to her about this book. And she and her family made the last stages of this project manageable by having my kids and me over for dinner every week when my life became even crazier than usual. Thank you, Wendy, for your friendship, encouragement, and—as necessary—tough love.

My family has lived with this project for almost a decade, and I am very grateful that they have only occasionally asked me to stop talking about civil rights trials. In 2002, in my very first tentative steps towards developing this project, I packed up my infant son, Owen, and my daughter, Sabine, then just six years old, for a two-week driving tour of civil rights sites in Alabama and Georgia. Owen spent those weeks charming strangers in restaurants, and at twelve, he is still charming, and has even become interested in the historical sites that Mom drags him to. Sabine spent the entire trip singing the soundtrack to *Mamma Mia*, and now, as a senior in high school, she is still entertaining me with her singing and dancing. They have made me laugh, kept me grounded, and provided a constant reminder of why it is so important to keep working on making this world a better place. My husband, Sean, has been my most important supporter during the many years I have been working on this book, years that witnessed family moves, new jobs, and major surgery, among other life challenges. I am grateful for his emotional and intellectual partnership, his constant encouragement, and his unwavering faith. Finally, I must thank my parents, Marcia and Joseph Romano, whose intellectual curiosity, generosity, and commitment to their family and community have served as a model for me to aspire to. I dedicate this book to them.

Index